Beyond Universals
in Cognitive Development
Second Edition

Beyond Universals in Cognitive Development

David Henry Feldman
Tufts University

Ablex Publishing Corporation
Norwood, New Jersey 07648

Library of Congress Cataloging in Publication Data

Feldman, David Henry.
    Beyond universals in cognitive development / David Henry Feldman.
 —2nd ed.
      p. cm.
    Includes bibliographical references and indexes.
    ISBN 1-56750-031-5. — ISBN 1-56750-032-3 (pbk.)
    1. Cognition in children.   2. Cognition and culture.   I. Title.
BF723.C5F44 1994
155.4'13—dc20   94-16334
                                                          CIP

ABLEX Publishing Corporation
355 Chestnut Street
Norwood, New Jersey 07648

For My Parents, While There Is Still Time

Table of Contents

Acknowledgments ix

Preface to the Second Edition xiii

Introduction to the Second Edition 1

1

Universal to Unique—Mapping the Development Terrain *15*
David Henry Feldman and Samuel S. Snyder

2

Unique to Universal—The Role of Novel Behavior
in the Evolution of Knowledge *39*
David Henry Feldman and Lynn T. Goldsmith

3

Individual Developmental Transitions—
A Film Metaphor *57*
Samuel S. Snyder and David Henry Feldman

4

Developmental Transitions a Decade Later   *103*
David Henry Feldman and Samuel S. Snyder

5

The Development of Expertise   *121*
David Henry Feldman

6

Creativity: Proof that Development Occurs   *145*
David Henry Feldman

7

Cultural Organisms   *161*
David Henry Feldman

References   187

Author Index   203

Subject Index   207

Acknowledgments

This is a Second Edition, so let me begin by saying that everyone who was thanked in the First Edition is still thanked. The years have not diminished my debt to the people who put so much of themselves into the First Edition of this book; if anything, that debt has grown, with compounded interest, over the years. I am very grateful to all of them, but the reader will have to find a copy of the First Edition of *Beyond Universals* to read the list.

I do want to mention by name two people who made valued, formal contributions to the First Edition: Seymour Sarason wrote a wise Preface, and Howard Gruber wrote a remarkable Afterword. These senior colleagues continue to have a special place in my heart, although, alas, no space in this edition of *Beyond Universals*.

With the publication of the Second Edition there are many more people to thank and many more benefactors to acknowledge. As for people, I first want to express my gratitude to my closest colleagues in the field of cognitive development, many of whom I did not know in 1980 but who have been a source of inspiration and support now for several years. It is impossible to say how much it has meant to find that the quest for a deeper understanding of the mind and its development is shared by a cohort of able scholars with views that complement my own.

Although this list could not possibly be complete, let me mention by name the following friends and colleagues: Bill Bart, Jeanne Bamberger, Harry Beilin, Marvin Berkowitz, Mark Bickhard, Marc Bornstein, John Broughton, Robbie Case, Mihalyi Csikszentmihalyi, Bill Damon, Robert Campbell, Susan Carey, Kurt Fischer, George Forman, Howard Gardner, Howard Gruber, Herb Ginsburg, Joe Glick, Annette Karmiloff-Smith, Lawrence Kohlberg, Deanna Kuhn, Jonas Langer, Lynn Liben, Frank Murray, David Olson, Bill Overton, Sidney Strauss, Lawrence Taylor, and Elliot Turiel. Each has had a significant influence on how I think about cognitive development.

Then there are people with whom I tend to disagree, but whose views I always find challenging and worth grappling with: Carl Bereiter, Charles Brainerd, Noam Chomsky, Jerry Fodor, Rochel Gelman, Fran Horowitz, Arthur Jensen, Frank Keil, Lauren Resnick, Sandra Scarr, Bob Siegler, Bob Sternberg, and Michael Wallach have been stimulating adversaries or foils in print and sometimes in person.

My students, coworkers, and collaborators are a hardy and talented bunch; several deserve special mention here. Among them, Margaret Adams, Ellen Band, Ann Benjamin, Ji Qie Chen, Ilda King, Lynn Goldsmith, Martha Morelock, Mark Ogonowski, Sam Snyder, and Ronald Walton made particularly important contributions to the work reported in this edition. Indeed, the most fun I have is arguing with these people.

Among my closest collaborators, one has become more than that: she has become my partner and my wife. There were aspects of the work that became clear only when Ann Benjamin and I began to explore our many dimensioned collaboration. These less obvious qualities reverberate throughout the pages to follow. True enough, many of these themes remain implicit even here, but we are committed to writing another book, and there the resonance between developmental theory and some of these broader (yes, broader!) themes will be portrayed.

Finally, there have been several agencies and foundations which have helped keep the work going. These include The Andrew W. Mellon Foundation, The Rockefeller Brothers Fund, The Jessie Smith Noyes Foundation, The Spencer Foundation, The Social Science Research Council, The Geraldine R. Dodge Foundation, The W.T. Grant Foundation, The Exxon Foundation, and the Eliot-Pearson Faculty Scholarship Fund at Tufts. The support of these agencies and foundations and their officers has been vitally important, so important that this book would not have seen the light of day without their help.

I hope that the work reported in this edition of *Beyond Universals* justifies, if only in a small way, the collective efforts of so many people, only a few of whom could be named in these Acknowledgments. I am grateful to all who have contributed, and apologize to those whose contributions are not as fully or explicitly acknowledged as they should be. Given my tendency to absorb indiscriminately, I can only assume that the debt will eventually be paid (e.g., see the Preface).

As is customary, I accept full responsibility for any errors of fact or interpretation that may be found in these pages, plus or minus the usual 3%.

Preface to the Second Edition
An Apology to
Lev Semenovich Vygotsky

In an interview with Piaget in 1979, a year before his death, J. Jacques Voneche attempted to question *le patron* as to how influential James Mark Baldwin had been on his work (Piaget, 1982b). In the introduction to that interview, Voneche wrote that "the unprepared reader could gain the impression that Piaget did not *want* to recognize Baldwin's influence on his work" (Broughton & Freeman-Moir, 1982). He then went on to show how Piaget was well aware of Baldwin's influence (it was Baldwin, for example, who first used the terms assimilation and accommodation, among others), but that Piaget's own way of constructing knowledge prevented him from accepting any external influence without making it his own.

The interview itself makes it clear that Piaget's memories are in places highly inaccurate. For example, he says that Baldwin was dead by the time he reached Paris; Baldwin died in 1934, several years after Piaget's Paris years. When it was pointed out to Piaget that he had written a long discussion of Baldwin's view of morality in *The Moral Judgment of the Child,* he replied: "Really? That's curious. I have no memory of that at all" (Piaget, 1982a, p. 84).

With this effort to show that I may be in good company for having forgotten how much I have been influenced by a long-dead predecessor,

I must now try to put right what was an egregious lapse in the first edition of this book. Although a citation for Vygotsky's *Thought and Language* (now retranslated and retitled *Thinking and Speech* (Rieber & Carton, 1987)) appears in the references, there is in fact not a single citation to Vygotsky in the text of *Beyond Universals*. This is a fact that I find hard to believe and even harder to explain.

The truth of the matter is that I was deeply and profoundly influenced by *Thought and Language,* and even hoped that the first edition of this book might be compared with that great work. I had fantasies about reading reviews that would draw such comparisons. In some of my earlier writing, in particular the 1974 article that anticipated much of the content of the present work, Vygotsky was cited, although not extensively. I was then just beginning to feel the full impact of the ideas in *Thought and Language,* which I first read probably between 1970 and 1972. It was (I believe) brought to my attention by my neighbor and colleague in Minnesota, Joe Glick, who was at the time working on *The Cultural Context of Learning and Thinking* (Cole, Gay, Glick, & Sharp, 1971). Somehow between 1974 and 1980 my conscious attention to the impact of Vygotsky on the ideas in *Beyond Universals* diminished to the point that they did not appear explicitly at all.

In 1974, I wrote this passage about Vygotsky's idea of cultural influences on development:

> The notion of reciprocal influence of cultural task on general intellec-
> tual development and intellectual advance on cultural knowledge is the
> point of view taken more than 30 years ago by the Russian psychologist
> Vygotsky (1934/1962). For Vygotsky, the causal influence relating uni-
> versal thought forms and specific knowledge is bidirectional whereas for
> Piaget the direction is always universal to cultural. Again little sys-
> tematic evidence bearing on the issue is available. Vygotsky's own
> experiments were methodologically weak, and subsequent research has
> been scanty (Sullivan, 1970; Wohlwill, 1970). Although no firm con-
> clusions can yet be drawn, the Piagetian stages become more comprehen-
> sible if the individual's readiness for their achievement is affected by
> specific knowledge previously acquired. The knowledge that one is able
> to acquire at any given point is still limited, of course, by the Piagetian
> operations that are available to him. However, the mystery of the source
> of such operations is less baffling if it is assumed that the individual
> constructed them from a set of existing concepts (elements) that can be
> taught and combined to form more powerful principles for organizing
> experience. (Feldman, 1974, p. 77)

It is clear from this passage that I was perfectly well aware of the profound importance of Vygotsky's idea of cultural influences on development. It is also true that I was consciously aware of and frequently cited the work of Jerome Bruner, whose related notion of cultural amplifiers of human capacities played (and plays) a major role in my thinking. What I was less aware of was how much Bruner's work during the 1960s was itself influenced by Vygotsky, a fact acknowledged by Bruner but apparently not acknowledged forcefully enough for me to grasp. It is possible that I simply combined Vygotsky with Bruner.

The other reason I may have been less aware of Vygotsky's importance in the formation of my framework is that I have little appreciation for language as the central human capability. As Roger Brown (1973) has said of those who are drawn to the study of language, there seems to be a "kinky gene" required, which I apparently do not carry in my pocket of genetic material. Because Vygotsky's work was so focused on language, I had difficulty paying sustained attention to it.

It is difficult to accept that probably the most powerful and pervasive influence on my work, other than Piaget, received almost no recognition in the first edition of this book. If I had it to do over (which in a sense I do), I would have had Vygotsky's ideas play a major role in the discussion. Universal-to-unique can be seen, for example, as an extension and elaboration of Vygotsky's notion of spontaneous versus scientific knowledge, as Strauss (1987) has pointed out. There are many places where Vygotsky's ideas would have enriched and deepened the presentation of the universal-to-unique framework.

There have been so many instances of Vygotsky anticipating or actually producing ideas very close to those presented in this book that it would be impossible to list them all. There seems to be an almost uncanny connection between my work and Vygotsky's; recently, in rereading an article which presented in translation certain of Vygotsky's notions about stage and transition (Zender & Zender, 1974), I was stunned to see that he had sketched an alternating sequence of "stable periods versus crises" that is amazingly close to our six-phase model (see Chapters 3 and 4). I am sure that I have read this work before, but had no recollection whatsoever of this material. It was as if I had read it for the first time this year.

I hope that my increasing awareness of a debt to Vygotsky can be at least partly rectified through explicit acknowledgment and incorporation of his ideas into this edition of *Beyond Universals*. But, I also find it interesting as a way of reflecting on how I go about my theory-building business. Not to draw too close a comparison with Piaget, but I do begin to understand better why Piaget might have forgotten how much James Mark Baldwin was part of his experience and why he might have found it irritating to be confronted with the similarity between some of his constructs and those of his predecessors.

For me at least, it was as if the work of Vygotsky was too catalytic and too close to what I was trying to construct to keep track. Part of me didn't *want* to keep track of it because, first of all, I was too absorbed in the process to take the time for the scholarly niceties, and second, because it would diminish the "originality" of my work if I constantly kept track of how it resembled that of someone else. In a sense, Vygotsky was too close for me to see, whereas Piaget, and even Bruner, were just far enough away for me to perceive consciously and use in constructing my own point of view. In a mind which has as powerful a tendency to transform and take liberties with existing theory as mine apparently does, the interplay between what is and what will be is continuous; keeping track of it gets in the way of the process.

Voneche explained about Piaget's "assimilation" of Baldwin that, given Piaget's constructivist tendencies, he would have been changing and transforming Baldwin's ideas before he knew it:

> There is no desire evident in Piaget to ignore his debt toward great predecessors. But in his reticence, one could read a certain position toward influences in knowledge which would be directly connected with his own version of genetic epistemology...[Piaget] believed strongly in *assimilation*. This means that he was convinced that the ideas of others became yours when they were truly digested or assimilated in the very same way, or to use one of his favorite images, that the cabbage became the rabbit once it was digested by the rabbit. (Broughton & Freeman-Moir, 1982, pp. 81–82)

Vygotsky was the greatest natural theorist in the history of developmental psychology. He has been called the Mozart of the field, perhaps to be contrasted with Piaget's Beethoven or Bach. Whether or not the work presented in *Beyond Universals* (either edition) is genuinely novel, it has been deeply and profoundly influenced by the works of others, especially Vygotsky. I only hope that some other rabbits will find the cabbage offered in *Beyond Universals* worth digesting.

Introduction to the Second Edition

This will be a somewhat unusual second edition; this should come as no surprise because the original *Beyond Universals in Cognitive Development* was an unusual book. The first three chapters of the original have been only minimally revised, whereas the rest is new (although two of the "new" chapters have or will appear elsewhere). We decided to keep Chapters 1, 2, and 3 relatively intact because they seem to have held up fairly well to the ravages of time, critical discussion, and second thoughts. There are certainly things my collaborators and I would change about these first chapters, but nothing about them seems utterly awful. And so, other than a few corrections, readers of the first edition of *Beyond Universals* will not find much that is unfamiliar until they reach Chapter 4.

Before turning to the new sections of this edition, I do want to reflect a bit on how things have gone for *Beyond Universals* during the first decade or so of its bookish life. Because its goals were ambitious, it seems appropriate to take stock of its accomplishments and short-comings. The avowed goal of the book was to change the face of developmental psychology; it is worth a glance at what the face of developmental psychology looks like at this point.

Has the face of developmental psychology changed, and if so, has it changed in the ways that *Beyond Universals* intended it to?

I believe that developmental psychology has indeed changed, and by and large it has changed in ways that I hoped it would. What is less clear is the degree to which *Beyond Universals* catalyzed that change. First, as to how developmental psychology has changed, there seem to be three important shifts in the hoped for direction. Developmental psychology has become at once more *applied,* more attentive to *individuality and diversity* (including interest in cultural and contextual influences on development), and more accepting of *stage and transitions frameworks,* although not traditional stage frameworks. In addition, there seems to be great interest in biological and even nativist interpretations of development. This last change might appear to be at odds with the track taken in 1980, but as should become clear in the version of this book you are about to read, a concern with biological matters is quite concordant with the overall framework proposed here (then and now), although the more radical forms of nativism are not consistent with my view (see Chapters 6 and 7).

APPLIED WORK

As for the movement toward applied work, the trend seems quite strong. In addition to a solid journal and a growing number of applied developmental psychology graduate training programs, the growth of policy and policy related concerns in child development circles has been dramatic. In the first sentence of a recent chapter about the importance of making cognitive development research more applicable to education, Deanna Kuhn (1989) wrote:

> It was not that long ago that relevant research was strictly second class. Research that related directly to real world issues and problems was labeled "applied" and strongly implied by that label was lack of rigor. Today, in contrast, we are concerned that our research be relevant. (p. 261)

Similar thrusts have come from the sectors of the field dealing with babies and children "at risk" for later learning and development problems (Bornstein & Krasnegor, 1989; Gallagher, 1989), and from the growing crisis in child care (Clarke-Stewart, 1989; Garwood, Phillips, Hartman, & Zigler, 1989).

Introducing a special issue on children of the influential journal *American Psychologist,* Horowitz and O'Brien (1989) contrasted the current publication with one from 10 years earlier:

The most striking difference between the two issues is not in the presence, absence, expansion, or contraction of specific topics, however. Rather, in this issue, as compared with the issue published 10 years ago, the difference is that a much more obvious effort has been made to relate the topics (even those oriented toward basic research) directly to issues of the health and welfare of children, especially as reflected in social policy. (p. 95)

As readers of the first edition of *Beyond Universals* know, this trend can only be seen as welcome. I wrote then that one purpose for developing a theory of nonuniversal development was to help developmental psychology serve applied purposes more directly: "The practical use is to help make developmental psychology more relevant to the professions, particularly those professions that concern themselves with the welfare and growth of children" (Feldman, 1980b, Preface, p. xv).

It appears that the identity of developmental psychology as a self-consciously applied field, as well as a basic research specialty, is well consolidated and likely to be stable for the foreseeable future.

DIVERSITY AND DIFFERENCE

With the population of the United States soon reaching a "majority minority," in which more than half of the people will not be of European origin, issues of education and development outside white, middle-class settings have been of increasing concern. Particularly intense have been discussions and studies of education, catalyzed into a major national political issue by the publication of the widely read report "A Nation At Risk" in 1983, which documented the decline of U.S. education in relation to its international competitor nations and called for fundamental school reforms.

It seems no coincidence that there has been a corresponding shift of interest to Vygotsky's work and decline in Piaget's hold on the field of cognitive development. Vygotsky, in contrast to Piaget, saw human cultures as the primary source of development; he also argued that culture actively constructs and largely determines both the course and the degree of developmental progress (Bruner, 1986; Vygotsky, 1934/1962, 1978). Although Vygotsky recognized that universal ("spontaneous" in the terms of the day) developmental processes are vital ingredients of progress and provide the source of a dialectic between individual and society, he gave enormously more importance to conscious, directed, culturally prescribed experience than did Piaget

(Glick, 1983). In other words, Vygotsky's stance is more didactically oriented and more consistent with the back to basics movement in education. It also allows for remediation of educational problems through direct intervention.

Of Vygotsky's theoretical stance, Glick (1983) wrote: "In opposition to the idealist view of things, this new approach represents a fundamental paradigm shift" (p. 45). It seems as if Vygotsky is everywhere, with books and articles appearing at an ever-increasing pace (e.g., Rogoff, 1990; Rogoff & Wertsch, 1984; Wertsch, 1985). The appearance in 1978 of a collection of some of Vygotsky's works in English probably provided the major impetus for the Vygotsky boom (Vygotsky, 1978). Although it cannot be claimed that *Beyond Universals* helped move things along more than slightly (particularly in light of the Preface to this book), it certainly was consistent with much of Vygotsky's theorizing, especially on the importance of systematic, active, directed intervention for acquisition of all nonuniversal developmental domains of knowledge.

Perhaps the most dramatic shift in the field has been toward a more context-oriented focus on "situated cognition" and "domain specific knowledge" in the fields of educational psychology and cognitive science (cf. Alexander & Judy, 1988; Brown, Collins, & Duguid, 1989; Dreyfus & Dreyfus, 1986; Ennis, 1989; Lave, 1988). There seems to be a growing consensus that thought is best understood within specific contexts and as domain specific. This is all to the good, although to my mind work in this area would benefit from the framework of *Beyond Universals*.

The key idea of nonuniversal development, after all, is that it will not occur without the availability and sustained deployment of cultural resources aimed to facilitate domain-specific developmental progress. Again, it is not possible to say that our book had much directly to do with the change, but shifts in the field have certainly occurred, shifts consistent with the line of argument taken in *Beyond Universals* circa 1980. It is gratifying that the universal/nonuniversal distinction laid out in *Beyond Universals* is being increasingly used by other theorists and researchers. In a valuable book on theory, for example, Frances Degen Horowitz (1987) made the distinction between universal and nonuniversal a centerpiece of her framework.

Closer to home, cognitive developmental research and theory has taken a decisive turn toward social and contextual influences on individual intellectual development. The great Vygotsky boom now in full force has of course been the most potent source of this shift, and will no doubt continue to influence it as more of Vygotsky's work, and works of those inspired by Vygotsky, become available.

To give some of the flavor of the shift, now a virtual fait accompli, here is a quote from Barbara Rogoff's (1990) recent, but already influential, book called *Cognitive Development in Sociocultural Context:*

> In the past decade or so…there has been widespread recognition that cognitive processes may differ according to the domain of thinking and the specifics of the task context. Cognitive development is now considered to involve advances in skills and knowledge in particular domains, rather than increases in general capacity (Feldman, 1980b; Fischer, 1980; Rogoff, 1982; Siegler, 1981). Hence, research in cognitive development has become much more grounded in the specific problem definitions and goal structures of the skill being developed, and has grown to include topics such as language, reading, writing, and mathematical development, which had been considered separate from "basic" cognitive processes, such as memory and attention. (p. 6)

Relatedly, workers in the field of intelligence and its assessment have begun to reach consensus around the notion that intelligence is best thought of as having several distinct and independent aspects, rather than as a single overall quantity (Gardner, 1983; Sternberg, 1986). These more "multiple intelligence" oriented views help reinforce the idea that the days of general, all-purpose, universal, learning and development theories seem numbered, although there continue to be many interesting issues to be explored in distinguishing among varieties of learning and development (Bereiter, 1985; Brown, 1982; Liben, 1987a, 1987b).

It will continue to be true that univeral *aspects* of development are essential ingredients of any theory aspiring to be comprehensive. After trying to prove otherwise in my prodigies research (Feldman, 1980a, 1980c, 1986a, 1986b), I am now quite convinced that there are broad shifts in thought that occur a few times during the first two decades, much as Piaget claimed, and that these broad sets of changes have profound impact on the rest of development, even in extreme cases such as prodigies.

STAGES AND TRANSITIONS

Perhaps the most gratifying change in the field since 1980 is the improved status that stage-theoretic frameworks have achieved. For example, the first Tel Aviv University symposium on Human Development chose as its topic "Stage and Structure: Reopening the Debate" (Levin, 1986), and the Jean Piaget Society sponsored a meeting on

"Development versus Learning" in which stage conceptions were central (Liben, 1987a).

Interest in transitions has also dramatically increased. A volume, *Mechanisms of Cognitive Development* (1984b), was edited by Robert Sternberg. Its entire contents were focused on the issue of transitions in cognitive development, albeit from an "information-processing" point of view. One of the contributors to this volume, Frank Keil, a radical nativist trained in the Chomsky/Fodor way of thinking, showed in his contribution to this conference that he had begun to shift toward a stage-theoretic framework because his data demanded it. And I am pleased to note that it is a stage-theoretic notion in some respects similar to our notions of stages in domains rather than stages in people's heads. For transitions in using higher order relations such as hierarchies, Keil found that domain specific changes in bodies of knowledge were a better candidate for accounting for major shifts than either preexisting rule structures or knowledge acquisition processes (Keil, 1984).

Two other contributors to the Tel Aviv conference presented stage theories that aimed to integrate information-processing and cognitive-developmental approaches (Case, 1984; Fischer & Pipp, 1984). These theories have gained considerable visibility and stature in the past 10 years, particularly in more educationally oriented child development circles. Both theories adhere quite closely to some of the Piagetian criteria of stages (i.e., of universality and spontaneous appearance, along with hierarchical integration and transition processes), although both also try to make more precise the actual mechanisms that might account for proposed stage-to-stage change. Another noteworthy stage theory, based on "knowing levels" that increase with reflective capabilities, has also proven itself worthy of the most serious attention from fellow scholars (cf. Campbell & Bickhard, 1986; Commons & Morse, 1988).

A contemporary theory with striking resemblance to the phase model presented in Chapters 3 and 4 is Annette Karmiloff-Smith's (1986) "Phase/process" model based primarily on work in language acquisition. In particular, Karmiloff-Smith makes dintinctions virtually identical to ours between stage, level, and phase, although the emphasis in her theory is more on process and less on changing structure, as is the case with our work. Where we tend to infer process from structure, Karmiloff-Smith tends to infer structure from process. To have reached such similar conclusions from such disparate data sources and analytic preferences suggests that the distinctions made in both theories may be quite deep, or maybe just a coincidence!

As for our own work on stages and transitions and how it has fared in the marketplace of ideas, Chapter 4 will review in some detail the efforts in our group to further refine and test our transitions framework. There have been others who have joined the fray, some applying our framework to other developmental domains, others putting the six-phase model (Chapter 3) to demanding empirical test. Chapter 4 was prepared to bring together in one place research bearing explicitly on work presented in the first edition of this book.

Chapter 5 summarizes more recent research done on what is best described as "expertise." Most of what is presented reflects efforts of our research group to expand into domains other than map drawing and also to conceptualize the work along lines more akin to what other researchers are doing. There is some discussion of research done in other groups which has been influenced by our work or was done with similar purposes; studies of programming in a language called Smalltalk are presented in the greatest detail. The purpose of this chapter is to bring the reader up to date on where things are currently going in our research program.

Chapters 6 and 7 are somewhat modified versions of works that have appeared elsewhere, but which seem to benefit from and enrich each other by appearing in the same place. Chapter 6 continues my tendency to theorize about creativity; this time the agenda is to use the reality of a changing cultural world of humanly crafted new things as an argument against increasingly strident radical nativist views that deny the very possibility of development, let alone its vital role in human experience.

Chapter 7 ("Cultural Organisms") presents some of my most recent speculations about context, environment, and how these forces seem to play their role in developmental change. In somewhat different form, it was presented at the 1989 Symposium of the Jean Piaget Society; Robbie Case was the discussant. Professor Case characterized the work as being poised between the past and the future, a good account of where I have come from and where I might be going at midcareer. Aside from the middle-ageishness implied by these remarks, they seemed to me at the time (and now) quite on the mark. The idea of a cultural organism created and maintained by people committed to the development of potential within a given field is one that has found a stable place in my thinking.

As for the work with prodigies, which was summarized in the first edition, it has been reported in detail elsewhere (Feldman, 1991; Feldman & Goldsmith, 1989; Goldsmith & Feldman, 1989). The idea of coincidence, introduced in 1980 in the prodigies chapter, is the central organizing theoretical notion of the prodigies research presented in *Nature's Gambit*. It continues to play a powerful role in my approach to development, and is reflected, albeit indirectly, in the work presented here. Research on prodigies does not have a chapter of its own this time.

Nor does the "craftsman" idea, which was explored in a separate chapter in the first edition. I would like to think that the notion of the child as craftsman was a predecessor and anticipated the current interest in "apprenticeship" (cf. Rogoff, 1990), although the line of influence is not altogether clear. I do think there is a good deal in common between the two notions, although the latter is based on more empirical work and grounded directly in Vygotsky.

UNIVERSAL TO UNIQUE TEN YEARS LATER

It remains to record a few reflections about how the central theoretical construct of *Beyond Universals*—the universal-to-unique continuum—has fared since 1980. I wrote then that I hoped that the face of developmental psychology would change as a result of bringing nonuniversal developmental domains into its mainstream. The push by Michael Cole, John Lucy, Robert Rieber, Aaron Carton, Vera John-Steiner, James Wertsch, and others to bring Vygotsky's work to the attention of western scholars undoubtedly has had greater impact, with our efforts perhaps helping move things along.

Where the specific influence of universal-to-unique can be documented, however, it seems to have made quite a difference. The fields of gifted education, creativity research, and art education have moved a lot in the past 10 years; at least some of the changes in these fields have occurred as a consequence of our work.

"Gifted" Education and Creativity

In gifted education, for example, there have been several recent major publications that show that the field has begun to recognize two important changes in how giftedness is conceptualized: the first is that giftedness should be thought of as domain-specific and not simply a general indicator of intellectual ability; and, second, that the course of the development of gifts must be understood if potential gifts are to be actualized in actual real-world achievements (cf. Horowitz & O'Brien, 1985; Reis, 1989; Sternberg & Davidson, 1986).

The field of creativity research, which has stood remarkably separate from giftedness work, moribund when the first edition appeared in 1980, has had a remarkable recovery. I made the case then that the field had to break out of its narrow trait-based conception of creativity and embrace a broader, developmental perspective in order to move forward. Fortunately, others were thinking along similar lines. And even more fortunately, the Social Science Research Council and the Andrew W. Mellon Foundation requested that I chair a Committee of the Council expressly for the purpose of rejuvenating and integrating these fields.

Along with fellow SSRC Committee members Jeanne Bamberger, Mihalyi Csikszentmihalyi, Howard Gardner, and Howard Gruber, and with important contributions at various points from Yadin Dudai, Helen Haste, Robert Siegler, and Robert Sternberg, we pushed hard in new directions. At the same time, some remarkable younger researchers were entering the field, most notably Theresa Amabile and Dean Keith Simonton, adding new social and historical dimensions to the developmental perspective of our group and the field. Robert Sternberg, as he has done so often, edited an important volume that showcased much of this new work (Sternberg, 1988). Vera John-Steiner's important work on writers kept the momentum going in case-study research (John-Steiner, 1985), and Jane Piirto (1992) has added a provocative attempt at review and synthesis of where the field is. In the meantime, West coast colleagues Robert Albert and Marc Runco put together a new journal (*Journal of Creativity Research*) and helped provide coherence and leadership for the newly energized field.

Although once again it is impossible to say just how much *Beyond Universals* had to do with the rebirth of creativity research, there is little doubt that it has occurred, and occurred along at least some of the lines laid down in 1980. As readers of this edition will see, I have in the meantime had some new thoughts about creativity, but this time I hope they are more forward looking. There is simply no need any longer to show why the previous research tradition has gone dry. From a personal standpoint, the new vitality and productive energy going into creativity research probably is the most gratifying change I have seen since 1980.

Art Education

In art education, universal-to-unique has been embraced (or at least accepted as important) by significant figures in two of the three major camps currently dividing the field. There are the DBAEers (Discipline Based Art Education aficionados), who believe that domain knowedge (e.g., art criticism) should be explicitly taught in the schools. An article called "A Framework for Educating Artistically Talented Students Based on Feldman and Clark and Zimmerman's Models" (1986) attempted to combine universal-to-unique with a framework specifically designed for art education purposes. I also tried to use the framework myself to think about art education in an article for a DBAE-sponsored publication (Feldman, 1987a).

A second group, the more expressively oriented art educators, have yet to embrace universal-to-unique, although I have not seen any nasty criticisms coming from that quarter either. It is perhaps safe to say that our work does not seem to threaten their view sufficiently to warrant much of a reaction. This is in a way ironic since it probably challenges traditional expressive art education as much as it does traditional cognitive developmental theory, as "The Child as Craftsman" (Chapter 6 of the first edition) makes clear. It includes the specific point that letting children do what they please is not an altogether fitting way to educate them.

There is yet a third group, the more skills-oriented art educators, who have shown some interest in universal-to-unique, enough interest to invite two papers into their literature (Feldman, 1983, 1987a). My impression is that this group has been largely eclipsed by its better financed and more aggressive brethren in the DBAE movement, but will probably continue to play an influential role in the field by pushing for a more solid theoretical and research base regardless of where the field goes. Universal-to-unique and our expertise research (cf. Chapters 4 & 5) should continue to make a contribution to this rapidly evolving field.

Educational Psychology

Another place where I hoped *Beyond Universals* would have substantial impact, but has not seemed to, is the general field of educational research. In fact, the book was not reviewed in education journals like the *American Educational Research Journal,* the *Phi Delta Kappan,* or the *Harvard Educational Review.* I did write a piece for the *Educational Researcher* that attempted to show the importance of nonuniversals and the universal-to-unique continuum for educational research (Feldman, 1981b); apparently the article was seen as sufficiently provocative to have Carl Bereiter respond to it (Bereiter, 1982; Feldman, 1982e). Not much seems to have come of this, however. Although there have been instances where the ideas of 1980 and 1981 have been used by others (cf. Strauss, 1987), the educational research community has seemed remarkably unmoved by our work.

Perhaps this is a healthy sign; the field of educational research is bustling along in its own way and may have no need to be discombobulated by the likes of a maverick developmentalist. Needless to say I think otherwise, and the chapter on expertise in this edition (Chapter

5) is in part an effort to capture the interest of educational researchers. Happily, there are a few encouraging signs that some of the leaders of that field have begun to think along similar lines (cf. Berliner, 1987). It will be interesting to see if in another 10 years the field of educational research has moved, and if so in what direction. Stay tuned.

Theoretical Issues

Finally, and somewhat sheepishly, I must admit that there have been a number of theoretical issues that were left unresolved in the first edition of *Beyond Universals* and that remain substantially unresolved. Although we in the Developmental Science Group (the name of our research group) have discussed many of these issues among ourselves, not much new writing has seen the light of day. I will mention a few of the more intransigent issues for the record, but must admit that less has been accomplished than I probably believed would be in 1980.

One issue that still plagues me is raised in the evolution chapter (Chapter 2), and it has to do with the assumption that culturally transmitted knowledge may eventually become biologically transmitted potential for spontaneously acquired knowledge. This Lamarckian sounding notion seemed necessary in order to complete the universal-to-unique continuum's function as the source of both the universal and the nonuniversal knowledge structures that humans acquire. How such a "changeover" might take place was and is beyond me. At a conference in the mid-1980s, the prominent geneticist Luigi Cavalli-Sforza suggested a modification to the continuum that placed everything but universals on one axis, and the universals on an axis perpendicular to it, finessing the problem.

Although I am not ready to do what Professor Cavalli-Sforza recommended, it did set me to thinking that it may not require a process other than typical variation and selection to explain how nonuniversal capabilities become universal, *if it only had to happen during one period in the far distant past.* In other words, if the universals of thought became universal many hundreds of thousands of years ago, then all of the current nonuniversal changes that must be considered as candidates for universal status are, relatively speaking, a drop in the bucket. It is not necessary for nonuniversal knowledge to survive the selection process because we have become adept at making it possible for virtually all of our species to acquire treasured knowledge through cultural means.

This would have the effect of reducing the advantage of individuals or groups who happen to have a knack for acquiring the knowledge in question, making selection based on that quality irrelevant to human evolution. So there may be no need to worry about nonuniversals becoming universal unless competitive advantages accrue decisively for individuals with a specific trait that leads to acquisition of vitally important knowledge, *and that cultural innovation is unsuccessful in widening the circle of qualities sufficient for acquiring that knowledge.*

We have, in a very preliminary way, begun to explore ways in which human groups are able to transmit capabilities from generation to generation in ways that are not based on reproductive combinations. We have called these processes "transgenerational influences" and have examined them in one extreme family, that of the violinist Yehudi Menuhin (cf. Feldman & Goldsmith, 1986). In truth, however, there is not much known about how such processes work and won't be until more information is gathered.

A second set of problems has to do with the nature of developmental domains, and how to distinguish one set of domains from another. The term *domain* is itself quite a problem because it is used in so many different ways by so many different people. Our continuum posits five distinct regions of developmental domains, but it has not specified in sufficient detail just what makes one region different from the others.

We know that universal developmental domains are acquired by all individuals and that they are stagelike, but little else has been specified about them, nor have we tried to make criteria explicit enough to test the possibilities against the criteria, as Howard Gardner has done, for example, with his multiple intelligences (Gardner, 1983). The same can be said of the other regions of the universal-to-unique continuum. For the concept of nonuniversal developmental domains to be of optimal use, further refinement in how to conceptualize a developmental domain will be necessary. As with the evolutionary question, we have done some preliminary work, but our efforts to date have not progressed as far as we hoped they would by this point.

One change in the universal-to-unique continuum that I have proposed adds a region between universal and cultural; I label this region "pancultural." It seems to me that there are domains like speech, music production, drawing, and dance that appear universally but which require *human cultures* for their development. In contrast to the Piagetian structures, which require only a natural physical world, pancultural domains require a human culture that presents the child with examples of the various domains. Children can learn pancultural domains reasonably well by simply being around and imitating others in their group.

The theoretical framework presented in *Beyond Universals* also suffers (in both editions) from not being presented in a formal way. This may help explain why reviewers of the first edition generally praised the writing style, but often criticized the loose quality of the claims. In recent years, I have been using a set of criteria for theories of development that I borrowed from William Kessen (1962), adapting them for the purposes of teaching courses in intellectual development at Tufts. Kessen proposed that any theory of development must explain *Beginnings, States of the Organism, and Transitions.* I have added to this list the criterion of *Ends,* not necessarily a specified endpoint, but at least evidence that the question of endpoints had been explicitly taken into account in the proposed theory.

In the case of universal-to-unique, it would probably benefit from an attempt to present its claims in relation to the criteria of beginnings, states of the organism, transitions, and ends. It seems on first pass to be strongest in relation to the two middle criteria, has the potential to respond to the question of endpoints, but has not specified in any satisfying way what is distinctive about universal-to-unique at the beginning.

There are, in addition to conceptual and theoretical issues like those just discussed, methodological problems that still pose formidable challenges. As the reader will see in Chapter 4, the ability to analyze much of our data has been limited by the lack of suitable statistical procedures. Although the work has proven to be of substantial heuristic value, its promise cannot be fulfilled until better analytic procedures and statistical tests are available.

Not long before his death, Lawrence Kohlberg invited me to his home in Cambridge to discuss theoretical issues of common interest. I had admired his work for many years, but had never had a discussion with him. We talked about what he meant by universal and what I meant by universal. He meant a sequence that is invariant across all cultural groups; I meant a sequence that is invariant *and* where it is guaranteed that everyone will traverse all of its specified levels. It was a wonderful exchange, one which reminds me just how generous, generative, open, and committed a theorist he was. Perhaps if there is a third edition of this work, or in some other place, I will be able to discuss in greater detail and with more precision than I can yet muster a more fully evolved theory of nonuniversal development, but that of course will be another book.

1

Universal to Unique—Mapping the Developmental Terrain

The primary aim of this chapter is to provide the reader with a relatively brief overview of the frame of reference that has guided our inquiry for the past several years—the idea that developmental achievements range from "universal to unique." Its importance lies in recognizing that there exist developmental domains which are not of the universal variety that have been the stock-in-trade of cognitive-developmental theory. The argument for proposing nonuniversal regions of development is straightforward enough: universal achievements are acquired under conditions so varied that they occur in all environments in all cultures, and while these achievements may be described in rich detail, the nonspecific nature of experience presumed to engender them makes them of limited value in examining the processes by which they are achieved. Moreover, much of what people come to know simply cannot be characterized as universal in this sense. "Nonuniversal" achievements, in contrast, provide us with negative cases (only some individuals acquire them) and demand study of the specialized environmental conditions (such as instruction and available technology) by which they are achieved.

The view we present rests on the untested premise that universal and nonuniversal domains share suffcient common attributes that both may be labeled *developmental*. We explore this premise by examining the assumptions of developmental theory as it now exists and by showing how these assumptions can easily be modified to accommodate nonuniversal developmental achievements. Before turning to this "universal-to-unique" framework itself, we must first consider a matter that is central to our enterprise: the place of stages in theories of development.

STAGES IN DEVELOPMENT

Much debate about developmental theory has revolved around the issue of stages. For some developmentalists a concept of stage is fundamental to the very idea of development. For others, stage is considered an impediment to understanding the nature of development. Whether for or against stages, every developmentalist must come to grips with the place, if any, of stages in the theoretical edifice. In the view which guides the work of this book, developmental stages are utterly central. We hasten to add, however, that the particular notion of stage used in this work is different in certain respects from any previous notion.

When one of us (DHF) was a graduate student at Stanford in the late 1960s, he was taught that the concept of stage was no longer useful—stages could not be tested empirically, were mentalistic and axiomatic, and were of no heuristic value in guiding the work of developmentalists. In particular, the notion of stage was said to be untenable because it assumed a coherent, homogeneous, internal organization that in all likelihood did not exist. Finally, and perhaps most difficult to accept, this internal organization was assumed to transform itself into a qualitatively different organization in some almost magical fashion. Even if such a reorganization as this could possibly take place, the argument went, it would most likely be physiological in nature and thus outside the realm of developmental psychology.

Compelling as these arguments seemed at the time, there remained the intuition that some notion of stage was essential to the developmentalist's work. Kessen had supported this intuition in a paper published in 1962, but just what notion of stage was called for Kessen did not say. In the early 1970s, John Flavell (1970, 1971a, 1971b) presented a similar viewpoint, but took it somewhat further. Flavell argued that the Piagetian all-or-none assumption for stage change was neither theoretically tenable nor supported by the empirical data, and he opted for a much more gradualistic, process-based concept of stage. Flavell protrayed the different ideas of stage change with an illustration similar to Figure 1.1.

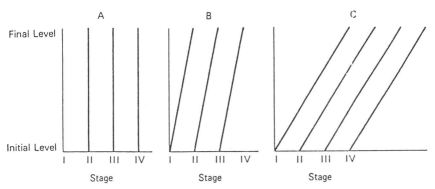

Figure 1.1   A representation of different notions of stage-to-stage movement (adapted from Flavell, 1971b).

The first illustration (A) in Figure 1.1 is of an early notion of stages which assumes both an abrupt change from stage to stage and the complete availability of all behaviors for a given stage from the moment of its onset. This notion of stages, which can be found as early as seventh century writings (Aries, 1962), has not been taken seriously in developmental psychology for some time. Nonetheless, as a caricature of stages, it serves as a useful starting point.

The second illustration (B) is Flavell's rendition of Piaget's view. This model assumes that the *capability* for all behaviors which reflect a stage is available at the moment of transition, but that the actual application of this capability to various problems takes time to unfold. Therefore, there is a gradual increase in the number of, say, concrete operational behaviors until a point is reached when all behavior comes to reflect concrete operations. This may take several years, as is the case with the various kinds of conservation which are acquired between about four and twelve years of age. But, as Flavell was moved to say, Piaget's view that this capability is complete when a single behavior reflecting the succeeding stage first appears is an untested and probably untestable assumption. Furthermore, empirical studies tend to indicate that mental organization is nowhere near as homogeneous or consistent as the Piagetian stage model would imply (cf. Turiel, 1966). Flavell therefore chose to present a much more gradualistic rendering, one like illustration (C), of how transitions between stages might actually occur. In this rendition, behaviors reflective of several stages are present at the same time; behaviors from new stages appear before the development of earlier stages is complete.

The concept of stage that we propose is based on Flavell's notion of stage construction as a gradual process, but to some extent our view takes the stage out of the child's "mind" and represents it as existing instead within a body of knowledge. In other words, when looking for the location of a stage ("Where would you find a stage if you were looking for one?"), theorists have tended to look for it inside a child's head. Piaget, for example, makes this argument:

> We have seen that there exist structures which belong only to the subject, that they are built, and that this is a step-by-step process. We must therefore conclude that there exist stages of development. (Piaget, 1970, p. 710)

While Piaget finds this logic compelling, other theorists have acknowledged that as long as stages are assumed to exist in the mind of a child, it is unlikely that we will ever be able to see what one looks like. Given this problem with traditional stage notions, we have found that concepts of development can be extended in useful ways when stages are defined not as holistic structures, but as levels of achievement within a specific field or domain.

Piaget's tendency has been to treat stages as independent of the content to which they are applied. It is clear, however, that stages of, say, map drawing are not the same as stages of general logical development, even though both are actively constructed by children. Yet by taking the location of a stage to be within a body of knowledge we do not mean to imply that the child does not participate in the qualitative changes we observe or experience in his stage to stage transitions. We do mean to suggest, however, that these successive constructions are linked in significant ways to the specific domains in which they are achieved (see also Turiel, 1977, 1983).

What is gained by conceptually placing stages within domains or bodies of knowledge? Why is it important to stop looking for stages exclusively within the child's head? It is important because critics of stage/developmental approaches have concentrated their arguments on the assumption of an internal, homogeneous, organized set of rules governing behavior (for example, Brainerd, 1977; Gagné, 1968). Charles Brainerd in particular has been unrelenting in his criticism of Piaget's concept of *structures d'ensemble,* the notion that a stage is a structured whole. Most of the empirical data seem to support Brainerd's view; a child at a single moment exhibits behavior reflecting several stages of development. In our own studies of map drawing, for example, it is rare for a child to exhibit reasoning from fewer than three of the six stages. Perhaps an even more compelling argument against a strict Piagetian interpretation of stage is the accumulated evidence that it takes children several years to achieve different concepts belonging to the same stage of development; a minimum of five to six years seems to be required for the acquisition of the various conservation concepts. Given such evidence it is harder and harder to argue that children are in the "same stage" from the appearance of conservation of number (at about four years) to the acquisition of conservation of area (which often does not appear until the early teens).

A critical aspect of the concept of stage we propose is that it does assume a structured whole, but not of the type that Piaget has proposed. Our notion of a structured whole is conceptually quite different from Piaget's in two significant respects.

First, we do not see structured wholes as ever existing in children's heads. Instead the structured whole represents the idea that a developmental domain can be characterized in terms of a set of idealized stages. The stages are ideal because the behavior of any given child (and the system that generates and governs this behavior) is never as consistent, orderly or stage-appropriate as the hypothetical ideal would predict. "Structures as a whole" therefore represents to us the ideal sequence of achievement in a domain of knowledge that never actually exists except as a model or template against which to gauge the actual behavior of actual children (this point is further elaborated in Chapter 3).

The second difference between our view of structures as a whole and Piaget's is that we do not see stages as restricted only to general, universal cognitive development. Indeed, we will propose that many domains of knowledge and skill may be fruitfully conceptualized as consisting of a set of ideal stages which are mastered in an invariant sequence. While the notion of a structured whole is thus at best loosely descriptive of a child's behavior, it is a powerful tool for conceptualizing the nature of the structure of developmental *domains*. It need not imply that any one person will ever behave exactly according to the ideal or hypothetical set of characteristics which comprises a stage. Such consistency could perhaps be artifically produced by designing a computer program to simulate behavior at a given level for a particular domain—for example, to play chess at the level of an Expert or a Master. The structure of chess (or any of many other domains) could therefore be seen as a series of increasingly sophisticated programs designed to play the game at succeeding levels. But the play of the machine would be much more consistent than any human being's play—and much less interesting.[1]

---

[1] As an expression of the view of stage to be taken in this book, the term *stage* itself will be generally used only to refer to universal reorganizations in thinking such as those described by Piaget. For all other developmental sequences the term *levels* is applied. Level is actually intended to be the more general term, with a stage being a particular kind of level (i.e., a universally achieved one). We are indebted to Deborah M. Levene of Tufts for suggesting this convention to us.

As does Piaget, we believe that structures are achieved through a "step-by-step" process. For Piaget, though, the incremental nature of the actual construction process contradicts the assumption of wholeness that is supposed to characterize the underlying system even at the first instance of more advanced behavior. Our view transcends this problem by using wholeness as a metaphor for characterizing benchmarks within domains, but not attributing this form of wholeness to the child's cognitive system. As we see it, the construction process is of the structures themselves, not of their application to various specific contents or problems, and the constructing is never of complete systems in a series of discrete jumps.

ASSUMPTIONS OF DEVELOPMENTAL THEORIES

We believe that, like the ancient all-or-none notion of stages, developmental views such as Piaget's (Piaget, 1970a, 1970b, 1971) require modification, elaboration and, to some extent, transformation if they are to continue to be useful. Simply reducing the number of assumptions about what can properly be labeled "developmental" accomplishes much of the necessary change. Currently theories of psychological development, it seems to us, share four basic assumptions which are outlined briefly below.

Universal Achievement. Simply stated, this assumption is that there are certain advances in thought which all children will achieve. It has been the major purpose of Piaget's empirical work, for example, to document the common achievements eventually attained by all individuals in all cultures. Piaget and his coworkers have thus attempted to isolate and describe those qualities that make us all cognitively part of the human family. From a developmental point of view, those aspects of thought which make us unique individuals have been of little interest relative to those aspects which we all share and which provide us with a common view of the world (Tyler, 1978).

Spontaneous Acquisition. The achievement of universals is assumed to occur *spontaneously*. By spontaneous the theories do not suggest that these achievements occur in the absence of an environment; this is certainly not Piaget's view. What is meant is that no *special* environment is required to guarantee that an individual will achieve a particular cognitive function or operation. Piaget uses the term "spontaneous" to suggest that children possess intrinsic tendencies to construct a view of the world and that sufficient environmental conditions in all cultures guarantee that, over time, each child will move through all of the stages and achieve all of the basic cognitive operations without specific interventions.

Invariant Sequence. A third assumption is that there are certain *sequences* through which all individuals must pass toward some final cognitive system (which in Piagetian theory is called *formal operations*). The steps in the sequence are usually seen as invariant (although not always, see Bart & Airasian, 1974); that is, it is not permissible for an individual to start at any step other than the first one, nor is it permissible for an individual to skip a step in the sequence. One begins at step one (in Piaget's scheme of things, at sensorimotor behavior) and moves through the succeeding steps in a prescribed order (for Piaget the order is: sensorimotor, preoperations, concrete operations, and formal operations). One does not skip stages and one does not move backward in the sequence.

Transition Rules. The fourth assumption of developmental theory is perhaps the most difficult one to describe: there are said to be transition rules governing movement from one stage in a sequence to the next. In principle these transition rules provide an explanation for how earlier steps in a sequence become incorporated into later ones. Stage one, for example, does not simply happen to precede stage two, sharing nothing in common with the latter; this type of description would be closer to a traditional maturationist view. Rather, the developmentalist argues that there are certain ongoing processes or mechanisms by which the steps in the sequence are first achieved and later reorganized as subsequent steps emerge. The fuel for these processes or mechanisms is the existing organization itself which is not only used as the basis for future steps, but which eventually comes to demand its own reorganization as it attempts to deal with the world's complexities.

The integration of earlier steps or stages into later ones through a set of transition processes is often referred to as *hierarchical integration*. A stage is not lost as the child moves to the next step in the sequence, but rather is transformed. The initial set of acquisitions and abilities is integrated into the succeeding set and in some important sense becomes part of it.

These are the four assumptions that seem to characterize most developmental points of view—universality, spontaneousness, sequentiality, and hierarchical integration through transition rules. These assumptions reflect the fact that developmental psychology has concentrated on understanding those changes in the child's behavior that occur without special environmental intervention. However, to provide a unifying set of principles for all of human intellectual development, cognitive-developmental theory has tended to ignore changes in thinking that fail to meet all four of the above assumptions (i.e., changes that are not inevitable, or do not occur spontaneously, etc.).

These assumptions have restricted the range of issues that have been viewed as "developmental," and therefore fitting for further study. Piaget, for example, has referred with derision to the preoccupation among American psychologists and educators with speeding up movement through the sequence of cognitive stages as "the American question," which he takes to miss the basic point of his theory. If one intervenes into the process then it is no longer "development" in Piaget's scheme of things. Similarly, trying to draw implications from Piaget's theory for curriculum formation is problematic because it seems futile to contrive a curriculum to provide conditions under which universal stages are achieved. These ways of thinking will be achieved naturally in any case. Therefore, to make contributions to curriculum development we may be inspired by existing developmental points of view, but for the time being we must seek guidance from elsewhere to build those specific curricula.

NONUNIVERSAL DEVELOPMENTAL DOMAINS

In light of the constraints of current cognitive-developmental theory, we propose to extend the theory in the following ways: by accepting only two of the four assumptions of the theory as is and modifying the other two assumptions by limiting their application. We continue to accept sequentiality and hierarchical integration as necessary characteristics of developmental domains, but we would limit the use of universality and spontaneousness as criteria for distinguishing developmental phenomena.

We propose that there are domains of knowledge acquisition that are truly developmental but have not been included in current theoretical treatments of cognitive development because these domains are neither universal nor spontaneously achieved. These nonuniversal domains are not necessarily mastered at the highest (or even initial) levels by all children in all cultures, nor are they achievements which can be acquired spontaneously, independent of the environmental conditions prevailing in a particular culture at a particular moment in time.

To provide some sense of the kinds of knowledge that nonuniversal domains might encompass we suggest the following provisional categories—these categories fall along a continuum from acquisitions that are universal to ones which are unique. We have already spoken of universals; they are the focus of developmental theory as we know it. As we move from universal achievements (such as conservation) to types of knowledge which fewer individuals will acquire, we begin to move along a continuum from universal to uniquely organized domains of knowledge (see Figure 1.2). These nonuniversal categories represent regions of cognitive achievement which satisfy the requirements of sequentiality and hierarchical integration, but which also require some form of outside intervention to facilitate acquisition.

Our aim here is to sketch major landmarks so as to convey the general lay of the developmental landscape rather than to specify details of the terrain. Our purpose is much like that of the early explorers of this continent who first charted the overall characteristics of the country and only later detailed the particulars. The difference is between noting that "there are some high mountains to the northwest" and that "the highest mountain in the northwest sector is 15,600 feet." In this same vein, we see the different regions demarcating the universal-to-unique continuum as provisional and approximate. They are not intended to suggest precisely where each region falls, nor even to provide clear boundaries between the various regions. With these remarks made, we now briefly describe these nonuniversal domains.

Cultural

There exist domains of knowledge that all individuals within a given culture are expected to acquire; these domains comprise the region of the continuum which we call cultural. Examples of cultural domains include reading, writing and doing arithmetic, understanding and drawing maps, and understanding one's political and economic systems. The expectation is that every child in the cultural group should be able to achieve a certain level of mastery of the designated domains, although not necessarily the highest level in each.

Obviously the domains which are important to master will vary from culture to culture, as will the level of expected achievement

Figure 1.2 **Developmental regions from universal to unique.**

within them. Equally obviously, for certain domains (such as mathematics) achievement at some level will be expected in many cultures, while for others (such as knowledge of democratic principles) achievement will only be required in some. Still other domains (e.g., certain religious observances, or techniques for navigation in sailing canoes) may appear as necessities in but a few.[2]

Discipline-Based

At the next major landmark are developmental domains that are based on mastery of a particular discipline. In some discipline-based domains such as chess or aviation, the different levels of mastery and the criteria for their attainment are clearly and explicitly established (e.g., Expert-, or Master-level play in chess). For other domains (such as medicine, carpentry, or political leadership) the levels of achievement are less clearly defined. One difference between cultural and discipline-based bodies of knowledge is that fewer people learn discipline-based domains than cultural ones. Primarily, however, the differences between these two regions lie in the extent to which the individual can exercise choice in selecting a domain to master and the extent to which one comes to share a distinctive way of thinking about the intricacies of the domains regardless of one's particular culture. Discipline-based thinking cuts across cultural boundaries; otherwise there could be no international chess tournaments or other forms of intercultural communication or competition within a discipline. As with cultural domains, instruction and a technology are part of the domains of this region.

Idiosyncratic

Still less frequently attained than discipline-based domains are those which lie in the idiosyncratic region of the continuum. Most idiosyncratic domains are probably actually subareas of a discipline, craft or profession. Not very many individuals within a culture will necessarily (or should necessarily) achieve a given level of expertise within such domains. Idiosyncratic domains represent one's specialty, one's *metier,* the particular work that a person chooses to master in a

---

[2] We should note that we do not use the terms domain and culture (or society) in a specialized or technical sense, but simply according to their everyday meanings. While anthropologists, sociologists, and others are more exacting in their use of these terms (cf. Geertz, 1973), our use of them here is conventional rather than technical.

particular way. Idiosyncratic though one's specialty may be, the process of mastering these kinds of domains is nonetheless a developmental one. If an individual elects to study mathematics he/she must begin at the beginning of mathematics and advance through its levels, progressing from novice mathematician to expert to master mathematician.

One of the most striking kinds of examples of idiosyncratic development is the child prodigy. Here we see youngsters who seem to connect with a domain in a most unusual way, almost as if they were pretuned to express their individuality through this one special field. Part of what is so compelling about performing at a very high level at a very young age is the apparent reciprocity between child and field. One gets the impression that such children were somehow destined to select a special domain by powerful natural and cultural forces. No matter how powerfully specialized or awesome a child's achievements may be, however, child prodigies move through the levels of the field to become specialists more or less as others do. What is so different about them is that they move at such an extraordinarily rapid rate. We consider the matter of child prodigies in more detail in Chapter 5. More typical idiosyncratic specialties are the particular subareas of a discipline practiced by adults (e.g., open heart surgery, Elizabethan music, Maserati repairs, patent law, ice sculpture, etc.).

Unique Achievements within Domains

Finally, moving as far from universal achievements as we can, we come to the region of unique developmental achievements. These represent a form of organization within a domain that has never before been accomplished in quite the same way. There is, to be sure, a certain axiomatic sense in which all behavior is unique, including all developmental changes; it is in the same sense that each of us is a unique physical organism. The kind of achievement we discuss here, however, goes beyond this sort of uniqueness. We propose that individuals may at times fashion out new levels of organization within a domain or, in the most extreme cases establish a new or radically altered domain by transcending the constraints of an existing field or discipline to establish a major new order. Those unique achievements that reorganize a body of knowledge are identified in our scheme as *creative* ones. From the many unique reorganizations of knowledge that occur, a small number which are perceived as particularly useful may eventually become incorporated into domains which enjoy wider popular exposure (see Chapter 2).

By including unique reorganizations in thinking, we have extended the range of developmental phenomena from universally mastered domains of knowledge to unique reorganizations of existing domains. But note that while all creative advances in thought are in some sense unique, not all unique advances should be called creative. Creative advances result in substantial new contributions to bodies of knowledge; most unique advances, in fact, do *not* do this and therefore are not considered here as creative.

ENVIRONMENTAL CONDITIONS FROM UNIVERSAL TO UNIQUE: CATALYSTS FOR REORGANIZATION

Flavell (1971a) observed that universal achievements emerge "assuming that the organism is a neurologically intact human being and assuming a *normal human environment*" (p. 122; emphasis in original). About this "normal human environment" Flavell said the following:

> I have trouble thinking clearly about the "normal human environment" part.... It seems to imply that there must be invariant features common to a wide range of...environmental objects and events...these higher order, invariant features which any and all possess constitute necessary nutriment or "aliments" for...development.... I personally take as a major objective for our field [i.e., developmental psychology] the search for possible *universal* outcomes of human cognitive development...which are common to all normal people in all societies....The [environmental] contributions to their genesis must consist of the aforementioned invariants of human experience....The [role of the environment]...is subtle and hard to conceptualize, but its conceptualization is a necessary task. (p. 122)

Flavell clearly sees the role of environmental conditions in bringing about developmental changes as a neglected but important topic. We offer a few suggestions below in the hope of moving toward a richer understanding of the conditions under which developmental advances take place. Not surprisingly, we extend Flavell's mandate to environmental conditions associated with nonuniversal as well as universal achievements. Our aim is to suggest some of the environmental conditions which may give rise to qualitative shifts in levels of development, whether they are universal or unique.

Universal Conditions

The environmental conditions that help to stimulate the acquisition of universal bodies of knowledge seem to be of two types: human conditions and nonhuman ones. An example of a nonhuman universal condition is the redundancy present in the physical environment, which leads the child to discover that the world consists of permanent, three-dimensional objects. Piaget has given considerable attention to such happenings, plotting sequences in the acquisition of the object concept, space, time, causality, and so on (e.g., Piaget, 1952/1963, 1954; Piaget & Inhelder, 1948/1967). Surely the fact that objects have weight and substance, that they drop to the ground, that they stand in topological relationships to one another, must provide experience necessary for building an adequate conception of the physical world. Also, regularities in time—changes during days, weeks, months, and years—are surely among the conditions that lead to temporal representation, causal inference, categorization, and so on.

While nonhuman conditions are usually external to the individual, human conditions include internal qualities of the changing individual as well as conditions created by social interaction with others. The facilitating effect of social interaction has been confirmed by recent research in moral judgment and conservation. This facilitation is particularly effective where a child at a lower level of development is confronted by others whose moral judgments are at the next higher level of the domain (e.g., Blatt & Kohlberg, 1973; Kohlberg, 1973; Kohlberg & Gilligan, 1974). Other researchers have demonstrated similar facilitating effects of social exchange with respect to the acquisition of conservation (e.g., Murray, 1972; Silverman & Geiringer, 1973) and map drawing (Levin, 1978).

These findings are consistent with Piaget's view that social interaction does not play a direct causal role in determining the nature of thought. Rather, in the course of social contact the child is confronted with a series of physical and social perspectives other than his own. Such conflicts are thought to motivate the child to seek a resolution of the disparate views, or what Piaget (1923/1974) called "verification" in his early work. By generating cognitive disequilibrium, the desire for change is energized:

> What then gives rise to the need for verification? Surely it must be the shock of our thought coming into contact with that of others, which produces doubt and the desire to prove....The social need to share the thought of others and to communicate our own with success is at the root of our need for verification. (p. 204)

Social interaction thus leads to motivation for the transformation of cognitive structures. In particular the desire to communicate with others and to have others accept one's views seem to energize the change process.

Other universal human conditions are more internally located. These include physical, perceptual, and neurological consistencies in response as well as regularities in bodily processes that may be related to time (e.g., sleep patterns), space (e.g., one's own movement and locomotion), and causality (e.g., crying), in much the same manner as are external patterns. Little more need be said about these universal conditions but that we know too little about them and we should know more.

Cultural Conditions

By definition, conditions that serve as catalysts for universally achieved thought patterns are available to all individuals in all cultures.[3] We believe that there are, in addition, sets of less pervasive conditions limited to members of particular cultures which give rise to mastery of the levels of cultural domains. Patterns of achievement and nonachievement for cultural domains are more varied than for universal ones. Perfectly normal members of a society may not achieve basic competence in all culturally valued fields, even in domains where competence is taken to be a critical aspect of cultural membership. Thus, the opportunities for investigating naturally occurring differences in cultural conditions and for examining the possible effects of intervention are potentially much greater than for universal conditions. One type of cultural condition has its roots in what Bruner (1971, 1972) has called culturally evolved "amplifiers" of human capacities. These amplifiers *carry* and *preserve* the knowledge that constitutes cultural domains of thought. The number and variety of cultural amplifiers is staggering: all of the symbol systems, models, tools, technology, and artifacts as well as the variety of cultural institutions and their products are examples (Gardner, Howard, & Perkins, 1974; Olson, 1974; Salomon, 1974, 1979).

A second set of powerful cultural conditions is the array of techniques involved in the *transmission* of knowledge. Although observa-

---

[3] It is true that there are instances where universal catalysts do not result in the formation of the related competencies, but these cases seem to involve organic causes (e.g., blindness, deafness), serious emotional disturbance (e.g., autism), or some devastating trauma (perhaps the result of an accident or an illness—for example, stroke or the side effects of medical procedures).

tion and imitation of an adult may be sufficient to acquire some of the simpler cultural skills such as bathing (Bruner, 1972), most such skills are acquired "nonspontaneously," that is, planned instruction using specialized techniques is requisite to their mastery. To be sure, schools and formal instruction by trained teachers have not existed for very long in human history, and much of what is learned about cultural domains may be acquired through other forms of cultural intervention (Bruner, 1972). Nonetheless cultural institutions, particularly schools, have been of major importance in introducing the child to the valued amplifiers of the culture, as Bruner has emphasized. Of special interest are the ways that instructional processes stimulate transformation and change in intellectual organization (e.g., Scribner & Cole, 1973). Despite centuries of experience we still know very little about why instruction works sometimes and not others, or about why some techniques affect some children positively and others negatively (Olson, 1972; Salomon, 1979).

Even one of our foremost thinkers about the nature of instruction, Jerome Bruner, frankly acknowledges that he has relatively little to say about the specific cultural conditions that might give rise to particular achievements. To the extent that he has written about this issue, Bruner's analysis tends to be in terms of general "cognitive conflicts" that must be stimulated as a precondition for intellectual advance. But as he notes, "the rub is that there are many cognitive conflicts...that do not lead a child to grow" as well as ones that do stimulate change (Bruner, Olver, & Greenfield, 1966, p. 4).

David Olson's recent work also considers the role of formal instruction in the development of knowledge and skill. In some of this research he focused on the concept of "diagonality" (Olson, 1970), or how the child learns to recognize and/or construct diagonal lines under varying instructional conditions. Olson has investigated with special care how the medium through which a concept is presented affects how well the child understands that concept (e.g., drawing, talking about, or building diagonals on a checkerboard). From this initial set of problems Olson has taken up the broader issue of why instruction works at all (Olson, 1972). Of particular importance in his view is that there are media-specific qualities in the transmission of knowledge (Olson, 1974). Although the underlying information or knowledge conveyed by various media may be the same (e.g., instructions presented via spoken words, sign language, or the printed page), they may not be equally effective in imparting that information because of fundamental differences in the media themselves (Salomon, 1979). The particular medium that carries the information has a structure of its own which is in part independent of the information it carries. If the knowledge transmitted through that medium is to be received, the child must be able to comprehend the structure of the medium along with the knowledge it conveys.

It follows that one fundamental purpose of instruction is to impart not only knowledge about the world but also skill in the utilization of various media. Noting that different cultures present the child with different information-carrying media, Olson (1970) has even defined intelligence as "skill in a cultural medium" (p. 193). Acknowledging that little is known about the processes through which skills in particular media are acquired, Olson speculates about the possible sources of skill in Euclidean geometry as an example:

> It is likely that the child's acquisition of skill in this medium has its beginning in such things as representational and geometric drawings, and building with blocks. As these skills are specific to our culture, people in other cultures or subcultures not sharing this medium can be expected to perform more poorly, as do, in fact...Kenyan children. (1970, p. 195)

Most cultural achievements require some form of instruction and, by virtue of being subject to modification and experimental control, provide a way to study conditions under which progress from level to level takes place. When more universal forces are at work, however, this is not a feasible strategy. The process of mastering cultural domains, then, is a layered one. The child's goal is to acquire some body of knowledge which is presented to him through some medium. In order to obtain the information, the child must first develop skills at extracting it from the medium in which it is embedded (Salomon, 1979).

Cultural conditions, then, tend to be those which directly instruct the child or which facilitate the acquisition of skills in a medium, facilitating (in Bruner's terms) the acquisition and use of a valued amplifier of human capabilities. As we have noted, though, we know very little explicitly about how this acquisition process works. If cultural domains are developmental, then it should be possible to learn something about how they are acquired by focusing on the environmental conditions prior to, during, and after a new level has been achieved. With this type of information we would then be able to specify which types of intervention might induce the cognitive conflicts that are likely to result in developmental advances and which are not.

In sum, cultural environmental conditions are different from universal conditions in that they are created, husbanded, preserved, and passed on by members of a culture. Many of these cultural conditions are transmitted through various media which have been evolved to amplify and extend human capabilities. They help organize and integrate the more spontaneously evolving concepts and ensure the acquisition of culturally valued knowledge that cannot be transmitted solely in the context of action. Tools, techniques, and models of aspects of reality are some of the ways in which knowledge becomes part of the cultural environment that is presented to the young.

Discipline-Based Conditions

Discipline-based environmental conditions may be distinguished in a number of ways from the other conditions discussed so far. In contrast to universal and cultural conditions, disciplined conditions help catalyze the acquisition of more advanced levels within a domain which are typically achieved by only a relatively small subset—sometimes a tiny subset—of the members of a given culture. On the other hand, disciplined conditions share with universal and with some cultural conditions the property that they are effective in facilitating such advance in practitioners from any culture. Professionals, students of an art or a craft, scholars, and tradesmen share with colleagues in other countries and in other cultures many of the skills and capabilities that are characteristic of their discipline. Needless to say there are also distinctive qualities to the expression of these skills; American Indian jewelry and Yemenite jewelry are both jewelry, but one would rarely be mistaken for the other.

It should be evident that disciplined conditions and cultural conditions overlap insofar as the exposure to certain discipline-based domains is available in many cultures. For example, there have been poets and musicians in virtually all known cultures; yet few in any culture will actually become poets or musicians themselves. We wish to focus for the moment on these and other disciplines whose acquisition would typically be considered optional within a given culture (i.e., where mastery is not necessary for participation in the culture).

Unfortunately, except for a few recent attempts in the field of the visual arts (e.g., Gardner, 1973; Getzels & Csikzentmihalyi, 1976) little is known about what makes a discipline a discipline, let alone how people advance through it. Our assumption that the acquisition of disciplines is sequential and hierarchical implies that they have distinct stages or levels of achievement. Master practitioners of the discipline might well be able to specify these levels (see Chapters 5 and 6). A paper appearing in a recent issue of the journal *Cognition* presents the sort of research that our conception of disciplined conditions seems to suggest. Hatano, Miyaki, and Binks (1977) studied the performance of expert abacus users for evidence that the techniques of calculation made possible by the device were eventually internalized by the users. Ten subjects at various levels of skill were given calculation problems with and without an abacus and were also asked questions both mathematical and nonmathematical in nature during their work. Imitative finger movements among abacus users of intermediate skill when solving problems without an abacus suggested that the technique of calculation utilized in the abacus was in the process of being "interiorized." Advanced users reported that they had used finger movements at an earlier time but no longer needed to do so. The "mature stage" users were also not disturbed in their calculations by prohibition of finger movement, nor by asking them to tap rhythmically, while "intermediate stage" subjects were. "In other words, abacus operation tends to interiorize into mental operation through a transition stage wherein the mental operation is not completely independent from the motor system and abacus-simulating finger movement gives important support" (p. 53). As the authors suggest, their results are quite suggestive of the development of levels of performance within this discipline, but "longitudinal studies are necessary to establish that individuals must make these qualitative changes" (p. 53). While mastering the abacus may not be the most compelling discipline to study, it does seem to meet our criteria as a discipline-based body of knowledge, and the results suggest that there are levels to the discipline that include qualitatively different ways of calculating.

A discipline has the effect of organizing reality, of suggesting certain possibilities and of foreclosing others. It becomes a set of controlling conditions in a person's psychological environment (Salomon, 1979). Indeed, the meaning of the term "discipline" implies that one's way of thinking, of organizing reality (or part of it) takes on a distinctive and traditional form as a consequence of acquiring that discipline. Moreover, individuals do not restrict their disciplined thinking to those problems which comfortably fall within the domain itself. When a disciplined way of constructing reality has become too confining, "breakthroughs" may be achieved by practitioners from other fields who apply a somewhat different perspective to longstanding unsolved problems (Ghiselin, 1952; Kuhn, 1962).

One of the advantages of studying developmental levels within a discipline is that most subjects are adults who can more readily reflect upon their experience (not always, of course; see Chapter 5). A second advantage is the likelihood that achievement of the levels within the discipline are compressed in time relative to the acquisition of broader cultural or universal domains; that is, more levels are covered in a smaller amount of time. In many disciplines one can, of course, continue reaching new heights for a lifetime, but the basic sequence of acquisition may not take as long as the acquisition of universal logical structures. This in turn offers the possibility of studying stage and sequence issues without some of the problems associated with more general developmental domains.

Metahobby. As a way of beginning to investigate further the nature of discipline-based bodies of knowledge, one of us (DHF) has given students at Tufts an unusual assignment; its purpose is to examine whether several fields are indeed developmental and are structured according to qualitatively different levels of achievement. The assignment is called "metahobby." The students (about 150 to 175 have participated thus far) are required to begin a hobby that they have always wanted to learn but have not had time to try. Their assignment for the semester is to spend a reasonable amount of time learning how to do something challenging with which they have had little experience. The only constraint is that the hobby they choose has to be sufficiently difficult that they are unlikely to master it fully in a semester's time. They are instructed to reflect upon the experience in a journal and try to relate their experience to developmental theory. And of course the "theory" these students learn is, more or less, the same one that is contained in this book.

It is impossible to tell the extent to which ideas about development are imposed upon the student's experience. The impression which emerges, however, is that the imposition, while no doubt a factor, is surprisingly minimal. Amazingly, almost all of the students thus far have been able to conceptualize their metahobby projects in terms of developmental levels and developmental transitions which seem quite plausible and natural. The metahobbies have ranged widely—belly dancing, ethnic cooking, sculpture, skiing, auto body work, calligraphy, radio broadcasting to name only a few. The range is remarkable but the common threads are, from our point of view, even more impressive. There is a real sense that the students' analyses are not simply a relabeling of experience. The notion of developmental levels and traditions within the variety of discipline-based domains selected seems to make a profound difference to these students as they reflect on their experiences. In other words, the approach does seem to lead to a different and fruitful frame of reference for organizing and understanding intellectual development, particularly in the nonuniversal domains that can be called disciplines.

Idiosyncratic Conditions

In the sets of environmental conditions considered thus far we have emphasized: (a) the importance of experience in the physical and social worlds, (b) cultural conditions and formal instruction, and (c) the meaning of acquiring a discipline. Moving from the universal domains, individual (internal) conditions become more crucial to the process of development in terms of both selecting domains to be mastered and responding to the available forms of instruction. Here, we focus on an even more restricted set of conditions which seem to have a unique personal flavor. The hallmark of these idiosyncratic achievements is the complimentarity between a field of endeavor and a set of individual predispositions or talents. As mentioned earlier, in some sense all individuals do what they do in unique ways, so there is an idiosyncratic aspect to all activity. However, *idiosyncratic conditions play a particularly crucial role when an individual has already progressed from novice to apprentice, to journeyman, to craftsman, to specialist, to expert, and is perhaps able to develop a singular expertise or preeminence in a field.* This progression conveys the development through levels we have in mind as an individual moves toward idiosyncratic expression within a domain. Obviously, when one has reached the most advanced level of a field, he or she shares with few others—or even no others—an individual way of organizing that field. Even when an individual never reaches the more advanced levels of a specialty, his approach or technique may be highly idiosyncratic.

The distinctive quality of idiosyncratic accomplishment in a domain is the extent to which achievement is a function of a highly specialized, joint set of personal and environmental conditions. Here the subtle interplay of individual and environment seems to reach its full expression. Perhaps the most telling examples illustrating such reciprocity between individual and field are to be found among child prodigies. Fascinating questions about sequence, mastery, the effects of instruction, predisposition to a field, and so on, tumble forth once the child prodigy has been provisionally admitted to the fraternity of developmentally lawful happenings. A paradoxical aspect of the prodigy's achievements is that they seem to arise with a minimum of formal tutoring, running counter to other cultural and discipine-based conditions which require prolonged and systematic exposure. These aspects of early prodigious achievement are less mysterious, however, when prodigies are conceptualized as examples of idiosyncratic developmental achievement for, as we shall see in Chapter 5, prodigies are actually no less (and perhaps more) dependent than others on appropriate environmental conditions for their achievements.

Another topic which, like early prodigious achievement, has tended to fall outside the boundaries of cognitive developmental theory is *creativity.* The same forces that lead us to extend developmental phenomena to include esoteric work within a discipline also impel us to consider creativity. Because creativity is discussed in detail in

Chapter 6, however, here we only mention that in accounting for creativity we must also extend our conception of developmental achievements since nontrivial creativity occurs only when a unique developmental advance within an idiosyncratic domain has been achieved.

Unique Conditions

For other developmental advances the fact of achievement is relatively straightforward to document. These reorganizations in thought are responses to reasonably well-understood problems, problems for which criteria of mastery and accomplishment are known. When a practitioner reaches the limits of his craft and yet continues to struggle with a problem that cannot be solved satisfactorily or an intention which cannot be suitably expressed, the likelihood of a unique reorganization seems greatest. In its more substantial forms a unique advance is made possible by truly transcending what has gone before, by appreciating fully the traditional importance of a problem and by sensing the limits of a known paradigm for dealing with it (Kuhn, 1962). By applying a combination of distilled experiences and knowledge to an unsolved problem an individual or group of individuals may move beyond the limits of existing knowledge in a way that changes their view of a field and reorganizes their way of thinking about it. This reorganization, if communicated to others, may become an important environmental condition itself, contributing to the achievement of the new level or reorganization by other individuals who have advanced to an idiosyncratic level of accomplishment in the domain compatible with the change. In other words, unique advances are most likely to themselves become incorporated into critical environmental conditions for facilitating developmental advances by others. By studying creative processes and products within this framework we may be able to understand better the conditions that give rise to unique developmental advances both remarkable and mundane.

CONCLUSION: RELATIONS AMONG
DEVELOPMENTAL DOMAINS

The universal-to-unique continuum represents the idea that many domains may be identified as developmental without having to be universally acquired. These different regions of nonuniversal cognitive endeavor meet the two key assumptions of sequentiality and hierarchical integration that we have suggested are necessary for a domain to properly be called developmental. The continuum itself is defined in part by differences in the kinds of environmental conditions which lead to each type of achievement and in part by the decreasing frequency with which advanced levels of each domain are achieved (i.e., by a set of regions which vary from achievement by virtually all individuals to achievement by perhaps a single individual), as in the case of powerful creative insights. Despite these differences, the regions of the continuum are similar in terms of the processes for advance from level to level within a domain. We would argue that the means by which individuals effect advances within domains of knowledge—the mechanisms of transition—are much the same for universal bodies of knowledge as they are for unique ones.

Once we have begun to make these conceptual links among the different regions of development and their domains, we are left with a number of questions. For example, are universal achievements prerequisite to all or only to some nonuniversal developmental achievements? Are universal domains the set from which all other domains are fashioned? Do the domains within the regions themselves constitute some form of a developmental sequence or are they organized in some other way?

In terms of the sequence of prerequisite functions it seems obvious enough that some of the universal achievements are necessary for cultural or more idiosyncratic pursuits to occur. Yet it does not appear that *all* universals need be acquired before *any* cultural mastery may take place. We are far from knowing, of course, but a reasonable guess at this point follows closely the line of argument put forward by Flavell (1971b). This guess is that achievement of at least certain elements of universal domains must precede initial mastery of aspects of cultural domains, but that there may also be parallel development in these two regions of thought. The same is true for cultural domains with respect to discipline, disciplined with respect to idiosyncratic, and idiosyncratic with respect to unique achievements.

Reaching the end or final level in a common domain is not prerequisite to beginning the process of mastery of a less common one, but it does seem likely that one cannot begin the latter until one has mastered at least some aspects of more basic, commonly achieved bodies of knowledge. It is not necessary, for example, to have grasped the full use of formal logic and reasoning to begin to learn to read, nor is it necessary to have mastered reading in order to begin to play the violin. It is necessary, however, to know that symbols can stand for things or ideas (a cognitive universal) in order for reading (whether words or music) to make any sense at all. And one can begin to play the violin only if one has been introduced to that part of cultural knowledge that makes violin playing possible. In a similar vein, Howard Gardner (1973) has argued that producing graphic art requires concrete but not formal operations and the Kohlberg group (Kohlberg, 1969, 1971) sees concrete operations as necessary for various levels of moral judgments or reasoning to occur.

When we ask the question about whether the domains in the less idiosyncratic regions of the continuum are included somehow in those of the more individualized regions, we face a thornier set of problems. In some sense and virtually by definition all other domains are dependent upon universal bodies of knowledge. Yet cultural domains are not really a subset of universal domains. While both are developmental in the sense that we use the term, cultural domains do not seem reducible to universal ones; there are universal aspects to cultural (and all other domains), but cultural domains also have their distinctive qualities as well. Cultural domains, however, do provide a set from among which disciplined, idiosyncratic and unique domains are fashioned. Perhaps this change from noninclusion in the case of universals to inclusion when we consider only the different regions of nonuniversal achievement is due to the increasing importance of individual qualities of mind and temperament in the selection and mastery of the more idiosyncratic domains. In fact, when we think about unique achievements we tend to think of them less as independent bodies of knowledge and more as unique *aspects* of an idiosyncratic domain (except, of course, in the extreme case of creative genius where a new domain may itself be fashioned). These rare instances of unique creative achievements are the cutting edge of new knowledge, some of which may even eventually become universal.

Thinking of a dynamic relationship between unique achievements and universal ones makes it possible to consider how the universal changes we have discussed come to achieve their status. A unique set of conditions gives rise to a unique mental reorganization of a domain in one or more human beings. If that reorganization is communicated or expressed in an effective way, it becomes a dark horse candidate for status as a universally important domain of knowledge. Thus a speculation can be offered: over evolutionary time *every* developmental advance may have once been a unique developmental advance. The unique advances of one generation have the potential to become critical environmental conditions for succeeding generations. It is this historical and evolutionary aspect of the universal-to-unique framework that is the focus of the next chapter.

2

Unique to Universal—
the Role of Novel Behavior
in the Evolution of Knowledge

Our purpose in this chapter is to further elaborate the universal-to-unique continuum by proposing another link among its various developmental regions. This is the link forged by time. The domains in the different regions share a common history, for they all originated from novel ideas—that is, they all began as novelties from the unique region of the continuum. Through the process of "cultural incorporation" of novel ideas described in this chapter, the various domains themselves may extend along the continuum, becoming bodies of knowledge to be mastered by larger and larger segments of the culture.

Each new body of knowledge begins as a unique reorganization of ideas by one or a few individuals. As these ideas become organized and reorganized, they are incorporated into the larger network of ideas. Over time, some sets become domains of knowledge and may begin to extend from the unique toward the universal regions. How far a domain moves toward the region of universal achievements (or whether it moves at all) is a function of the number, quality, stability, and utility of reorganizations it undergoes and also of the effectiveness with which these potential advances are communicated to others. Movement of a domain along the continuum is also a function of the extent to which the knowledge contained in a given domain becomes crucially important in some way to larger numbers of individuals over time.

The notion that a domain, once formed, may extend from the unique region of the continuum into one of the more universal regions reveals a number of characteristics of the continuum itself which are explored in this chapter. Perhaps the most important is that as a given domain develops, it may occupy a number of different regions along the continuum at various points in its history. This, in turn, suggests that domains located in different regions may represent expressions of the same processes of incorporation but at different points in the histories of the domains. Thus, universal and nonuniversal domains not only share attributes of having developmental levels and transition processes, but also share the common underlying process of cultural incorporation. What differs among the domains in different regions of the continuum is the span of time that this process has been operating and the importance (as of that moment) of the domain for human cultures.

NOVELTIES IN THOUGHT

A few years ago we asked a prominent Yale psychologist working within the Pavlovian tradition what research, if any, could be found in the literature of experimental psychology dealing with the issue of novelty in thinking. After a few moment's pause to consider the question, he replied that as far as he knew there really was not any recent work on the topic. He mentioned a few experiments from the 1940s having to do with problem solving and insight, making and breaking mental sets and so on, but said that on the whole nothing of any real significance had appeared in the literature during the past 30 years. He added by way of an exclamation point that there was more than enough to do just trying to understand predictable and mundane responses; as far as he was concerned, the science of psychology was by no means advanced enough to consider the problem of new responses.

We grant that rigorous experimental work on novelty in thought is well into the future, at least in the sense that our friend meant it. As the reader will see, some of the research reported elsewhere in this volume (especially in Chapter 3) begins an empirical line of study on the appearance and effects of simple novelties on individuals learning to master a particular cultural domain. However, for the present chapter, it would matter little if there were no work yet of an empirical sort; some important issues regarding the effects of novelties can be fruitfully discussed even though we are still in the dark about how novelties in thought come about. So for this discussion we take for granted that novelties in thinking somehow occur. It is what happens after they occur that is of interest. We are not so much concerned with what happens to the individual bringing about the novelty, but rather with what happens to the body of knowledge of which the new idea becomes a part.

Considering the effects of a novelty on an existing body of knowledge allows us to propose a plausible account of the origins and history of the universal-to-unique continuum. For the purposes of this discussion, a novelty in thought represents any idea (or ideas) that may have the potential to catalyze a reorganization in the body of knowledge. Not all novelties have equally powerful impact on their bodies of knowledge, of course. Novel thoughts can range from relatively trivial to relatively important in terms of their immediate or eventual impact on the domain.

Viewing the production and incorporation of novelties as part of a process of evolution within bodies of knowledge creates an interesting change in the character of the universal-to-unique continuum. With the addition to this notion, the continuum changes from a set of relatively stable categories or regions as presented in Chapter 1 to a representation of a dynamic process which has been captured at a particular moment in time. The domains which occupy the different regions may differ with time as they become more and more relevant to the functioning of the larger community, extending toward the universal end of the continuum. New elements are continuously entering the system at the unique end, and these become potential catalysts for reorganizing domains. Over time it may become increasingly important for some bodies of knowledge to be understood and mastered by more and more members of a culture. These will be refined and simplified so that they can be more effectively communicated. As this happens the domain itself develops, extending from the unique and idiosyncratic regions of the continuum toward the more universal ones. Each domain of the continuum may thus be seen to be more ancient than its neighbors to the right and more recent than its neighbors to the left. Over eons of time the novelties in thinking produced by countless individuals and shared with countless other individuals have been winnowed down to those that remain as the accumulated knowledge passed from generation to generation.

Novelties that effect changes in existing bodies of knowledge (or establish entirely new realms of endeavor) are to be our focus of interest (i.e., we are concerned with novelties that have significant impact). More frequent, but of less interest here, are advances which allow individuals to reconceptualize various domains of knowledge for themselves. While they are related, novelties that transform domains of knowledge and novelties that transform individuals' understanding of existing domains are not precisely the same. Thus, novelty can be considered within two contexts, both of which are "historical" in some sense. First, novelty may be judged in relation to the previous experience of an individual. Every behavior is novel to some degree as it never exactly replicates earlier ones, but we also judge novelty in terms of how unprecedented a given behavior is for a particular individual.

The second context within which novelty is judged is the field (or fields) of knowledge; we call this the context of the domain. Often the individual believes his behavior to be novel in relation to both contexts when in fact it is only novel in relation to his own experience—this is a form of egocentrism. Egocentrism of this type is typical of the universal cognitive changes that characterize development during the course of childhood. The changes allow the child to see new vistas opening as he develops more and more powerful cognitive structures, and he often feels as if he were the only person to ever have experienced the attendant alterations in thought and perception. And these changes unquestionably do reveal new vistas for the child, even though the adult knows that they are actually familiar views to fellow travelers of more advanced years.

From the point of view of a 6-year-old child the experience of reorganizing a universal domain, say seeing the conservation of a continuous quantity problem for what it is—a sleight of hand played on us by our own perceptual systems—may be as powerful relative to his own developmental level as evolving a new explanation for ion exchange in chemical reactions may be to a chemist. The 6-year-old's insight, however, has no direct implications for the domain, nor for the universal-to-unique continuum. It does assure us that yet another child has achieved yet another advance in his thinking, and this may mean that later on when he has mastered the levels of his specialty he may produce something of significance for his field. But a child's achievement of concrete operational thought has no direct implications for the future of the domain of logic. In contrast, a new explanation of ion exchange might stimulate a reconceptualization of certain chemical processes, and would thereby become a candidate for inclusion in the evolving body of knowledge about chemistry.

A Puzzle

As a domain extends toward the universal region of the continuum its transmission depends less on special attention from agents of the culture such as parents, teachers, priests, mentors, family members, older peers, and so on. And yet earlier, as the domain became more important for the culture, *more* attention had to be paid to make sure that as many members of the society as possible mastered its knowledge.

It is not clear just what accounts for the fact that certain kinds of knowledge are eventually acquired without specific environmental intervention, when at an earlier time a substantial amount of attention had to be paid to ensure their transmission. It seems that individuals must at some point have evolved a predisposition toward acquiring universal bodies of knowledge (e.g., time, space, and logic) and that this predisposition is now part of the biological inheritance of every human being. We know that by the time a domain has reached universal status it must be possible for virtually all of us to spontaneously acquire the valued knowledge. This suggests that the environmental conditions which support the acquisition of that knowledge are sufficiently varied and readily available that everyone will naturally encounter some of these conditions in their transactions with the environment.

This, to be sure, is a very different pattern from what seems to happen in nonuniversal domains. Unlike universally acquired domains of thought, the acquisition of nonuniversal bodies of knowledge is not necessarily supported by powerful tendencies which are part of one's biological heritage. These bodies of knowledge cannot be acquired through the normal, everyday experiences which seem sufficient for catalyzing the acquisition of universal domains. For those domains which extend into nonuniversal regions of the continuum, cultural resources must be brought to bear to teach them in some deliberate, systematic manner.

Lamarckian as it may seem, the capability to acquire certain levels of knowledge for certain domains must eventually become transmissible from generation to generation by some biological process. For example, some time long ago someone (or some few individuals) must have discovered the concept of number. Explaining this concept and illustrating its importance to one's peers, and later one's children, would have been no small feat. Now an understanding of the notion of number is quite a basic cognitive achievement, and provides the foundation for an understanding of mathematics and other domains (Gelman & Gallistel, 1978). We cannot yet begin to explain how a domain shifts from cultural to universal, that is, how it changes from a domain that is mastered only with the aid of some specific form of instruction or other intervention to a domain for which individuals are predisposed to master its contents without any deliberately imposed intervention. Nor can we explain how the original creative insight, say that the number of objects in a collection remains the same regardless of the physical shape of the collection itself, initially comes about. For now we must take these processes as given and direct our attention to those aspects of transformation and change about which we can say something more specific.

By doing so we follow a tradition perhaps best exemplified by Darwin's work. Darwin's thoughts about evolution rested upon the notion of variation despite the fact that he was never able to describe the mechanisms that produced it. Once presented, however, his notions about evolution guided the search for the mechanisms of variation. If we can show how novelty affects the process of developmental change, perhaps others will be stimulated to search for a plausible mechanism to explain how a novelty in thought is produced in the first place (Gruber & Barrett, 1974).

Since we have mentioned Darwin, we should note that much of our thinking about novelty and its effects on bodies of knowledge has profited from drawing analogies to biological evolution. The role of novelties in the process of extension of bodies of knowledge from unique to universal seems to us analogous to the roles of gene mutation and recombination in biological evolution. This line of speculation is not unprecedented, having been advanced as a model for the evolution of scientific thought (Campbell, 1974, 1975; Popper, 1959).

The basic outline of the argument is that novel thoughts are subject to "selection pressures" which are similar in some ways to those that operate in biological evolution. This similarity allows one to think of novel ideas as fuel for a mechanism for changing the structure of bodies of knowledge over time, and for influencing the importance of the domain for a culture. We do not embrace this argument without reservation; indeed some have argued that it is a precarious position to take (cf. *American Psychologist,* 1975, *31*(5), pp. 341–384). With full appreciation for the limitations of such an analogy, we hope to show that the comparison of variation, selection, assimilation, transformation, and maintenance in biological evolution provides a fruitful way to think about the role of novelty in the evolution of bodies of knowledge.

THE ANALOGY TO BIOLOGICAL EVOLUTION

It seems to us that selection and "incorporation" of novelties into domains of thought which, in turn, come to be mastered by larger and larger segments of the culture may occur by a mechanism analogous in some ways to that of natural selection. This analogy has been suggested before in several contexts. As noted above, Campbell (1974, 1975) and Popper (1959) have used the analogy in discussions of the progress of scientific knowledge. Also, 30 years ago the neurophysiologist R.W. Gerard (1946/1952) proposed the analogy of novelty to mutation, invoking "imagination" as a cognitive process equivalent to the spontaneous alteration of genetic material:

> Imagination, not reason, creates the novel. It is to social inheritance what mutation is to biological inheritance; it accounts for the arrival of the fittest. Reason or logic, applied when judgment indicates that the new is promising, acts like natural selection to pan the gold grains from the sand and insure the survival of the fittest. Imagination supplies the premises and asks the questions from which reason grinds out the conclusions as a calculating machine supplies answers. (p. 227)

Gerard thus compares imagination to mutation and reason to selection, arguing that some novel ideas which are candidates for inclusion in a body of knowledge eventually prove to be useful and some do not. It is the role of reason, or judgment, to decide which are which. In biological evolution, selection works through a reproductive advantage for those individuals who display certain behaviors (or physiological or morphological characteristics). In the evolution of bodies of knowledge, selection works through the active incorporation or rejection of novel ideas into domains of knowledge; the impact of the selected novelty is to make the knowledge carried in the domain more important to the culture at large. Some initially novel ideas or behaviors influence a field of knowledge in such a way that their inclusion becomes important for the further development of that field and these further developments may, in turn, make it important that more and more members of the culture learn some of the contents of the domain.

It is likely that at least since the beginnings of human tool use some novel ideas and behaviors have been recognized as important and valuable. New contributions have been incorporated into existing bodies of knowledge and skill and, when integrated into an ongoing tradition, have become part of the accumulated knowledge and wisdom that we identify as part of culture. On some basis that we do not fully understand decisions are made by parents, educators, clergy, and others that certain information must be passed on to future generations through socialization and instruction. Other knowledge is judged less important and less effort is made to ensure that it will be transmitted.

While there are interesting similarities between the processes by which novel ideas are incorporated into the knowledge base of a culture and by which physical and behavioral characteristics are selected, they are also different in important ways. These differences also merit our attention. For example, the two differ strikingly in the mechanisms by which change occurs as well as in the speed with which changes are effected.

Biological evolution is an extremely slow process spanning many generations; it operates at the level of the individual organism by favoring certain individuals with slightly higher rates of reproduction and survival of offspring. In contrast, cultural evolution may proceed at a far faster rate; a new discovery or idea can revolutionize a field of knowledge in a matter of a few years. Furthermore, the selective advantage conferred by novelties is more likely to occur to groups rather than to individuals and through mechanisms that are quite distinct from those considered to be normally involved in biological evolution. These differences notwithstanding, processes of biological and cultural selection are not totally distinct. Indeed, they are inextricably intertwined.

For example, Dobzhansky (1962) and others (e.g., McClearn, 1972; Wilson, 1975) have noted that it is naive to maintain that cultural achievements occur only after biophysical evolution is complete—the two processes occur reciprocally. In a related vein, Cavalli-Sforza and Feldman (1973a, 1973b) have begun developing a quantitative model for genetic inheritance that includes a cultural component. They suggest that cultural factors contribute to the phenotypic development of each individual, primarily through the influence of parental phenotypes on the child. Although conceptual and empirical work relating cultural to biological change is not widespread, there does seem to be increasing recognition within the biological research community of the necessity to consider those cultural factors that may affect the course of biological evolution.

THE ROAD FROM UNIQUE TO UNIVERSAL

Figure 2.1 represents the universal-to-unique continuum, adding several features regarding the effects of novelties. Most unique reorganizations of domains by individuals fail to impact on a wider audience. This may happen for a variety of reasons. Such novelties may not be communicated to others or perhaps are communicated ineffectively, expressed in terms that are idiosyncratic, obscure or arcane, may be of no real interest, or may be just plain wrong; these constitute the

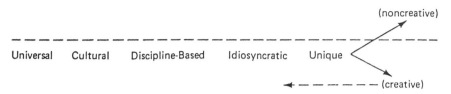

Figure 2.1   The universal-to-unique continuum illustrating extension of a domain after creative reorganization.

category of noncreative novelties in Figure 2.1. By "noncreative" we simply mean that a particular novelty, however unusual, daring, expressive, satisfying or individually meaningful, does not contribute in any significant way to others' understanding of a field. Because they are not perceived as useful, noncreative novelties simply tend to fade out of existence, as the culture makes no effort to ensure that they are acquired by members of the society.

Only a small proportion of the novelties that are produced are creative; once expressed, they are recognized as useful by other individuals and are adopted by them. Creative novelties thus contribute to the accumulated knowledge of a field. A unique novelty begins its trek toward universality at the point when it is perceived as creative—when individuals other than its originator find it to be a useful idea, when it fills a gap in existing knowledge, or when it opens up new avenues of thought. Only a tiny number of novel thoughts are ever perceived as useful at all, even a tinier number continue to be useful for very long, and even a smaller number yet become continuing parts of an evolving field. For every plausible atomic theory developed there must have been many more explanations of the composition of matter that were eventually discarded.

When a novelty becomes a significant part of a domain or body of knowledge, its fate and the fate of the field of which it is a part become linked. When the novelty stimulates a reorganization in the body of knowledge as a whole two events take place. The domain is reconsidered and reevaluated within the larger culture, and the novelty sheds its uniqueness as it becomes integrated into the domain—even while transforming it.

Figure 2.2 illustrates the proposed relationship between time and domains occupying various developmental regions. Universal achievements have been part of the human cognitive repertoire longer than cultural, discipline-based, idiosyncratic, and unique ones; Figure 2.2 plots the history of a single developmental achievement that has become universal. It may take a very long time for a novelty (and its

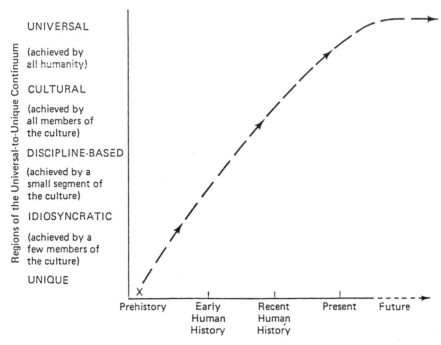

Figure 2.2   History of a developmental novelty from first occurrence (X) to extension into the universal region.

domain) to extend into the cultural and universal regions of achievement, if this actually occurs at all.

The speed of incorporation and extension does not necessarily *have* to be slow, although this may be the rule, particularly as the domain extends into the cultural region. An example where communication of a novel achievement was relatively rapid and its assimilation into a body of knowledge almost immediate was Linus Pauling's presentation of the structure of RNA:

> During the summer of 1937 I devoted a good part of my time, perhaps half-time for a few weeks, to the attempt to find a way of folding polypeptide chains that would account for the x-ray pattern of keratin. I worked a little on the problem during succeeding years, and, of course, we had a large program of experimental investigation of simpler substances, amino acids, and peptides, going on. I think that it took me about a day to discover the alpha helix in the Spring of 1948, when I settled down to work on the problem again.

David Olson comments:

> Yet in the space of a brief scientific report, which could be read in about 15 minutes, he was able to describe his discovery to the scientific community. What had taken Pauling years to learn took colleagues and students only minutes. (both quotes from Olson, 1972, p. 9)

If a novelty transforms a body of knowledge and skill in the way that Pauling's certainly did, it is likely to be incorporated into the field almost immediately. Other sets of ideas, also novel, will be discarded or ignored if they are not perceived at the time as valuable. The long period of obscurity of Mendel's formulation of particulate inheritance illustrates how novel reorganizations may fade if they are not perceived as important for a body of knowledge.

If, upon incorporation of the novel idea a field of knowledge becomes more valuable, complete, interesting, or germane to some aspect of living or knowing, it may be deemed important that larger and larger numbers of individuals learn about it.[1] Thus, depending on the perceived significance and communicability of the reorganized domain, a society may place greater emphasis on becoming proficient with the new knowledge; this is typically accomplished through instruction.

For example, in the 40 years or so since computers were invented hundreds of people in this country have learned how such machines operate and many thousands have learned to use them to perform calculations. This latter group (which includes the authors) is able to make use of the computer as a tool without having to know its theoretical underpinnings or its more technical aspects. This has been made possible by increased communicability of knowledge and better instruction in how to use the tool. Other (more specialized) professionals who learn the technical aspects of computer use not only can keep current machines functioning but can try to improve their design. Because knowledge about computers is perceived as important for some segment of the society (and also for the smooth and efficient functioning of the society itself), it becomes the task of the culture to find ways to instruct key individuals to use the technology of computers.

---

[1] It should be evident that very little is known about the factors that contribute to the "perceived significance" of an idea at a particular point in time. This problem is of course worthy of the most careful study.

Some bodies of knowledge may become so integral to operating successfully within a society that virtually all members of the group are expected to achieve competence in these domains; these were called cultural domains in Chapter 1. In Western societies simple arithmetic and communication skills (e.g., reading and writing) are examples. Such capabilities as these may have once been achieved by an exceedingly small "educated" proportion of the human population, but over time they have become so basic that they are integral to cultural membership. As the technology and pedagogy of a body of knowledge become more powerful, more varied ways to achieve mastery are made available, and more and more members of the society can acquire the valued knowledge. A program like "The Right to Read" is a recent example of an attempt to extend the tool of reading to a greater number of members of this society.

The circumstances under which various epistemological advances or achievements are found valuable (become "selected for") are not well understood. It is possible that for bodies of knowledge which have become very valuable to the culture—those that all members of the society must learn—pressures to acquire the knowledge take place at both the individual and the cultural level. Pressures may be brought to bear against those individuals who have difficulty developing these critical abilities by identifying them as "abnormal" in some way; possible forms of such pressure could be ostracism, ridicule, segregation into institutions. Pressures on the society may lead to efforts to devise more ways to transmit the knowledge, resulting in a wider range of environmental conditions supporting the mastery of the domain. At some point along the way biological processes may "take over" by selecting against those individuals who do not seem to be predisposed to acquire the valued skills through the range of environments available (and adequate for most people). In practice, this may mean that there is selection (in terms of reduced fitness) against those who do not seem "educable" with respect to the desired ability (Dobzhansky, 1970). Selection would operate against those individuals who did not possess a predisposition to construct the skill from the existing environmental inputs.

It is possible that cognitive abilities which are initially nonuniversal might become part of the human biological program by a process that Waddington (1953, 1957) has called genetic assimilation. This is a mechanism by which a characteristic which is initially expressed only by certain individuals in response to certain changed environmental conditions becomes programmed into the genomes of more and more members of succeeding generations; the characteristic changes from being environmentally induced in a few members to becoming biologically programmed and elicited in many individuals without special exogenous treatment. Wilson (1975) has suggested that human social behaviors may have evolved in this way. Whether by Waddington's mechanism or some other, a major change in the manner of transmission of knowledge takes place when a domain extends into the universal region.

Simply put, our argument is that the selection of novelties over evolutionary time occurs at every point along the continuum from unique to universal; in the few most successful instances, the novelty (and its attendant domain) travels the entire route. In the process, there is a shift from deliberate, systematic instruction to transmit the body of knowledge to a spontaneous (most likely biologically supported) predisposition in the individual to construct the knowledge from his or her everyday experiences in the environment. Although most novel ideas at the unique end of the continuum never become part of the universal human repertoire, a small number that are valuable for one purpose or another will be incorporated into the body of knowledge and will begin to extend into the more universal regions of the continuum. This incorporation process does not have to be a conscious one in the same way that biological selection is neither conscious nor deliberate. Novelties in thought which are likely to be valuable in the sense intended here are expressed in the form of various tools, technologies, communication skills, and conceptual models that members of a culture learn to use. Given sufficient importance for human adaptation, a few novelties will eventually become part of the human program, as common across cultures as within them.

PROGRESS OF NOVELTIES OVER TIME

To carry the discussion of incorporation a bit further we consider additional aspects of the process. Emphasizing the dynamic aspect of development draws attention to the fact that any description of intellectual skills and capacities can provide only a "stop-motion" picture of intellectual development. We cannot know for sure what bodies of knowledge our species will develop in the future, nor precisely what human abilities existed in the past; we can, however, speculate about the history of knowledge based on our assumptions about its dynamic character.

Figure 2.3 is an attempt to convey the sense of continuous movement and ongoing change that emerges when a temporal component is added to the universal-to-unique continuum. Our earlier illustration

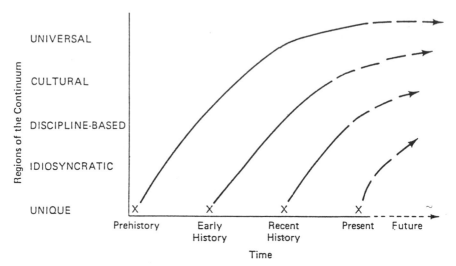

Figure 2.3   The extension of novelties (and their domains) as a function of the historical era in which the novelty first appeared (X).

(Figure 2.2) showed the hypothetical history of a developmental novelty which has become universal. In that example we assumed that the first appearance of the novelty must have occurred many thousands of years ago for the incorporation process to have had time to do its work. Consider for a moment the fact that novelties in thought are occurring all the time, novelties that are unique in only a statistical sense as well as those that are truly creative. Sometimes novelties occur which transform ideas from trivial to practical. For example, Leonardo DaVinci had invented the bicycle except for a mechanism that transfers energy from pedals to wheels. What was perhaps a whimsical notion became a practical one with the achievement of a technological advance (i.e., a pedal-drive mechanism), although many years later.

Figure 2.3 simulates histories of developmental novelties which appeared at various points in human history, including the present. The leftmost curve is the same as in Figure 2.2; it indicates the history of a developmental novelty that appeared at some early point in history and that subsequently extended into the universal region of achievements. The other curves show the progression of unique achievements which occurred later in human history. The process of cultural incorporation—of communication and selection—begins anew for each novel behavior or idea. If the novelty is valuable, it begins the long journey from unique to universal, from unusual to common expression, from environmental to biological transmission. The ellipses are included in this figure to suggest that the entire process is a continuing one. However crudely, Figure 2.3 tries to capture the dynamic quality of the process of cultural incorporation.

In the idiosyncratic and unique regions of the continuum a relatively large amount of planned intervention is required for the achievement of more advanced levels of mastery of the domain. At all points along the continuum, however, the role of environmental conditions on the acquisition of knowledge is crucial. What changes as the domain extends toward the universal region is the "naturalness" of the environmental input and the proportion of individuals mastering the body of knowledge. The amount, variety, and quality of instruction carried on in a culture is an indication of the number and variety of unique developmental achievements that have become requisite to full participation in the social life of the culture.

HOW MIGHT NOVELTIES OCCUR?

In his mid-20s, Charles Darwin signed on as the naturalist for the HMS "Beagle" and spent the next five years sailing around the world gathering notes on the variety of natural forms he encountered. It was this voyage and his response to it that made manifest Darwin's dissatisfaction with the creationist explanation of how the earth came to be populated by living matter. Darwin saw a plausible alternative to the theory that a Divine Creator had produced the enormous variety of life forms he encountered during his voyage. For example, in the Galapagos Islands Darwin saw a multitude of avian species that seemed pecularily suited to their unusual and varied environments; it occurred to him that reciprocal relationships between environments and the kinds of organisms populating them must exist, and that these very relationships might explain the origin of new species (Gruber & Barrett, 1974).

Although we have taken no voyage comparable to Darwin's, it occurred to us that the variety of human inventions seems in its own way as overwhelming and inexplicable as the infinite variety of life forms that Darwin saw. Just as Darwin rejected Divine intervention as an explanation for the relationship between organisms and environments, we were compelled to see novelty as the natural consequence of individuals' intellectual interactions with their environments rather than as a miraculous and inexplicable cognitive gift.

As to how the individual actually *produces* novelty, while we do not know very much about it, two requirements seem crucial to the process: a new insight into some aspects of the problem (Feldman, 1974; Henle, 1975), and a reorganization of a field as it exists, which allows the individual to produce new combinations of reorientation toward old facts in one which has been documented by many inventors, and will be taken up in greater detail in Chapter 4. Familiar examples are Watson and Crick's construction of an intertwined pair of spiral staircases, which in turn stimulated them to seriously consider a double helical structure for DNA, and Kekulé's dream of a snake turning to bite its own tail, which led him to consider a ring structure for the benzene molecule rather than a chain.

Considering these two requirements of insight and reorganization in terms of our analogy to biological evolution, an "insight" might represent genetic mutation or reorganization, and the reevaluation and reordering of existing knowledge might refer to selection processes favoring the new genetic structure. It is important to recognize that there are limitations to the amount of change or novelty that a system can sustain in either biological or cultural evolution. Those genetic mutations which are radically atypical generally result in such drastic dysfunctions of the organism that it does not survive. Furthermore, some genetic reorganizations (inversions, for example), seem to be far more frequent than expected by chance, while others apparently cannot physically occur (Dobzhansky, 1970). In like manner there are clear limitations on the degree to which a body of knowledge can be successfully extended or reorganized. Those discoveries that move so far beyond the current state-of-the-art of a field are often considered unintelligible and dismissed as useless or even crackpot. While such ideas do not cause the "death" of an entire body of knowledge or render a person nonviable in the same way that certain mutations or recombinations of genes do, novelties in thought which are too far in advance of their time may "die off," sometimes to be "resurrected" at a later point in time when they fit more closely into the prevailing paradigm of a domain. Leonardo's fantastic inventions, Aristarchus' computation of the earth's circumference (Thrower, 1972), and the Arab invention of algebra, are examples of novelties that were available long before any widespread appreciation or practical need for them existed. They are examples of a mismatch between the appearance of a novelty and a society's readiness for cultural selection and incorporation. Only those discoveries which make sense to others and which are comprehensible extensions of existing knowledge will have a chance of reorganizing their associated domains and being incorporated into more universal regions of cognitive achievement.

Human invention can thus be viewed as having much the same

place in the evolution of bodies of knowledge that gene mutation and reorganization have in the evolution of biological characteristics. Novel behavior assumes great importance because it represents the most powerful psychological force in the formation and evolution of human cultures, particularly in the evolution of cultural bodies of knowledge. Without the continued production of novel ideas, the diversity of intellectual endeavor which it ensures would disappear. Mayr (1970), Dobzhansky (1970), Clarke (1975), and others have argued that the maintenance of genetic diversity is extremely important for the evolutionary success of any species; an underlying flexibility is essential in order to survive and adapt to changing environmental conditions. This seems to be no less true of ideas than it is of genes.

The message seems clear. Diversity both within and across bodies of knowledge should be valued and encouraged, or as Clarke (1975) has expressed it: "We should, perhaps, ask for polymorphisms in our institutions to match the polymorphisms in ourselves" (p. 60). Maintaining diversity of intellectual endeavor seems of paramount importance, since often what is required for survival is change that responds to uniquely human dilemmas. It can be assumed that within limits a society producing a greater number of usable novel achievements will be better off than a society producing fewer, for it will have the capability for continued evolution and may be better able to respond to changing environmental conditions.

CONCLUSION

Young Charles Darwin was overwhelmed by the variety he found in nature. We are overwhelmed by the variety of achievements and inventions that we have found in human thought. That we would find Darwin's explanation for the evolution of species a fruitful analogy to pursue in making sense of the evolution of bodies of knowledge should not be surprising. And Darwin was not unaware of the possibility of our analogy; Gruber and Barrett (1974) have shown that from the very outset Darwin included man and his unique mental powers in his musings about evolution. Our discussion of novelties is in keeping with this Darwinian tradition; it is an attempt to make human behavior more comprehensible by considering it as part of a natural process. Where there are living beings there is novel behavior; when these living beings are human some of their novel behaviors catalyze reorganizations in culturally valued bodies of knowledge. This is a most startling fact of mental life. The function of novelty in human behavior is to provide the raw material for the evolution of developmental domains, of bodies of knowledge and skill.

In this chapter we have proposed that, over time, novel ideas may become incorporated into the mainstream of human thought so that what is a unique achievement today may be a universal one in the far-flung future. Whether or not this observation turns out to be true in some scientifically defensible sense, it leads to some interesting implications for developmental psychology. The view of the place of novelty in the evolution of knowledge offered in this chapter leads to the proposal of plausible time bound relationships among domains of knowledge at all points along the universal-to-unique continuum (cf. Chapter 3). These connections remain to be made fully explicit, but the sense of the extension of domains over time from unique to universal should be clear.

It can be reasonably said of Darwin's insights about evolution that they lessened the remarkableness of humanity when man became simply another expression of a natural process rather than a special creation of God. Similarly, it can be said that our discussion of the evolution of knowledge may also detract from man's "special place" in nature. By viewing the production of novelties as a normal aspect of human behavior they lose some of their mystery, as do the individuals who produce them. On the other hand, the processes through which novel thoughts are expressed become even more remarkable as they become more comprehensible.

It is perhaps accurate to say that in the future, when we reflect upon creative works, greater credit will go to the countless individuals who have contributed to and husbanded the smaller, cumulative achievements of earlier generations, but who themselves never shared center stage with those fewer, more remarkable individuals responsible for major new syntheses or discoveries. While the view offered here may detract a bit from a *specific* individual's achievements, it seems to us to enhance the overall achievement of humanity.

Our guess is that the dynamic process of evolution of domains of knowledge sketched in these pages makes things a little less mysterious but no less awesome. It is as if Loren Eiseley (1946), in discussing the incredible improbability of life existing on other planets in anything like the form it does here, had added cultural as well as physical factors to his equation. He did not, but the case for human uniqueness and creative accomplishment is, if anything, strengthened by the observations put forward here. We cannot help but believe that Eiseley would have agreed.

3

Individual Developmental Transitions— A Film Metaphor

In Chapter 2 we were concerned with the fate of a cognitive novelty after it had occurred and had begun to be communicated to others. The purpose there was to present a plausible history of the universal-to-unique continuum: where it came from over eons of time, what kinds of cultural selection processes might have governed its growth and where it might be headed in the future. We did not worry a great deal about how *individuals* came upon novel ideas. Yet is is of course true that every novel idea must come from the mind of someone. In this chapter we examine the general set of processes that govern the production of new ideas. These processes are sometimes called *transition mechanisms* because their function is to transform mental organizations (Flavell, 1971b; Kessen, 1962; Langer, 1969a, 1974). As we noted in Chapter 1, an assumption about the universal-to-unique continuum is that fundamentally similar transition mechanisms govern movement in all of its regions. In this chapter we illustrate these transition processes with reference to relatively mundane reorganizations in thinking; in Chapter 6 we will look at the more powerful reorganizations which may contribute to our store of knowledge. Reorganizations in regions of the continuum other than the unique may be less dramatic than those which revolutionize whole bodies of knowledge, but they reflect a set of processes that are occurring continuously during an individual's lifetime—in all kinds of transitions.

We chose an analogy in Chapter 2 based on biological selection processes to express and explore ideas about the history of the universal-to-unique continuum. For somewhat similar purposes we elect here to use the device of metaphor. The metaphor pursued in this chapter is that of a motion picture film. Ideally, we would like to have a camera able to record every individual reorganization in every region of the developmental continuum. Needless to say we have no such camera, but if we did we would probably begin by focusing on one region, or perhaps even select a single domain within that region so our enterprise would be less overwhelming. This is (metaphorically speaking) what we do in this chapter. We attempt to shoot two films of transitions in a single domain—map drawing. While the images thus produced do not reveal the actual mechanisms that govern reorganization, they do reflect the consequences of this process in rich enough detail to guide the search for more adequate accounts of the mechanisms themselves. In tracing the sequence of transition states as a child moves from level to level in map drawing, we will glimpse: (a) the *conditions* that give rise to novelties, (b) the *changes in organization that seem to accompany* novel behavior, and (c) the *consequences* that follow from getting a foothold in the next level of the domain.

Before we get too far into the discussion, we want to assure the reader that our efforts are based on data gathered on children's map drawing over the past several years. What we present therefore is not a flight of metaphorical fancy—although we confess that there are fanciful aspects to it—but rather an attempt to use the idea of a motion picture film to organize our data and to guide theory construction.

The first film uses group data to construct a sequence of steps in the transition process that is consistent with theory as we understand it and predicts reasonably well changes in map drawings for individual children. The second film takes a closer look at some more subtle changes that give rise to the general picture constructed with the group data.

Not surprisingly we choose to focus our efforts on capturing certain specific changes in map drawing that seem theoretically important. In the first film our metric is a shift in "modal level," an approximation to the traditional definition of stage and stage change. The second film examines specific changes in the map drawings, for example, from representing buildings "straight on" to representing them in consistent 90° perspective (i.e., from above). This kind of change reflects movement to a more advanced level of spatial representation.

If 90° perspective is the first problem that the child has solved at a higher level, this kind of change comes as close as anything in our data to what seems to be meant by a developmental "novelty." Taken together the two views of change in children's map drawings aid our understanding of developmental transitions as continuous transformations in the organizational state of the child's mind.

Before we present our two films, it is necessary to place them in their proper theoretical context. For this purpose we will review some of the thinking of Piaget and others in the cognitive-developmental tradition about the problem of developmental change. We will assume that the reader is familiar with the basic ideas in Piaget's system (for those unfamiliar with Piaget's work, we recommend Cowan, 1978; Flavell, 1963, 1977; Ginsburg & Opper, 1979; or Gruber & Voneche, 1978). A second purpose in reviewing Piagetian and neo-Piagetian research on developmental change is to introduce some of the concepts, measures and techniques used in gathering the data upon which our film efforts are built.

PIAGET ON CHANGE: AN OVERVIEW

It was Piaget who is credited with discovering that child thought is not simply an imperfect copy of adult logic, but rather a series of qualitatively different "logics" each consistent within itself, but different from adult thought. Moreover, Piaget argues that these stages in cognitive development are neither biologically programmed nor given by the environment, but instead are *constructed* or created by children as they actively attempt to understand the world. They cannot be given by the environment because at times they are factually incorrect (preschoolers often believe that the moon follows them around, that the wind is alive, and that dreams come in through the window at night). Nor are they innate because these "wrong" ideas are later given up. To illustrate the process of construction, Piaget tells this story about a mathematician friend of his:

> When he was four or five...he was seated on the ground in his garden...counting pebbles....He put them in a row and he counted them...up to ten...and started to count them in the other direction....Once again he found ten. He found this marvelous that there were ten in one direction and ten in the other direction. So he put them in a circle and counted them in both directions and found ten....So he put them in some other direction and...in some other arrangement and kept counting them and kept finding ten. There was the discovery that he made. (Piaget, 1964; in Gardner, 1978, pp. 231–232)

And exactly what was discovered? Piaget asserts that it was neither a property of pebbles (i.e., not given by the environment) nor a property of his friend (i.e., not biologically given), but instead a property of the action of ordering: specifically that the sum is independent of order. An action, then, clearly requires something to act on and someone to do the acting. In the absence of either there is no knowledge created or constructed; in the coordinated presence of both there is cognitive development.

Within Piaget's framework every action (or perhaps transaction is a more descriptive term) has two aspects: adaptation and organization. Adaptation, which refers to the interplay between a child's cognitive system and his experience, in turn has two complementary aspects: *assimilation* and *accommodation*. Assimilation refers to "taking in" the environment and relating it to existing mental models, while accommodation is noticing aspects of experience which are *not* easy to interpret with existing models and changing the models to effect a better "fit." Roughly speaking, assimilation is the "molding of experience to fit the mind" and accommodation is the "molding of the mind to fit experience." Each process operates only in conjunction with the other; neither ever operates in total isolation. Organization may be understood as the strictly internal parallel to adaptation. Not only do the cognitive models assimilate and accommodate to each experience, but they also assimilate and accommodate to each other. The results of this "mutual assimilation and accommodation" among mental models are coherent, well-organized ways of thinking. Piaget calls them *les structures d'ensemble* or "structured wholes," and for him they are a defining characteristic of cognitive developmental stages.

Structures d'ensemble are at the heart of Piaget's theory. The child is neither a blank slate nor a solipsist but rather a *scientist*. He is constantly building models of the world and testing those models against his experience, often in ways that facilitate changes in the models themselves. These changes, Piaget argues, are universal, invariant, and spontaneous. Each successive set of models is a coordinated mental system that grows out of, enriches and incorporates aspects of previous stages to generate a more powerful and more satisfying overall system.

Conditions Giving Rise to Change

Why is it that cognitive systems change? *How* do they change? *When* do they change? For Piaget the why question is not a question at all. Asking why cognitive systems change is much like asking why a fish swims or why lungs breathe. Swimming is part of what it means to be a fish and breathing is part of what makes a lung a lung. Swimming and breathing are two functions which help to define fish and lungs, respectively. From Piaget's biological perspective the motivation to function is not a separate force which requires separate explanation, but rather a part of the inherent nature of the structure itself. It is the nature of fish to swim, of lungs to breathe, and of cognitive structures to change. Thus for Piaget the why question is really contained in the how question, and the answer to the how question lies in describing structures and functions.

The structures in Piaget's framework are of course the stages which characterize human cognitive development from infant sensorimotor intelligence through adult formal operations. The functions most directly related to change are assimilation and accommodation. How do assimilation and accommodation facilitate development? Simply stated, every assimilation is accompanied by a complementary accommodation, and every accommodation is cognitive growth which makes possible new assimilations, further accommodations, and so on. This dynamic interplay of assimilation and accommodation is called *equilibration* and is seen by Piaget as the fundamental mechanism of cognitive developmental change. When appropriately discrepant, new or unexpected experience upsets equilibrium (upsets the balance of assimilation and accommodation), facilitating cognitive activity aimed at restoring equilibrium and leading to intellectual development. In this "dialectical" fashion, new intellectual abilities solve old problems and also make possible the appreciation of new ones in a dynamic, never-ending process.

While we have not directly addressed the when question, Piaget would probably argue that the answer is implicit in the above discussion. Structures are likely to change when they are in disequilibrium, when the assimilation/accommodation balance is upset. And this is about as far as Piaget goes in detailing the specific conditions giving rise to change. To be sure, if one is concerned with only those changes which are universal, invariant, and spontaneous, then describing the stage sequence and declaring an inherent, progressive force toward the final stage might be considered an adequate treatment of the change process. But because we are concerned with changes that are neither universal nor spontaneous, we see a more elaborate treatment of disequilibrium as crucial to our work (see also Langer, 1969a, 1969b, 1974; Strauss, 1972; Turiel, 1969, 1974). We have found it useful to distinguish at least three aspects of disequilibrium: one related to adaptation (external), one related to organization (internal), and one which Langer (1969a) has called the "energetic parameter" of disequilibrium.

External Disequilibrium. When a child confronts and tries to deal with an environmental event, adaptation occurs. If the child's current models of the world permit interpretation of this experience with relative ease (i.e., if it can be assimilated without significant changes in the models themselves), the cognitive system remains in relative equilibrium. If it is too discrepant to be processed at all, the child will ignore it as best he can. In contrast, there sometimes occur situations where an event is sufficiently novel such that no readily accomplished interpretation is possible within the bounds of the existing cognitive system. If this discrepancy is recognized and responded to, the result is external disequilibrium. We call it external disequilibrium because the source (the "perturbation" in Piaget's terms) is external to the child. The disequilibrium itself, of course, derives from the interplay of child and environment, from attempts at adaptation.

Thus, external disequilibrium arises from experiences which are sufficiently discrepant to facilitate significant accommodation and restructuring of a child's cognitive system. Exactly what constitutes "sufficient discrepancy" and "significant restructuring" are very difficult and largely unresolved issues. Typically, providing an experience which requires thinking skills characteristic of a more advanced developmental stage, followed by evidence that the child begins to reason at that stage, are criteria for restructuring taking place. Many Piaget-based training studies use this approach and criteria such as these (see Brainerd & Allen, 1971, or Flavell, 1970, for reviews).

Internal Disequilibrium. In contrast to external disequilibrium with its focus on adaptation and child/environment interplay, internal disequilibrium refers to the child's intellectual organization itself. It reflects what might be called contradiction or competition among the child's alternatives for dealing with experience. For example, logical inconsistency between two cognitive rules or models, if recognized by the child, would be an instance of internal disequilibrium.

While Piaget has written about internal equilibrium, internal *dis*-equilibrium has not received as much attention. This may be in part because internal disequilibrium is somewhat difficult to reconcile with Piaget's notion of *structures d'ensemble.* A stage is a structured whole, so the argument goes, and because children are "in" stages, their mental organization should reflect that same unity of process and product. Variations in consistency, *les décalages,* have been called by Piaget (1971) a "negative" aspect of development, a nuisance to him in his search for universal, integrated structures. But such variation need not be a negative quality, particularly when considered as a possible impetus for the child to build new cognitive systems. About this possibility we will have more to say later.

The Energetic Parameter. An obvious difficulty in moving from the world of theory to the world of children's behavior is that even the most cleverly encouraged putative contradictions between child and environment, or among child-produced responses, may not be noticed—let alone be used—in the creation of new structures. Therefore, recent treatments of disequilibrium and developmental change have begun to emphasize the child's realization that "something here doesn't quite fit." Langer (1969a) calls this realization the "energetic parameter" of disequilibrium and describes its importance as follows:

> Here the concern is with the affective character of disequilibrium between mental acts as a source of cognitive reconstruction....Piaget presents evidence that suggests the child must be cognitively "ready" to assimilate contradictory information and *to feel that something is wrong,* if there is to be any cognitive reorganization and development. (p. 30; emphasis added)

The idea of wanting to make things fit as a source of motivation for intellectual achievement appears often in the psychological literature; it is generally called *intrinsic motivation* (see Deci, 1975, for a review of related work). Most approaches, including Piaget's, emphasize the importance of "optimal discrepancy"—neither too little nor too much—but nowhere in the literature is there much detail about how to arrange this match (Hunt, 1961). Finer grained analysis of internal, organizational aspects of a child's developmental state, we believe, may provide a way to predict the set of conditions that will energize the child's system and prepare it for progressive developmental change. Our vehicle for approaching these issues empirically has been children's map drawing.

MAP DRAWING: A NONUNIVERSAL DOMAIN

Map drawing is an especially appropriate domain with which to begin the study of nonuniversal domains and the conditions under which their stages or levels are achieved. Although Piaget and Inhelder (1948/1967) used map drawing to study universal aspects of spatial reasoning development, there is considerable evidence that modern cartographic skills are acquired neither universally nor spontaneously, and mapping techniques are undeniably a creation of culture. Yet research by Piaget and others (e.g., Feldman, 1971b; Feldman & Markwalder, 1971; Snyder & Feldman, 1977) does indicate that map-drawing ability progresses through a hierarchical and invariant sequence of levels. Map drawing, then, is an example of a culture-linked, nonuniversal developmental domain, one which has evolved from a discipline-based domain to its current cultural status over the last five or six centuries. In the 15th century few individuals could read geographic maps and even fewer could construct them (McLuhan, 1964). Today, the basic principles of modern cartography are easily communicated, and maps have become commonly available in many cultures (though the science of cartography remains a discipline and retains its esoteric aspects).

Additionally, the production of a map calls upon a variety of spatial and logical-mathematical skills—for example, topological, projective, and Euclidean concepts and how to use them to represent geographical features. As a task which requires the coordination of these concepts, map drawing may be used to diagnose both the developmental level of several different sets of skills as well as their integration into a representational system. For this reason, Piaget and Inhelder (1948/1967), in a book on spatial reasoning development, used a map-drawing task to summarize the trends they had noted on other tasks:

> In practice, the construction of a [map] entails (1) the selection of a particular point of view, together with certain pictorial conventions intended to express it....(2) A system of co-ordinates—whose function should be self-evident—along with the implied concepts of straight lines, parallels, and angles. (3) Reduction to a specific scale, which entails the concepts of similarity and proportion. Hence the construction of a map incorporates in a single entity all the concepts examined [in the previous 13 chapters] and at the same time shows how they are related to one another. (p. 426)

In studying a map drawing, then, we are able to gather information about the child's developmental level in handling numerous aspects of this domain—perspective, spatial arrangement (e.g., a system of coordinates), proportion, and the symbolic (i.e., pictorial) conventions through which they are expressed. From that same drawing we can also evaluate the way in which these several aspects are coordinated into a representational system.

Finally, before describing the map-drawing task we have used in our research, we note that mapping may be considered to be one of the categories of cultural conditions mentioned in Chapter 1 and also similarly described by Piaget and Inhelder (Inhelder & Chipman, 1976). Learning to draw a good map involves using shared conventions for representing, organizing, and communicating the features of a geographical landscape.

Mapping, then, is a symbolic model for representing and transforming parts of reality, a cultural amplifier in Bruner's terms (cf. Chapter 1). It is a system of rules and procedures which draws on a variety of spatial and logical skills, requires their integration and coordination, and does so in a way which could hardly occur spontaneously.

A Map-Drawing Exercise

The mapping exercise we have used requires the child to draw a map of a miniature village landscape, one similar to the small models used by Piaget in his research. Since our work gives greater attention to symbolization than did Piaget's, the landscape model we use is constructed from relatively realistic model railroad paraphernalia rather than from the more stylized trees, buildings, and so on, used by Piaget and Inhelder (see Figure 3.1). The children draw only with a pencil on an eight and one-half inch square paper, which we provide.

In their study of maps produced by similar procedures, Piaget and Inhelder describe the development of map drawing as the successive coordination of two sets of correspondences between a model lanscape and the map: (1) LOGICAL-MATHEMATICAL correspondences concern the way in which logical classes of objects (e.g., houses, trees, etc.) and numerical collections (e.g., *three* houses, *ten* trees, etc.) are represented. As we shall see, a given drawing may emphasize shared logical qualities without regard to number, include both logical and numerical correspondence or, at the most primitive level, be essentially devoid of either logical or numerical correspondence. (2) SPATIAL correspondence concerns the representation of objects as they are integrated within an overall spatial framework (i.e., how well the sizes and distances on the model are maintained on the child's map. On a good map the objects correspond both logically and numerically and are arranged so that spatial relationships are properly maintained as well. The successively more sophisticated attempts to achieve this coordination have been cast by Piaget into a six-stage developmental sequence. An adaptation of that sequence (Table 3.1) guides our scoring procedures. Figures 3.2 through 3.7 provide examples of map drawings generally representative of each of the six developmental levels outlined by Piaget.[1] The maps reproduced in Figures 3.3 through 3.6 were drawn by children in our studies; those in Figures 3.2 and 3.7 have been modified somewhat for illustrative purposes.

The *level one* map in Figure 3.2 shows priimitive logical correspondence to the landscape model; there are some trees and buildings

---

[1] We say "generally representative" of each level because none of the examples is a "pure type." Each of these maps is predominately at one level and shows more characteristics of that level than of other levels, but all exhibit aspects of several levels or what Piaget has called *décalage*.

Figure 3.1 The landscape model photographed from about 45 degrees.

Table 3.1   Levels of spatial reasoning development as revealed in map drawing (adapted from Piaget & Inhelder, 1948/1967)

Level 1: No spatial correspondence except for a few elementary proximities

Characterized by child's inability to distinguish between spatial proximity and logical resemblance or between spatial separation and logical difference. Yields objects on map which do not appear on model and objects on model which are not represented on map. Arrangement appears virtually arbitrary.

Level 2: Partial coordination.

Characterized by recognizable but inconsistent logical and numerical correspondence. Spatial correspondence often confounded with logical resemblance or limited to small groups of proximal objects and isolated left-right relations without an overall spatial plan. Representation limited to one dimension (i.e., uses frontal view) with detail and proportion essentially unrelated to model.

Level 3: Midway between partial and beginning of general coordination

Characterized by inconsistent coordination (i.e., reasonable logical and numerical correspondence but with a mixture of perspective (e.g., frontal, 45°, 90°) and viewpoints), in poor but recognizable proportion to model. Larger groups of objects now linked together to produce primitive overall representations of model, often with "photograph-like" detail.

Level 4: Beginning of general projective and Euclidean coordination

Characterized by items in good logical and numerical correspondence and arranged according to a crude two-way system of reference (i.e., width and depth) with a consistent 45 degree or 90 degree perspective. A legitimate two-dimensional representation of the model often with some evidence of abstraction, but with as yet inaccurate scaling—relative sizes of objects often proportional, but distances (especially heights in the 45° perspective) remain distorted.

Level 5: Mastery of distances and proportions

Characterized by complete coordination of logical and numerical with spatial correspondences. Although not formally scaled with metrics and fractional reduction, an adequate diagrammatic representation of the model. A consistent 90 degree perspective with clear evidence of abstraction and symbolization.

Level 6: The abstract plan with metric coordinates

Characterized by complete coordination, totally accurate scaling, a consistent 90 degree perspective, and use of abstract symbolization.

---

represented as well as some crisscrossing lines which might be roads or perhaps a road and a river (which do intersect on the model). Numerical correspondence is entirely absent, and spatial relationships are limited to elementary proximities such as the crisscrossing lines, the buildings on the ends of what could be a road, and the large, centrally located circular object. The trees are represented in a vertical line indicating that logical resemblance has here completely overridden spatial correspondence. In short, although there is enough in the way of correspondence to suggest that this is a map of the landscape rather than a picture that has been simply made up, we can say little more than that. The young map maker producing a level one

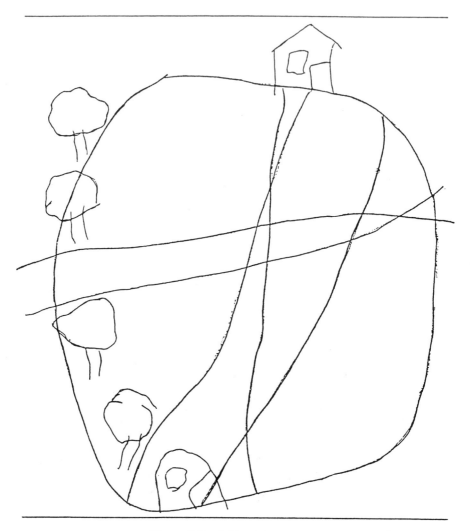

Figure 3.2   A level one map.

drawing has only begun to grasp the idea that a map and the place being mapped must somehow correspond.

The major advance of map drawing at *level two* (Figure 3.3) is that there is evidence of logical, numerical, and spatial relation between landscape model and map. However, they tend to be treated in relative isolation with first one aspect being emphasized, then another. The ability to integrate the separate sets of correspondences simultaneously is poorly developed. For example, Figure 3.3 shows the hill, lake, and river each marking an edge of the map, but only the river

Figure 3.3   A level two map.

marks the appropriate edge. Similarly, the bridge is part of the road, but the river does not pass under it; instead the road seems to go on right into the lake! There are some trees on the hill and some more in other places, but both numerical and spatial correspondence are imprecise. There are buildings in only three of the four quadrants, and they are represented identically and idiosyncratically. The central rotary is missing entirely, and while each house is surrounded by a fence, there are two separate fences rather than a shared one as on the model. Finally, the map is largely in "front-on" perspective, almost as if one were standing on its bottom edge, and proportion is poor—notice that one of the vehicles and several trees are shown as large as the bottom-most building.

Figure 3.4   A level three map.

As logical, numerical and spatial correspondences begin to be coordinated at *level three* (Figure 3.4) larger groups of objects become linked in an overall spatial plan. Thus, if the miniature landscape were an actual hamlet you could use a level three map to find your way around. However, you would often be surprised by the actual distances between things, their real sizes once you found them, and you would find that some things mapped are not present, as well as others present but not mapped. Still, as Figure 3.4 shows, things found would be relatively easy to identify because of the photograph-like detail in which they are often represented. While proportion remains inaccurate in that it does not correspond well to the model, it is more real to life than the rather incredible proportion characteristic of level two (e.g., these houses may not be this size, but this size is a reasonable one for real-life houses somewhere). Piaget describes level three as "transitional" between partial and general coordination and the drawing in Figure 3.4 does reflect some of the inconsistency characteristic of the transition. For example, the two buildings on the right side are roughly in proportion, as are the two on the left side. But when all four buildings are considered together the proportion is poorer—the two houses in the upper part of the landscape, for example, should be the same size. Similarly, the two areas of elevated land are placed at appropriate corners of the lake, but are shown inside the lake rather than along its edges as they really are. Finally, we note a mixture of perspectives (some 90°, some 45°, and some "front-on") as well as some inconsistency in viewpoint (e.g., parts of the fence are seen from the front and other parts are seen from one side). In sum, a level three map maker seems to recognize the purpose of a map and is able to coordinate bits of appropriate information in some rough form. He or she does so, however, inconsistently and idiosyncratically, without applying representational conventions. A level three representation often looks more like a picture than a map.

A *level four* map (Figure 3.5), in contrast, is marked by more consistent coordination of logical, numerical, and spatial relationships. The overall spatial plan incorporates improved arrangement of objects, more appropriate proportion and more accurate numerical correspondence. In short, a trip around this hamlet guided by a level four map would include far fewer surprises than with the level three drawing. Most of the mixture between partial and general coordination is gone. There is but a single viewpoint and except for some "incidental" features (e.g., trees, vehicles, etc.) the map is drawn from a consistent 90° perspective. A level-four map, then, conveys better information because it does so in a more efficient, more consistent way. Improved scaling and placement render the full, photograph-like detail we noted in level three less necessary for positive identification of objects. What something looks like is redundant with where it is—if where it is relative to other things is represented with some accuracy. Even so, there is only a partial loosening of the "pull of perception" toward realistic representation. A level four map incorporates little in the way of the domain's symbolic conventions; abstraction is typically limited to what is inherent in a realistic 90° perspective. While drawings at this level are not as "picture-like" as those at level three, neither are they as abstract and symbolic as those at more advanced levels. In sum, a level four map has many of the characteristics of a rough aerial photograph which, after all, is a common first step in the construction of a modern map.

Figure 3.5   A level four map.

Figure 3.6 shows a *level five* map drawing, one which clearly merits the label of a geographic map. There is complete coordination of logical, numerical and spatial correspondences; spatial arrangement, and proportion, though not mathematically exact, are quite good, and for most practical purposes this representation is a serviceable map. In addition to increased accuracy, level five begins to incorporate more systematically the conventions of the domain. Relevant information (e.g., where and what an object is) is differentiated from largely irrelevant information (e.g., exactly what it looks like) and the former is represented in a more efficient, more abstract manner. Labels and/or icons substitute for the realistic presentation of detail more common at the earlier levels, and the conventional use of 90° perspec-

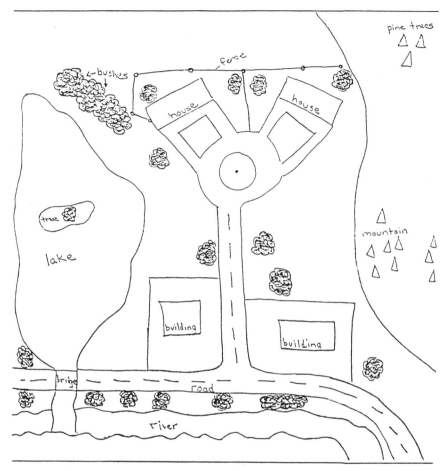

Figure 3.6   A level five map.

tive is adopted.[2] In sum, a level five map does everything a level four map does, but does it more consistently, more accurately and with greater utilization of the domain's abstract conventions. A level five map maker seems to know quite well the purpose of a map, knows which information is relevant to that purpose and is beginning to adopt the conventions which make its abstract representation possible.

The *level six* map drawing shown in Figure 3.7 requires little comment. The two principal improvements over the level five example

[2] Although the pine trees in Figure 3.6 may seem to violate the consistent 90° perspective, our interpretation of these is that they are stylized representations, or icons, intended to identify the object and its location, not a realistic "front-on" perspective.

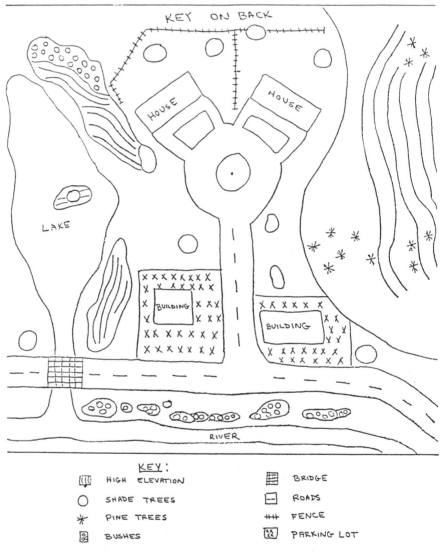

Figure 3.7   A level six map.

are accuracy, which approaches perfection, and increased use of abstract symbolization. Although a few labels remain, the icons characteristic of level five have been replaced by more arbitrary symbols in conjunction with a key. Gradations in elevation, for example, are indicated by means of topographical contours, a sophisticated use of an abstract convention. While the mapping task we have presented is a relatively crude one in comparison to the vast array of complex information which can be incorporated in modern maps, the ability to draw a level six map indicates real appreication for and considerable skill in applying the fundamentals of cartography.

DEVELOPMENTAL STATES

Having now described the six idealized levels of map drawing, we move to a consideration of transition processes as revealed in the actual drawings produced by groups of children. In Chapter 1 we argued that developmental stages do not exist in the minds of children; instead, we suggested that developmental *levels* exist in the psychological structure of domains. Having removed stages from children, we also removed children from stages and placed them instead in developmental *states*. A developmental level, then, is not a representation of a child's overall cognitive system. Rather it is one idealized system for dealing with certain kinds of knowledge which, in conjunction with other such systems or parts of systems, can be used as templates against which to gauge the child's intellectual repertoire—his or her present developmental state. Once the notions of developmental level and developmental state are thus established, we can begin to test the extent to which children do or do not conform to the ideals. Moreover, we can also explore how the various developmental states are transformed from one system to another, including the internal conditions under which a new level begins to appear.

The focus of Piaget's work on map drawing was to classify children as being "at" or "in" an overall developmental stage. Although it is certainly possible to describe map drawings—and therefore children—as generally representing one stage more than others (as we have just done in the preceding section), our experience with maps and children is that such typologies do not reflect children's actual performance: no two maps judged to be at the same stage are identical, nor does any child ever produce a "pure" map representing a single stage.

In contrast to Piaget, the premise for our studies was that the variability normally present in children's map drawings would lead us to a more powerful conception of transition mechanisms (Feldman & Snyder, 1977). Rather than classifying each map as belonging to a single developmental stage, we divided the domain of map drawing into the four spatial concepts and skills that Piaget and Inhelder identified in their own research: (a) spatial arrangement, (b) proportion, (c) perspective, and (d) symbolization. Building upon the general

Piagetian stage descriptions, we were able to construct four parallel sequences of developmental levels, one for each of the sets of concepts just mentioned.

Our experience also indicated that for a given child, different features of the miniature landscape tended to be represented at different levels. Roads and other flat surfaces, for example, were represented in 90° perspective before buildings were. And while virtually all the children's maps included the lake, far fewer represented the proper number of trees. We therefore separated the specific topographical components of the landscape model into four "feature clusters," where each cluster is a set of items which shares logical and/or physical properties. A scoring procedure was developed (see Snyder, Feldman, & LaRossa, 1976) such that a trained judge could evaluate the developmental level at which each spatial concept was applied to each of the four feature clusters. In addition, the judge evaluated the level at which each spatial concept had been applied overall to the "map as a whole." This procedure yields a total of 20 developmental-level classifications for each map: (4 feature clusters + 1 map as a whole) × (4 spatial concepts) = 20. The general developmental levels are presented in Table 3.1; the spatial concepts and feature clusters scored are summarized in Table 3.2.

Applying our scoring procedure to a single map drawing permits us to obtain data on four aspects of spatial reasoning as they are applied to five sets of problems in mapping. When the 20 developmental-level classifications are plotted in histogram-like form (see Figure 3.8) we

Table 3.2 Spatial concepts and feature clusters used in scoring map drawings

SPATIAL CONCEPTS (adapted from Piaget & Inhelder, 1967)
  I. ARRANGEMENT—emphasizes topological concepts in lower levels and Euclidean concepts (i.e., systems of coordinates) in advanced levels.
  II. PROPORTION—emphasizes Euclidean concepts (i.e., similarity)
  III. PERSPECTIVE—emphasizes projective concepts
  IV. SYMBOLIZATION—emphasizes pictorial conventions

FEATURE CLUSTERS
  A. *Buildings*—easily identifiable logical class; regularly shaped; obvious third dimension, but relatively easy to represent.
  B. *Hill, bridge, island, other elevated land*—among major features of model; relatively large, irregularly shaped; three-dimensional; more difficult to represent.
  C. *Lake, river, roads, driveways, parking lots*—major flat surfaces of model; easily represented.
  D. *Trees, fence, motor vehicles, flagpole, bushes*—relatively small, more "incidental" features of model; obvious third dimension; relatively difficult to represent.
  E. *All-inclusive score*—the mape as a whole.

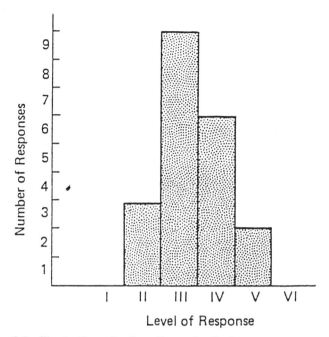

Figure 3.8   Illustration of a "configuration" of responses to the Map Drawing Task.

have a schematic representation of a child's developmental state with respect to map drawing—we call it a "configuration." Configurations tell us about variation in a child's behavior across developmental levels—the relative sophistication of each spatial concept and the consistency with which it is applied to various features of the landscape model. Additionally, a set of calculations can be applied to each configuration to yield a variety of quantitative indices related to internal and external disequilibria.

Modal Level

Typically the majority of a child's responses fall at one developmental level; this we call the modal level. The remaining responses are usually distributed more or less widely but almost always with decreasing frequency at levels one step from the mode, then two steps removed and even three steps away in some cases (see Figure 3.8).

Modal level is an index of central tendency or a best estimate of the child's most commonly used organizational structure. It is the basis for a qualitative classification of the overall map into one of the six developmental levels, an evaluation akin to the ones Piaget made on the basis of clinical judgment. As an estimate of a child's usual way of thinking, modal level is useful in research on external disequilibrium. External disequilibrium arises from a comprehensible but problematic discrepancy between a child's usual way of thinking and his recent experience. One way to express the degree of discrepancy (too little? just right?) is in terms of the difference between the child's modal level and the level of the events he or she encounters in the environment. Thus, researchers (ourselves included) have explored the effects of different interventions aimed at levels *below* the child's mode, *at* the modal level and one or more levels *above* the mode. While results are not entirely consistent, it is fair to say that experiences above the mode have generally facilitated developmental advance, whereas experiences below the mode have usually resulted in little change (e.g., Arbuthnot, 1975; Kuhn, 1972; Snyder & Feldman, 1977; Turiel, 1966, 1969).

Modal level, however, is a relatively crude estimate of a child's developmental state when used alone, and while we sometimes refer to "level three children" for the sake of convenience, there are often significant differences among children who share the same modal level. Additional aspects of developmental states, especially the distribution of other responses around the mode, provide valuable information not captured in the modal level measure.

Level Mixture

The tendency for children to exhibit responses indicative of more than one developmental level (Piaget's *décalages*) has been termed by other researchers "stage variation" (Turiel, 1966, 1969), "structural mixture" and "transitional reasoning" (Strauss, 1972), and "level mixture" (Snyder & Feldman, 1977). Level mixture (as we will call it) has theoretical import because of its relation to internal disequilibrium. In contrast to external disequilibrium (structure/environment discrepancy), internal disequilibrium is thought to arise from discrepancies or inconsistencies within the child's internal system itself; hence its relation to level mixture. As an index of the amount of competition among elements in a child's intellectual repertoire, level mixture reflects general instability in the system (Strauss, 1972). The degree of instability reflected in level mixture provides a useful measure of readiness for developmental change (i.e., of disequilibrium).

A potential source of instability and thus readiness for advance is the increased likelihood that children with greater degrees of level mixture will produce contradictory responses in a series of related tasks. For example, in some situations a child may exhibit logical or concrete operational solutions to problems, while in other similar situations preoperational or intuitive strategies may be applied. Because level mixture reflects the presence of thinking at several different developmental levels, the likelihood of moving back and forth between two conflicting strategies (and presumably the chance of developmental advance) is greater than if mixture were minimal. A number of researchers have demonstrated this positive relationship between level-mixture or level-mixture-like measures and change: in classification of objects (Kuhn 1972), map reading (Markwalder, 1972), map drawing (Snyder & Feldman, 1977), conservation of area (Strauss & Rimalt, 1974), and moral reasoning (Turiel, 1969). Presumably, past a certain point, increases in level mixture are unrelated or inversely related to advance, but this remains to be tested empirically.

In our own empirical work we quantify level mixture in a child's map drawing according to a procedure suggested by Turiel (1969). The number of responses at each developmental level is multiplied by the number of steps separating that level from the mode; these products are then summed and divided by the total number of responses. Level mixture thus adds a measure of variability to the indication of central tendency provided by the modal level estimate. There remains to discuss another measure which provides still finer discrimination among transition states.

The Bias Index

Just as there are differences in level mixture among children with the same modal level, there are differences among children who share both mode and degree of mixture in their map drawings. For example, in the extreme case of two mirror-image configurations, perfectly symmetrical patterns of response occur but on opposite sides of the modal level (Figure 3.9). While the two configurations in Figure 3.9 are indistinguishable with respect to mode and level mixture, common sense suggests that they represent two quite different types of developmental states. The bias index was devised to capture this difference (Snyder & Feldman, 1977). Bias focuses on the distribution of nonmodal-level responses: a greater number of responses above the mode is designated *positive* bias; conversely, a greater number of responses below the mode is termed *negative* bias.

To ground the notion of bias in our conceptual framework, recall that Strauss (1972) equates level mixture with "transitional reasoning." While variation in use of developmental levels is certainly indicative of transitional reasoning, the bias index speaks directly to a

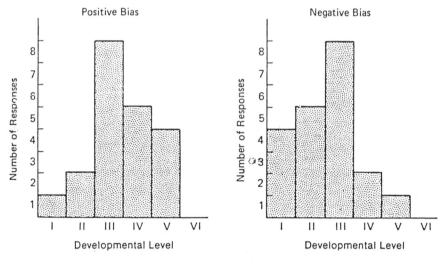

Figure 3.9 Illustration of positive and negative bias profiles.

most pertinent question: transitional between what and what? Bias distinguishes those children moving toward strengthening a currently existing modal level (negative bias) from those children moving away from the current mode and toward the succeeding developmental level (positive bias). This difference between being on the way into a modal level and on the way out of one relates to the question: how much discrepancy (i.e., how much external disequilibrium is just right for inducing change)? It suggests that intervention experiences *at the modal level* might be most appropriate for stimulating advance in negative bias children (who still respond to a variety of situations with strategies less advanced than the modal level), whereas positive bias children would be expected to profit more from experience at levels above their mode (because these more complex strategies are already emerging). In the empirical tests we know of, positive bias, in concert with experience at levels above the mode, was strongly related to advance in modal level (Levin, 1978; Snyder & Feldman, 1977).

Elaboration and Consolidation

Our conceptual analysis of how modal level, level mixture, and bias in various combinations describe phases of developmental transitions has by and large been confirmed by results from the experimental studies mentioned above. These results suggest that development proceeds through alternating periods of internal equilibrium and disequilibrium, as well as through periods of "elaboration" and "consolidation," which are related but not identical to the equilibrium/disequilibrium states (cf. Flavell & Wohlwill, 1969). As new higher level cognitive skills emerge, level mixture (i.e., internal disequilibrium) increases and continues to increase while these new skills are elaborated or extended to a wider range of situations. The process of elaboration then becomes reflected in a positive bias index. As the application of these newer skills becomes the child's usual approach to problems in the domain, an advance in modal level occurs and is followed by a period of decreasing level mixture (i.e., less internal equilibrium) as the system consolidates around the new mode. The process of consolidation is signaled by a negative bias index, and when completed, the system is prepared for creation of a still more advanced level as the cycle begins once more.

When a child begins to consolidate a new, more powerful system, there is typically a tendency to overapply it (Langer, 1969b). The application of well-consolidated skills to new situations will tend to reveal new problems which require the creation of still higher order skills for their solution. Thus a developmental state, even a well-equilibrated one, does not remain stable for long, but rather moves in a dynamic cycle from one state of disequilibrium to another, with periods of stability and consolidation setting the stage for the emergence of more sophisticated cognitive strategies (Piaget, 1970).

By this time the reader may have begun to sense that our description of various transition states is leading up to a proposed sequence of phased changes in the child's system for representing space in map drawings. This sequence is the plot of our first film, an empirical illustration of a provisional sequence of states of transition in children's map drawings over a three-year period.

DEVELOPMENTAL STATES AND DEVELOPMENTAL TRANSITIONS THROUGH A LONG-RANGE LENS

We began our study of map drawing by collecting maps from 96 fifth graders, scoring them by the procedures described earlier and calculating modal level, level mixture, and bias for each child's drawings. The 63 children who exhibited modes at level three were split into positive and negative bias groups and also divided by level mixture (i.e., amount of internal disequilibrium). The children were then assigned to interventions which presented different degrees of external disequilibrium: instruction with map drawing techniques at the child's modal level, one level above or two levels above the child's mode.

Our results detailed in Snyder and Feldman (1977) are easily summarized: the bias index was the most powerful and consistent indicator of progressive developmental change—positive bias children advanced in modal level nearly three and one-half times as often as did negative bias children. Instruction at levels higher than the pretest mode also increased the frequency of modal level advance. The effect of level mixture was less easily interpreted. The findings upon which we began our "film" of transitions, however, are best captured by outlining more specifically the patterns of change observed in three different groups of children.

1. Consolidating children (those with negative bias) typically did not change modal level, but did move from consolidation to elaboration (from negative to positive bias) following the interventions.
2. Elaborating children who had received instruction at their modal level also did not change modes, but did retain a positive bias index.
3. Elaborating children receiving instruction at levels higher than their mode tended to advance in modal level and at the same time shifted from elaboration to consolidation (from positive to negative bias) at the succeeding developmental level.

These patterns of change suggested that a more systematic examination of intermediate steps in the process of transition from one modal level to the next would prove useful. Might not this accomplishment be profitably described in sequential terms itself? Toward this end we collected additional maps from all available children two years after the original study and again one year later. The two- and three-year-follow-up groups included 76% and 70% of the original children; no further instruction in map drawing had been provided during this time.

Figure 3.10 presents a protocol of one child's performance on our map-drawing exercise over the three-year period. The first three configurations come from the intervention study just described and reflect pretest, posttest, and delayed posttest performance respectively. The fourth and fifth configurations show maps collected in the follow-up studies. Configurations, then, are like snapshots or "still frames" reflecting a child's cognitive system with respect to the domain of map drawing at a particular point in time. The process of taking repeated snapshots over time provides a more dynamic representation, a "film" of how the sequence of transformations in these developmental states may occur. Of central interest is the study of how particular developmental modes are built up or *strengthened* and then torn down or *weakened* as they gain or lose responses.

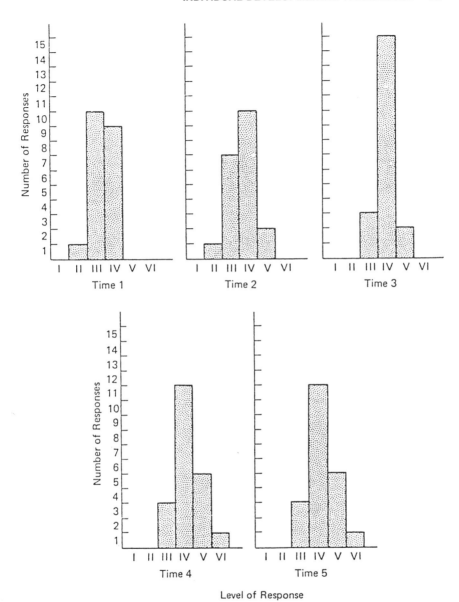

Figure 3.10   Five configurations for a single child over three years time.

Elaboration and consolidation are both key in the strengthening of developmental levels. Elaboration is the extention of newly acquired skills to a wider range of situations. Consolidation is the strengthening of "older" abilities until their application becomes routine. We therefore define consolidation as the strengthening of levels below the current mode, while elaboration refers to the strengthening of levels above the mode. Because the elaboration process strengthens levels above the mode, however, levels below the mode are concomitantly weakened.[3] Our operational definitions of elaboration and consolidation rest on the straightforward assumption that development is generally progressive. Thus, on the average, abilities at lower levels will tend to have been part of the cognitive repertoire longer than abilities that have emerged at higher levels. Similarly, the emergence of a new mode indicates that this higher level has now become the child's typical way of dealing with problems; it thus seems a reasonable marker for the end of elaboration and the beginning of consolidation. We assume also that positive bias indicates an overall tendency toward elaboration, while negative bias denotes a tendency toward consolidation. Finally, we take the degree of level mixture to be an index of instability, with higher mixture indicating relatively greater instability.

Even with these operational definitions of stability, instability, elaboration and consolidation, however, the classification of changes within individual protocols remains a difficult task. To provide a general picture against which to gauge each child's changes, we have combined and transformed the individual protocols into a more manageable set of group composites. First, the immediate and the delayed posttest configurations for each child were averaged since these were separated by only five weeks during which no map drawing instruction occurred. We reasoned that their combination offered a more reliable representation of the children's knowledge of map drawing at a point in developmental time than did either single drawing. Second, using the pretest configurations from the intervention study, children were separated into four groups distinguished by various combinations of level mixture and bias: (a) a low-level mixture group, (b) a middle mixture/positive bias group, (c) a high mixture/positive bias group, and (d) a middle-level mixture/negative bias group.[4] The data from those children in each group who had received instruction at levels above their mode were then combined and the percentage of all

---

[3] Since this definition was written, we have had some second thoughts about it. In more recent work, including research reported in Chapters 4 and 5, somewhat altered notions of elaboration and consolidation have been used. We now define elaboration as extensions of elements beyond the existing mode, and we define consolidation as the movement of elements from *either* side of the mode toward the modal level. This definition of consolidation incorporated backward movement, an aspect of transitions of great interest to us.

[4] There were too few high mixture/negative bias children to permit reliable interpretation of progress in this group.

responses falling at each developmental level was calculated. Four histograms were plotted for each group to show the changes in map drawing performed over the three-year period: pretest, posttests, first follow-up (two years later), and second follow-up (three years later).

Oversplicing

With but four "frames" for each group and three years for development to occur, our filmmaking efforts were somewhat limited. To increase the number of frames we adapted the film editor's technique of splicing. Figure 3.11 presents an example of our method, which we call *oversplicing*. Oversplicing involves following one group of children from pretesting onward until one of their subsequent histograms could be superimposed on the pretest histogram of a second group. Matched points in developmental time may then be compared to check the success of the overlapping splice and the film is able to continue to trace the course of development beyond a group's last histogram by following a second group, and so on.[5] In Figure 3.11 for example, histograms (b) and (d) show the point at which two groups were "joined"—the similarity in shape of histograms is striking. Histograms (c) and (e) are also part of the overlap. While the comparison here is somewhat less striking, it is still reasonably clear; the patterns of performance of the two groups changed in quite similar ways. Histogram (f) shows the second group at a later point in developmental time—our assumption, of course, is that subsequent testing of the first group would have eventually produced a histogram very similar to this one. Applying the oversplicing technique to the data from the four groups described above yielded a six-step film of progress from one modal level to the next (see Figure 3.12).

How well do the data fit the kinds of changes we expected? Recalling that level mixture reflects the degree of stability or instability in the system and that the bias index distinguishes elaborating systems from consolidating ones, it can be seen that the group data, when spliced together this way, outline a sequence of developmental transition phases which is remarkably congruent with the theoretical account presented earlier. We begin at Step 1 with a state of high stability and high consolidation around the modal level (the

---

[5] The "over" in oversplicing thus refers to the "overlap," the period of developmental time shared by both groups in the splice. It thus contrasts this method with simple splicing (as in a cross-sectional design) and a true film (which requires a longitudinal study). In some respects, then, oversplicing is similar to cross-sequential methodology (cf. Schaie & Strother, 1968).

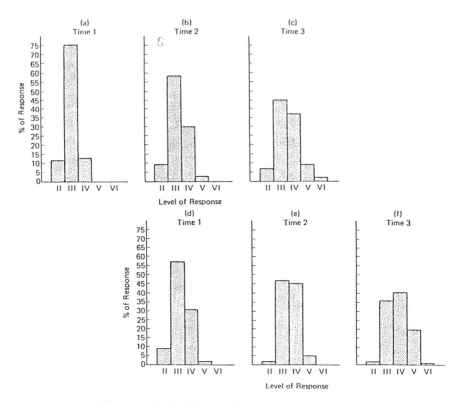

Figure 3.11 An illustration of oversplicing.

"zero" level as a reference point). Step 2 shows increased instability (i.e., higher level mixture), a weakening of the mode and of the minus 1 level, and concomitant strengthening of the plus 1 and plus 2 levels. This process of elaboration has yielded a clear positive bias index. At Step 3 we see continued elaboration—the plus 1 level is now nearly as strong as the mode—and with it a further increase in instability. Together these suggest that the system is ripe for modal level advance.

Step 4 shows the most important event (at least traditionally) in the process of developmental transition—a new modal level has emerged. Concurrent with the appearance of the new models is the continued high-level mixture, but with a shift from positive to negative bias. These suggest a relatively unstable developmental state, as would be expected in the case of a newly achieved mode, but consolidation of that new mode will strengthen it as development proceeds. At Step 5 the consolidation process is clearly underway. Both extremes of the con-figuration have weakened, while the more central "minus one" and modal levels have strengthened to produce increased stability (i.e.,

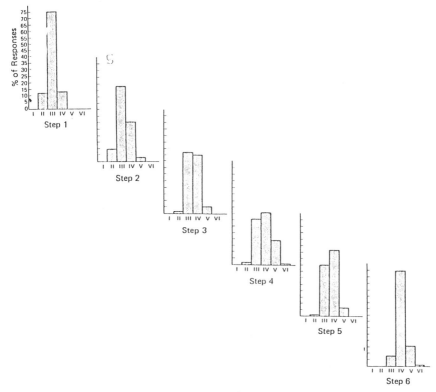

Figure 3.12   An illustration of the six steps in the transition process based on group data. (Note that Steps 1 and 6 are essentially the same shape, indicating a complete transition cycle.)

lower level mixture). Finally, at Step 6 the film "loops" back on itself; once again we see a state of high stability and high consolidation, but this time at the succeeding developmental level. These six "scenes" provide some empirical support for our theoretical speculations about the succession of states that characterize movement through a developmental transition.

To determine whether the four group composite sequence shown in Figure 3.12 reflected the sequence of changes for the individual groups themselves, we checked each group's sequence of steps against the composite. The changes made by each group over the three-year period of the study are summarized as follows:

Group 1: Low-level mixture   Step 1—Step 2—Step 2—Step 3
Group 2: Middle mixture/positive bias Step 2—Step 3—Step 4—Step 5
Group 3: High mixture/positive bias   Step 3—Step 4—Step 4—Step 4
Group 4: Middle mixture/negative bias Step 5—Step 6

Except for repeating steps, all groups conformed to the sequence generated by the oversplicing technique. There are of course dangers in this kind of analysis. All the children in the study began at modal level three, all children received some instruction in map drawing, and each group was composed of children who had received one of three different treatments. Also, many of the same protocols used to construct the film were then used to "test" it. Additionally, the histograms are group composites which do mask to a certain extent individual variation in the transition process (but see below). Still the sequence is more than hypothetical; it is revealed in the data. The suggested sequence of states is not only plausible but follows from theory. The alternation of phases of relative equilibrium and relative disequilibrium, the periods of elaboration and consolidation, the systematic changes in stability are all consistent with the theoretical account. In the next section we again examine the plausibility of the film sequence by assessing the extent to which individual children conform to predictions based on the group data.

Individual Changes

Having constructed a broad film sequence to highlight (if in somewhat idealized form) the phases involved in advancing from one modal level to the next, we began the task of reviewing the changes made by individual children to see how well they agreed with the group-based data. In order to accomplish this we sought to formalize the sequence of transition states in a set of possible *principles* through which developmental states change (see Table 3.3). The heart of the transition process as we see it is the alternation of periods of elaboration and consolidation.

The bias index and level mixture together define these two developmental states, with positive bias and higher mixture indicating elaboration, and negative bias and lower mixture indicating consolidation. Elaboration prepares the system for modal level advance; thus a shift from negative to positive bias precedes an advance in modal level. Modal level advance, in turn, signals the transition from elaboration to consolidation and should therefore be accompanied by a shift from positive to negative bias and perhaps a decrease in level mixture. Finally, modal level changes are progressive and are limited to one level at a time.

Comparing these principles as outlined in Table 3.3 to the changes observed in the configurations of the individual children yielded a 75%

Table 3.3   Proposed principles of developmental change as abstracted from the group-based film

A. *Consolidating systems—Negative bias:*
   1. *Level mixture generally remains constant or decreases until a shift from negative to positive bias occurs.*
   2. *A shift from negative to positive bias precedes an advance in modal level and may be accompanied by an increase in level mixture suggesting the beginning of elaboration.*

B. *Elaborating systems—Positive bias:*
   1. Level mixture generally remains constant or increases until bias shifts to negative.
   2. Positive bias is maintained until a modal level advance occurs.
   3. A modal level advance is accompanied by a shift from positive to negative bias and may also be accompanied by a decrease in level mixture suggesting the beginning of consolidation.

C. *Modal level:*
   1. Modal level does not revert to lower levels.
   2. Modal level advances only one level at a time.

incidence of agreement between predictions and data.[6] Of the 134 possible changes, 100 of them were in accord with the predictions of how developmental states should change.

To summarize the results of our group-based film effort, we have constructed a sequence of phases of transitions based on the Piagetian equilibration model which emphasizes the role of disequilibrium. Using histograms showing performance over time, our "film" illustrates the intermediate steps in moving from one modal level to the next and to some extent tests the plausibility of our conceptual analysis of change processes. Principles of change in developmental states derived from the group-based film yielded good agreement with changes in individual children's map drawings, thus further supporting our sequence. In the next section we apply an even finer grained lens to these data; we begin to examine level-to-level movement of individual responses from children in the sample, adding texture to the systemwide changes we have observed thus far.

---

[6] In applying the principles to changes in level mixture, "remains constant" was operationally defined as change of less than eight points of mixture in either direction. The empirical basis for this range is plus or minus less than one-half a standard deviation as calculated on our sample. Also, as was the case in constructing the group-based film, the two posttests for a child were combined to represent a single point in developmental time.

A LOOK AT TRANSITIONS THROUGH
A CLOSE-UP LENS

The crucial conceptual advance that made the second film possible came about because of an almost trivial technical change in the way we represent level mixture. One of us (DHF) was preparing for a colloquim at Tufts and was deciding which among many possible tables and figures to present. It was important to say something about level mixture, both because it was an idea which was not widely enough circulated and because it was so central to the way we thought about internal disequilibrium. Level mixture as first introduced by Elliot Turiel is usually represented as a histogram showing the percentage of a child's responses that reflect various developmental levels.

The histograms we had been using were based on raw frequencies, not percentages (see Figure 3.8). In order to prepare the more standard level-mixture histograms it was necessary to count the number of responses children had made at various map-drawing levels. Doing this was rather tedious. To make the counting easier, horizontal lines were drawn through the columns. This small modification made for convenience sake has turned out to be extraordinarily important for our work. Almost instantly it became clear that each of the individual responses that made up the columns in the histogram reflected the child's solution to a specific map-drawing problem. In other words, we discovered that it is possible to consider not only the number of responses at a given developmental level, but also that *each response is itself distinct and identifiable*. For example, the spatial arrangement of buildings is a specific problem with which the child must deal, achieving a solution at a certain developmental level. As long as the child's solution to this problem is not obliterated by simply counting it as a member of a column of other responses, the movement of this response across levels can be tracked over time. This movement can also be compared with changes in solutions to other specific problems over the same time interval.

Psychological Elements

The realization that each of the twenty separate indicators of map-drawing ability could be tagged and their movements traced led us to produce configurations like that in Figure 3.13.[7] The individual

---

[7] Since each element is an identifiable response the term histogram is somewhat misleading, as histograms represent frequencies only. We therefore have called these representations of developmental states "configurations."

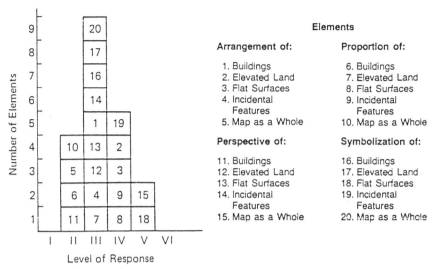

Figure 3.13   The 20 "elements" of the domain of map drawing. (Note that the vertical position of each of the elements within a level is arbitrary (i.e., it has no meaning). There were for this child at this time 4 Level II responses, 9 Level III responses, etc.)

responses were termed "psychological elements" because an element is the typical term used to refer to the individual parts of a cognitive structure. A structure is often defined as a set of elements governed by a set of rules, a definition compatible with our purposes.

Our elements were called psychological because they exist only as a result of a child's actual attempts at spatial representation. For example, drawing a map of our model landscape requires that the buildings be arranged on paper in some fashion, but it is only when a child actually attempts to arrange the buildings that the "element" exists. Arrangement as a spatial concept thus occurs only when a person attempts to do it; it is not an abstraction that exists apart from a child's activity, but is dependent on the child's attempts to deal with particular spatial problems.

To have conceptualized the domain of map drawing as 20 psychological elements would have served little purpose if our impirical work had not been longitudinal. A Turiel-type level mixture histogram and a configuration of psychological elements say much the same thing about the child's psychological state at a given moment in time. The advantage of analyzing psychological element movement becomes clear, however, when a longitudinal series of protocols is available showing different points in development for individual children. Here the opportunity exists to trace the movement of specific elements over time. This kind of analysis has led to conceptual and empirical advances in our understanding of developmental transitions, particularly those aspects of transitions having to do with novelties, which are defined here as the appearance of an element at a level unprecedented for a given child.

To illustrate why this is so, we must again consider the notions of *décalage,* resistance, and their relation to novelties. For Piaget the basic intellectual capabilities of a stage are constructed all at once. The first appearance of reasoning at a new stage signifies that the child's "competence" to reason in this manner is basically complete. A novelty, then, is an initial behavioral manifestation of an overall internal shift in structure. Although Piaget assumes internal consistency, he acknowledges inconsistency in performance. The various conservations, for example, are achieved over several years, but formally they are seen to require the same underlying logic. *Décalage* is Piaget's label for this phenomenon of delays in the appearance of behaviors, and resistance is his explanation for *décalage.* Some problems or tasks are said to be more resistant to the application of logical structures than others. Therefore, easier problems emerge from competence to performance more quickly than the more resistant ones. But these resistances are not relevant to a theory of transitions because transitions occur in the realm of competence, according to Piaget (1971a, 1971b).

Our view of transitions as a series of element movements leads to a radically different interpretation of novelties and a different notion of structure as well. Instead of a transition occurring all at once, we assume that transition is an ongoing process of partial structural transformation (cf. Flavell, 1971b). We make no assumption that an overall structure is somehow in place when the first behavior reflective of that new level appears. There is therefore no specific point at which a transition has occurred; transformation is occurring continuously. Resistances of different contents are also not irrelevant; the overcoming of resistances reveals some of the workings of the system in the child's head. The system that makes possible this repertoire of responses is the child's "structure" at that moment.

For Piaget a transition has occurred whenever a novel behavior appears in sturdy form, reflecting the existence of a more advanced stage. For us a novelty is only one (albeit an important one) of many changes in a system which are suggestive of the organization of the child's cognitive functioning at that point in time. The difference is subtle but important. Piaget's conception of transitions leads to no obvious empirical test, since structure is assumed to be complete at its first behavioral manifestation; our view of psychological elements is testable, and we have begun to examine it empirically. (It should be noted, however, that our use of novelty here captures only some of the meaning of novelties as described in Chapter 2.)

Once the domain of map drawing had been represented in terms of the 20 psychological elements, a provisional definition of a developmental transition became possible, to wit: *a developmental transition is the transformation of any set of psychological elements making up a structure such that each element advances one level.* This definition is illustrated in Figure 3.14. As the reader can see, the shape of the configuration in Figure 3.14 is unchanged from Time 1 to Time 2. Each element has moved one level in advance of where it was at Time 1. As the simplest, most straightforward definition of a developmental transition, Figure 3.14 specifies what happens to each element of a structure (in our sense) when a developmental transition occurs.

While we do not believe that this illustration necessarily shows inner workings of transitions, the definition offered here is a useful template against which to gauge our findings. For example, we suspected that elements do not always move one level at a time. We already knew in fact that some aspects of map drawing moved more

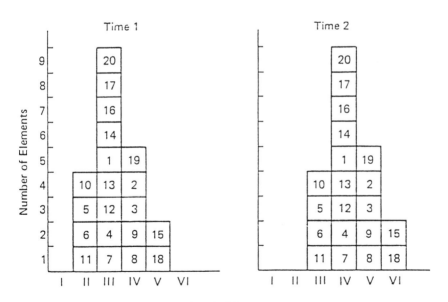

Level of Response

Figure 3.14   Illustration of the formal definition of a developmental transition: All elements move + 1 level.

rapidly forward than others (i.e., covered more levels than others over the same unit of time). We also knew that some elements tended to move backward as well as forward (Feldman & Snyder, 1977).

The true complexity of the problem of specifying "lawful" movements is not readily apparent. Even taking the simplest model of transitions, as in Figure 3.14, where all elements move forward at the rate of one level per unit time, there are nearly 2,500 trillion sequences of element movement in map drawing that could lead to the same result.[8] If differences in the number of levels covered and the direction of movement are added to the system, the number of sequences is still larger. If we do allow for these more varied movements among elements, as both theory and our empirical results indicate is the case, a more accurate (and even more complex) model of transitions emerges. But with the method of tracking psychological elements and their movements over time, we are able to begin to study transitions at a level of detail sensitive enough to chart some subtle aspects of the transition process.

Some Movements and Positions

A perfectly consistent map drawing would yield a configuration showing a 20 element stack at one level and no elements at any of the others. Many types of deviations from this "ideal" could be studied, but we focused on two sorts of unusual movements and two unusual positions of elements. The two movements were: forward more than one level, which we called *leaping*, and backward more than one level, which we called *deep reversion*. The two positions that first attracted our attention were those at the extremes of the configuration. At the extreme left or lower bound we studied elements which seemed to lag behind the rest of the configuration; these were termed *laggards*. At the extreme right or upper bound we noted with obvious interest the appearance of an element at a developmental level beyond anything the child had exhibited previously—a *novelty*. We expected that elements at the extremes would be the least stable and would therefore be more likely to leap and deep revert, if for no other reason than because they were the least well integrated into the overall configuration. In general we found that the system of map drawing is a stable one; between any two points in time almost two-thirds of the elements did not move at all. And when there was movement, almost two-thirds of the elements moved forward, and one-third backward.

---

[8] The actual number of possible sequences is 20! or 2,432,902,008,176,640,100.

Not surprisingly, we center the present discussion around an examination of novelties. For the purpose of studying novelties we analyzed the four maps drawn by each of 48 children between their fifth- and seventh-grade years.[9] By examining a child's configuration of elements prior to, at the time of, and subsequent to the appearance of a novelty, we were able to carry out the first empirical study of the conditions under which a developmental novelty occurs and to examine the consequences of a child's having achieved this kind of developmental advance (Feldman & Snyder, 1977). An example of a child's protocol including a developmental novelty is shown in Figure 3.15, where the novelty appears at Level VI (Time 4). Because a novelty was defined as a single element appearing at a developmental level unprecedented for that child, it was necessary to know something about its history. As Figure 3.15 shows, the novelty appears only in the fourth protocol, making it possible to infer with some confidence that no element had previously appeared at this level. Situations similar to this one in other children's protocols enabled us to study the movement of novel elements both before and after they become novelties.

What have we learned about novelties? First of all we know now that (at least in map drawing) novelites are not common; they occurred only in roughly ten percent of the configurations. We have also learned that novelties tend to occur more frequently among some elements than others; this suggests that certain "contents" of the domain are regularly at the vanguard of developmental change, while others are relegated to bringing up the rear. In map drawing it appears that the concepts of symbolization and perspective are more likely to yield novelties (more than 70% of the novelties reflected these two spatial concepts) while arrangement and proportion were less likely (about 30%). Thus, when a child first apprehends a higher developmental level, he or she begins to advance the cognitive structure more commonly with some elements than others.

We have also started work on other problems in structure/content relationships prior to, at the time of, and following the appearance of a novelty (Feldman & Snyder, 1977). We have begun to answer questions such as these:

- From where (in a configuration) does a novelty typically come?
- What are the effects on the rest of the elements in a configuration when a novelty appears?
- What happens to a novelty after it has appeared?

---

[9] At the time of this writing, analysis of element movements from the fourth to fifth map was just beginning.

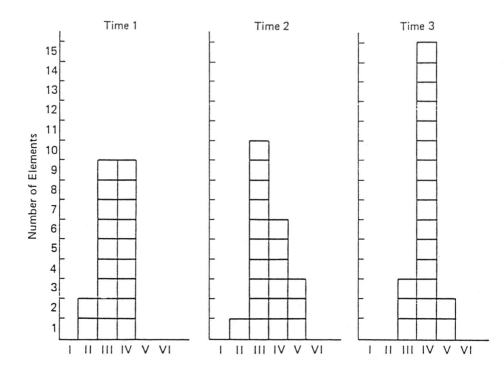

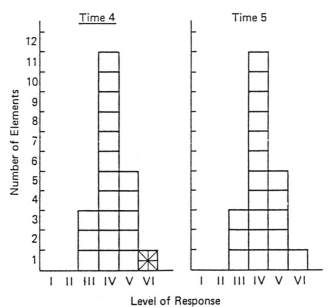

Figure 3.15   Protocol for a child in the longitudinal study showing changes in map-drawing configurations over three years with a novelty shown at Time 4.

Novelties, as it happens, are frequently leapers. This means that the element which is to become a novelty tends to leap out of the middle of a configuration to take its place at the leading edge. For novelties, leaping occurs more than 70% of the time, although for other elements the frequency of leaping is only about 4%.

As discussed earlier, the element that becomes a novelty has a specific identity; it reflects a certain spatial concept applied to a specific map drawing problem. What of the fate of those other elements that share a spatial concept or a map-drawing problem with the novel element? Suppose, for example, that our novel element is *perspective of buildings*. What happens to the other elements that also deal with say, perspective of trees, or of roads? What seems to occur is that the novelty has a strong "pulling" effect on other elements dealing with the same map-drawing problem or feature (in this case the feature cluster of *buildings*). Figure 3.16 shows how a novelty "pulls" other elements sharing its spatial concept. An element that shares a spatial concept with a novelty is likely to move forward with a probability of about .60, whereas other elements move forward at a rate of about .30 during the same time interval.

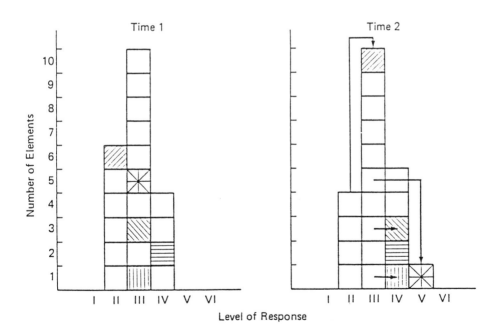

Figure 3.16 "Pulling" effect of a novel element on other elements sharing its spatial concept. Also shows "leaping" of a novelty.

Finally, we may ask what happens within a configuration after a novelty has appeared? Here our results are sketchy, but we have found some fascinating leads. Perhaps most striking is the fact that novelties are relatively unstable; they tend to *revert* back one or more levels after their appearance. Almost 80% of the novelties reverted at least one level during the next time period, and 56% showed deep reversion (they reverted more than one level). This rate of deep reversion is remarkable when compared with the overall reversion rate for all elements, which is about 15% for all revisions and only 1.6% for the more pronounced deep reversions.

From results such as these we have begun to piece together a picture of the role of novelties as catalysts in the transition process. Novelties seem to leap out of the middle of the pack to take their place at the highest level of a configuration. Novel elements also exert a pulling influence on other elements sharing the same spatial concept. Once a novelty appears, it often subsequently reverts back into the configuration, almost as if the child found the new level a bit too heady a brew and decided to be somewhat more conservative so as to regroup cognitive forces.

Also of interest in our analysis was an examination of elements reflecting certain contents that may play other roles in the transition process. We saw, for example, that novelties tended to come from among elements involving the spatial concepts of perspective and symbolization. We also found that spatial arrangement provided a high percentage of the deep reversions, and laggards more often than not reflected a map-drawing problem related to proportion (see Feldman & Snyder, 1977). As we continue to unravel the mysteries of the structure-building process, we will have to learn more about these specific spatial reasoning problems because of their potential special roles in developmental transitions in the domain of map drawing. With the techniques for tracking element movement, it is now possible to study these matters empirically.

ON THE MEANING OF MOVEMENTS

We would of course like to specify precisely which elements move and why they move as a configuration is transformed from level to level, but the complexity of the task remains staggering. At some later point we would hope to integrate our observations of single element movements into the more global view of transition states that was the outcome of our group oversplicing enterprise. For now we are limited to juxtaposing the two views. Still, it seems appropriate to comment in a preliminary way on the relationships we perceive between types of element movements and some traditional issues relevant to developmental transitions.

There is ample speculation in the literature about backward movement—what we have called reversion—as part of the transition process. Heinz Werner (1957) is the theorist who has perhaps been most explicit about this aspect of development and Jonas Langer (1969b), a theorist in the Wernerian tradition, has elaborated upon Werner's views. Both Werner and Langer stress the idea that development is not all progressive, but that preparation for movement to a more advanced level of functioning may well include some "dedifferentiation" or temporary reversion to earlier levels. "Regression in the service of the ego" (Kris, 1958) is the phrase that expresses somewhat the same notion within the psychoanalytic tradition. We use the term *reversion* rather than *regression* because, like Strauss (1972) and Turiel (1974), we believe that the individual's overall developmental organization does not move backward. More plausible from our point of view is that various elements in a generally forward moving configuration are drawn back temporarily in order to consolidate a level or enhance elaboration of an emerging level. The term reversion seems to us to capture this aspect of backward movement better than the term regression.

Rapid forward movement, similar in some respects to leaping and novelty, also has a time-honored place in the developmental literature. Perhaps the idea of *readiness* best captures this notion. Given an individual with a certain set of capabilities at a certain point in time, we can predict relatively rapid progress if the appropriate conditions are met. Most earlier views of stage-to-stage progress also partook of this notion. Piaget's *structures d'ensemble* is often interpreted as precipitous movement from one state to the next, although recent discussions of the stage issue (particularly Flavell, 1971b; Gruber & Vonèche, 1978; Piaget, 1975) place less emphasis on this idea. It is now our interpretation that Piaget means his notion of stage advance to be taken only in a most metaphorical way. Perhaps it is accurate to say that for Piaget a new stage is *glimpsed* at the appearance of a novelty, but the full range of capabilities must be constructed and consolidated over an extended period of time. This way of dealing with the issue might even eventually resolve the paradox between *structures d'ensemble,* which seems to demand rapid movement of an entire set of elements, and gradual transition, which is more likely to be what actually happens, even in Piaget's view of things (Gruber & Vonèche, 1978).

To summarize, a novelty does seem to signify the first solid behavior reflecting a new, more advanced level. This new level, however, has only a foundation and a few joists; it is far from complete at the appearance of the novelty. This may be what Piaget means by *décalage;* although the child has apprehended a more advanced level of thinking, he has done so only in a limited area of the domain. It follows that a novelty, once it has appeared, may be drawn back into the center of the configuration because the child has no way to integrate this new-found apprehension into his already well-established ways of thinking within the domain. But the fact that a new, more advanced solution reverts to an earlier level or is abandoned under countersuggestion, does not (contrary to Piaget) necessarily mean that "mere learning" has taken place. Our data suggest that an essential part of the transition process seems to be reversion of novel elements; reversion thus may be seen as integral to development. The significance of reversion may lie less in the fact that it represents a failure to resist countersuggestion (as Piaget has argued) than in understanding where in the transition process the reversion takes place. Under some conditions reversion may indeed indicate "mere learning," under others it may signify development at work.

To push this line of speculation one step further, we would expect that the appearnace of a novelty in the sense it is defined in this chapter, signifies something like the occurrence of "insight" in problem solving, but it is not clear just what happens following this insight. There seem to be two possibilities, and these may manifest themselves in different ways in terms of element movement. One possibility is that the novelty is the "missing link" in an almost complete structure. Once this link is in place, the structure coalesces, becoming more complete and irreversible. Piaget seems to suggest something very much like this when he reports that a child who had solved a problem of recurrent reasoning exclaimed: "Once one knows, one knows forever and ever!" (Piaget, 1971, p. 5). A second possibility, one which seems more plausible, is that a novelty is probably not the final truss in a well-evolved structure, but rather the first hint that a grand new structure will be built in the future. Indeed, if it were possible to conduct an interview at the exact moment when a novelty appeared, we would predict finding a child who is both exhilarated and anxious, excited and troubled. And we would expect on this basis that novelties would be rather short-lived behavioral phenomena, not the stable, irreversible, unshakable reasoning of a newly achieved, well-consolidated structure.

Unfortunately, we do not have data on the reactions of children to the appearance of a novelty in their own thought. It does seem, however, that the event which makes a structure unshakable is probably not a novelty, not a single element pushed beyond the prior boundaries of a configuration. The "once one knows, one knows forever and ever" phenomenon, we believe, is more likely to be precipitated by moving a lagging element up so that the mode becomes really well consolidated, achieving a stable equilibrium state. A novelty on the other hand is more likely to be an ephemeral, fleeting insight, a glimpse into the future.

We confess that these speculations about the meaning of various element movements go well beyond our data. Nothing presented here can yet reveal the true meaning of a novelty, nor the function of laggards, nor the significance of rapid forward and backward movement. But the techniques described in this chapter show that the study of specific movements among specific elements adds fine grain to the broad picture of transition states presented earlier.

REFLECTIONS OF TWO NOVICE FILMMAKERS

In this chapter we have tried to deal with issues of individual developmental change through two "films" of the transition process. Since we see change as a continuous process of transformation, we chose to feature two traditional indicators of qualitative advance: modal level shifts and developmental novelties. A modal shift is as close as we could come to a measure of "overall stage change." We wanted to construct a sequence of changes in developmental state that would lead up to, include, and then follow a shift in this most frequent level of response. We produced a set of six phases of transitions that did just that. Following a modal level advance, this film would simply be rewound and run again, but with the whole configuration having advanced to the next level.

By distilling from these data a set of principles governing developmental transitions, we could account for changes among nearly three-quarters of the individual children in our sample; not bad for a first try. Still, these children were the same ones who provided the group data upon which the sequence was built. We would have more confidence in the accuracy of our scenario if we had another set of map drawings with which to test this sequence. We are working on this, but in the meantime we must be content with what seems to us a respectable first outing. Obviously there are many more subtle changes that occur between modal level shifts than are reflected in our six frames. It must be something like an actor finding that his or her best scenes ended up on the cutting room floor.

As a complement to this necessarily general picture, we moved in for a closer look at specific movements among the psychological elements that comprise a child's map drawing. The kind of movement that has interested us most is the developmental novelty, the first appearance of reasoning at a level unprecedented for a child. We were able to trace the conditions preceding and following the appearance of novelties in individual children's protocols. While we cannot yet say why a novelty does what it does, we can at least begin to shed a little light on the matter.

It seems that novelties leap out of an elaborating configuration, pulling a number of other "like-minded" elements with them to more advanced levels. It also seems that novelties frequently revert back into the middle of a configuration after they have made a first, dramatic appearance. We are not sure why this is so, but it may well have something to do with the child consolidating his gains before taking too great a further risk. A novelty seems to show the child what is possible, to set a new but somewhat dangerous carrot out in front of one's cognitive donkey; but then the carrot jumps back on the wagon and somehow helps move the rest of the load.

We have obviously just begun to explore this enormously complicated but fascinating process called developmental transitions. By studying a relatively slow-moving, stable domain-like map drawing, we have been able to capture on "film," if only in grainy, jerky, and primitive scenes, some of the movements of cognitive systems as they proceed from level to level. Future efforts will necessitate refinement of our tools and techniques for studying both the general and the more specific aspects of transition processes. This will undoubtedly require that we branch out into other domains as well as study map drawing, but we would not, after all, want to become typecast after only two films.

4

Developmental Transitions
A Decade Later

In this chapter we report on empirical work done on our transitions model since the publication of the first edition of this book. The research has in some respects been quite continuous with what was reported in 1980 (and beyond), including a bit of further work on map drawing. But it has changed directions in some significant ways as well. This chapter will focus on the research directly related to the transitions studies previously reported. Chapter 5 will summarize some of the more recent studies moving into a number of new developmental domains, including juggling, aesthetic judgment and reasoning, computer programming, and teaching. Much of this work was done in our own research group, but a significant amount has been done by others as well.

The major shifts in the work have been twofold: We have moved from map drawing in the cultural realm to other domains, particularly some from other regions of the universal to unique continuum, and we have recast the work somewhat in the language of expertise, hoping to establish more common ground with colleagues in cognitive science.

Map-Drawing Research

The major study of map-drawing research was longitudinal: five maps were drawn over a period of three years. In the first edition of this book, we reported analyses of the first four drawings. The fifth map has since been scored and added to the data set. Results from analyses of these data will be briefly summarized, as will some methodological issues that have arisen since we first reported our findings. The methodological issues are particularly troublesome for the analyses having to do with individual element movements.

A nasty problem with some of the data we are analyzing is that they lack an acceptable unit of analysis. By focusing on movement among individual elements in many analyses, we preclude use of virtually all existing statistical procedures. These procedures, as most readers know, are designed to compare individuals or groups. The element analyses are contaminated because the 20 elements from a single subject are not independent. However, the statistical techniques which might otherwise be used to analyze novelties, leapers, laggards, and so on, assume that all data points are independent. It is not clear how to carry out statistical procedures other than descriptive ones on our data set, as long as individual elements, rather than individual people, remain our focus.

This does not mean that we are unable to report findings based on element movements, only that we are not able to test the statistical significance of these results. We have found, for example, that novelties (single elements appearing at an unprecedented developmental level in the system) are infrequent, occurring about 14% of the time (10% was reported in Chapter 3), or about 3 times in 20 opportunities. We are unable to say if this frequency exceeds chance or random occurrence for at least two reasons: the first is that, as already mentioned, independence among opportunities can not be assumed, and second, there is no obvious way to estimate what chance distributions of novelty occurrence might be even if opportunities were independent of each other. These methodological points were driven home by sympathetic but demanding critics who read manuscripts we submitted to journals for publication. In general, our groups analyses were published, our element analyses have not been.

What this means is that for the elements analyses we are able to legitimately report only summary statistics, frequencies, and percentages, but not able to test their power against chance models. As was true in our earlier reports, we believe that the findings are highly suggestive, but our optimism at finding good statistical procedures for analyzing our findings about element movements turned out to be misplaced. Still, we think the results are worth reporting for descriptive purposes.

Adding a fifth drawing to the protocols reduced the subject pool from 48 to 44 subjects but changed little in the way of results. Not reported earlier is the fact that the protocols on the whole tended to be stable over time. Almost 60% of all elements remained stable from one drawing to the next, independent of the amount of time between drawings. This is a difficult number to interpret without knowing if simple test-retest reliability exists with this Map-Drawing Instrument. Although interjudge reliability has been established in several studies using the scoring system developed for our earlier studies, test-retest reliability had not been established prior to our earlier report.

It is in one sense reasonable to expect our instrument to prove its reliability across testings. Any psychometric instrument should be shown to yield substantially similar scores when given to the same group of subjects on two occasions. And yet, the map-drawing test is not really a psychometric instrument; it is a *developmental* one. There is therefore an inevitable conflict that arises between the goals of psychometric and developmental testing. Psychometrics requires stability, while development predicts transformation and therefore lack of stability. The key here is to do test-retest reliability with a relatively brief interval between testings so that the expected changes in the system will not be expected to have taken place during the interval between testings. Since we have determined from prior work that map drawing is a relatively slow-evolving system in most children, an interval between testings of a month or two should be short enough to test the overall stability of the instrument without compromising its developmental character.

If the instrument did not have stability over time at least as much as is usually expected of a standard psychometric (80% is a rule of thumb widely accepted), then it is unclear what the predicted changes in performance would mean. Would they mean simple unreliability in the instrument? It is impossible to tell without an idea of how the instrument performs under the usual test-retest conditions. In order to find out, we carried out a small study in three fifth-grade classes in Somerville, MA in 1983–1984. Four weeks separated the two administrations of the Map-Drawing Instrument, and 59 children completed the task. Of the children completing the task, a random set of 25 pairs of map drawings was scored. The correlation between Reasoning Levels on the two sets of scores was .82, thus exceeding the criterion of .80 for test-retest reliability. Because only 3 of the 25 subjects had the same score at both testings, we decided to use the Pearson correlation rather than the less sensitive rank order, although the results are not appreciably different with the two techniques for calculating a correlation.

Having established reasonable stability for the instrument, we now move to the question of whether change in the system is simply random fluctuation or more systematic movement. To show that change is not random, it is necessary to show that distinctive *patterns* of movements occur, patterns that could be predicted and interpreted theoretically and that would be unlikely to occur by chance. In the study of map drawings, a number of interesting patterns did occur, although as has often been our fate, we have been unable to test these patterns formally against chance or random variation.

Among the more than 3,500 opportunities for movement (44 subjects × 20 elements × 4 intervals), forward movement was found to be nearly twice as frequent as backward movement (26% vs. 14%). The cliche "two steps forward, one step back" describes the system fairly well, except for the fact that most of the time, as mentioned earlier, neither forward nor backward movement occurred. The ratio of forward to backward movement suggests that progress toward a more sophisticated map-drawing system proceeds with systematic backward movement as part of the process, as Werner (1957) emphasized, although with more of an emphasis on deconstruction than in our framework.

Using the mode as the measure of change rather than element movement, we find a similar picture. Of the 176 opportunities for modes to change (44 subjects × 4 intervals), 69% remained unchanged from drawing to drawing, 23% advanced, and 8% reverted. Once again, it appears that there is regular, orderly movement toward more advanced map-drawing levels. What is less clear is how much this picture would change if the drawings were more frequent, less frequent, or if there were more drawings in the set (cf. Berkowitz & Keller, in press). What we do know is that the interval between drawings varied from one month to two years, but the patterns observed seem to occur similarly regardless of interval. On the other hand, there were interventions between the first and second drawings for some subjects which might have affected the pattern of movements (Snyder & Feldman, 1977).

Novelties. For theoretical reasons, we were especially interested in elements that appeared at the leading edge of a child's map-drawing system. Although we could have defined novelties in a number of ways, we chose to examine the most clear-cut of definitions (i.e., an element appearing alone at the leading edge of a configuration). We expected such events to be rare, and they were, but it is not possible to estimate if their occurrence was different from chance. We do know that nearly half of the subjects' protocols (21 of 44, or 48%) contained a novelty, as defined above, that most subjects produced only a single one during the three-year course of the study (three children produced two), and that novelties appeared 14% of the time when they could have.

Our hope was to track the movements of novelties before, at the time of, and after their appearance, so that we might gain insight into the conditions under which novelties appear. Based on the grouped data and on our guesses based on theory, we expected that novelties would tend to appear when the system needed energizing, when the possibility of a new mode was real (i.e., when there were several elements at that level), but when progress toward a modal shift was stalled. Based on informal experience over several years with metahobby (see Chapter 3), where we have been asking students to stop doing their projects for a week or so, we also expected novelties to appear after a period of respite.

We did see novelties coming from the stable center of the map drawing system, leaping forward to energize the system, and catalytic to the forward movement of other elements. Psychologically, we believed that subjects would be aware of the greater movement of an element relative to other elements, and that the exhilaration from that experience would tend to stimulate renewed activity in extending the system forward. In fact, based on these kinds of guesses, we have for the last few years been also asking metahobby students to keep track of their *emotions* as well as their learning experiences. We have found some interesting patterns of emotions that seem to accompany movements in the more cognitive aspects of change. More will be given on this later.

We also pursued the idea introduced in Chapter 3 of "pulling" by the novelty of other elements sharing the same spatial concept (e.g., proportion). In the longitudinal study, we found that 53% (53/100) (vs. 60% reported in Chapter 3) of those elements sharing a spatial concept with a novelty also advanced, while 33% (122/371) (vs. 30%) of other elements in the same configurations progressed during the same time interval. For example, if a novelty occurred in a proportion element, other elements reflecting the use of proportion were more likely to advance than elements reflecting the use of perspective, arrangement, or symbolization. So a novelty is not simply moving itself; it seems to be part of a more general progressive change among related elements, with the novelty out front leading the way.

Because of the difficulty in gauging what chance movements would be in a system like ours, it is not possible to estimate the statistical significance of the leaping rate among novelties. What we can and have done is to do other analyses to see if they are consistent with our best guesses about how processes of developmental change seem to work (Feldman, 1986). We found, for example, that 52% of the elements that became novelties leaped from the subject's current mode. This is a plausible finding based on our understanding of novelties as catalysts; their movement from the center of the system to a place where they are likely to be perceived as dramatically advanced seems appropriate given what we know. On the other hand, as said several times already, we are unable to tell just how much 52% is relative to other possibilities.

Because novelties are assumed to signal cognitive reorganization, we expected to find a strong relationship between the emergence of novelties and other indices of change—specifically, modal shifts and changes to positive bias. While we did find some relationships between novelties and these two indices, these relationships do not seem to be as clear-cut as we expected. In one-third of the instances where novelties were found, they co-occurred with shifts in modal level, and in another 14% of the cases the novelties proceeded the shifts by one interval. Novelties were coincidental with shifts to positive bias in another 20% of the cases. Fully one-third of the novelties failed to yield any obvious relation to stage changes. In addition, many modal shifts were observed without a novelty in the protocol at all. We did find that a significantly greater proportion of subjects who had produced novelties sometime during the three years of the study had advanced by one modal stage by the end (48% vs. 6% of the rest of the sample).

Reversion. Another finding described briefly in Chapter 3 was the observation that novelties, as defined here, tended to move backward in the interval following their appearance. The rate of reversion (as we call it) was high among novelties, and high compared with other elements which had moved forward during the preceding time interval. For novelties, the rate of reversion was 14 of 17 or 82% and for other forward moving elements 37% (232/629). (Novelties at times could of course not be followed.) Even though novelties have more opportunities for backward movement than other elements (by virtue of their position in a configuration), the contrast in backward movement between them and other elements seems striking. Perhaps more striking is the finding that 59% (10/17) versus 56% based on Chapter 3 result of the novelties "deep reverted" (i.e., moved backward more than one level), whereas 5.2% (33/269) of other forward-moving elements did so. The patterns of movement for novelties do seem to separate them from other elements, as theory would predict, and their movement does not seem to be due to the way they are defined as singular, leading edge phenomena.

Finally, in a further effort to draw together the two sets of analyses reported in Chapter 3, we examined the relationship between the appearance of novelties and positive "bias" (the appearance of more elements above the mode than below). We predicted that novelties, as catalysts for change, should be systematically associated with changes in mode. And since mode changes occur more frequently among configurations showing positive bias, we expected novelties to be more frequent among such configurations. These predictions, while supported, were not as clear as was generally true in the other analyses. In 64% of the configurations where novelties appeared there was a positive bias in the overall system. We would have expected a higher percentage. If it is true that a third or more of the novelties in a transforming system appear in negative bias configurations, our notions about the conditions favoring novelties might have to be revised.

Overall, the effort to study transitions in map-drawing configurations at the microlevel has been fruitful, but it has been limited by the lack of appropriate statistical tests. While the results produced for element movement, novelties, leaping, and reversion are plausible in terms of our theoretical framework, we are unable to say at this point how strongly the data support our theory. And since the theoretical framework was in part built from the empirical findings of the longitudinal study, an independent effort to predict change in this or another domain would help determine how productive this line of analysis will be.

Nonetheless, the analyses of element movement, mode shifts, bias, and novelties convince us that we are not dealing with random fluctuations in a random change system. Too many patterns are consistent with theory, and especially with a sequence of events that theory would support, to dismiss the data as simply chance. For example, the fact that the system as a whole tends to remain stable, the fact that elaboration toward new modal levels seems to proceed in a plausible, orderly manner, the fact that novelties seem to catalyze the system by "pulling" other elements (although, to be sure, we cannot say what is pulling what without further study), the fact that many novelties seem to revert or deep revert after leaping to take their place as novelties, all seem to suggest meaningful patterns of movement.

Yet, even if we are able to demonstrate that the transition patterns in map drawing are theoretically compelling and empirically systematic, it will still be true that we are limited to map drawing in what we can say about transitions. We can *believe* that similar mechanisms and processes of change will prevail in other developmental domains, but until there are data to show the comparability or incomparability of various domains with map drawing, our findings are quite limited.

We have more recently begun to study several other domains, but the results of these studies are still quite preliminary. Some of our work has been done using Kohlberg's well-known sequence of stages of moral judgment and reasoning (Kohlberg, 1971; Snyder & Norcini, 1982a; see also Walker & Taylor, 1991). It was intended to test certain aspects of the six-phase model, as well as to continue our efforts to study the effects of interventions aimed at stages above or below the center of a child's system of thought for dealing with a particular domain. We will first summarize the work with moral judgment and reasoning, as well as some work done by other researchers who have attempted to put our model to empirical test. This latter work includes some additional research on moral judgment and reasoning using the Kohlberg scale (cf. Walker & Taylor, 1991). Then we will move to our most recent research which deals with the development of expertise in several disparate domains: juggling, aesthetic judgment and reasoning, and teaching, including as well a summary of research done by Robert Campbell and his associates on developmental levels in computer programming.

The Snyder–Norcini Study of Moral Judgment and Reasoning

In research carried out by Norcini and Snyder (1983, 1986) 87 junior high school students in the Philadelphia area were administered a multiple-choice-format adaptation of the Kohlberg Moral Development Interview. Using prototypic statements from the scoring manual, stage-typed responses to the probe questions were generated at moral stages one through five for each of four moral dilemmas. The dilemmas, probe questions, and stage-typed responses were edited, pilot tested, and reedited to remove ambiguity and redundancy and to achieve a reading level equivalent to approximately grade six. The moral reasoning measure was then bound in booklet form, complete with instructions, and administered to the students by their regular classroom teachers. The students worked self-paced through the booklets, selecting for each of the 22 probe questions the "best" response from among the stage-typed statements which had been prepared previously.

The students' selections, which comprised the pretest, were cast into frequency histograms (similar to the configurations of Chapter 3) displaying each student's use of moral reasoning levels one through five, and three indices were calculated: modal stage, level mixture, and bias, all determined in the same way as in the map-drawing studies. Based on pretest data, students were put into groups balanced for gender, grade, modal stage, bias, and level mixture ("high" vs. "low" based on a median split), and randomly assigned to treatments designed to present moral reasoning either one stage *above* the pretest mode or one stage *below* that mode.

The treatment was incorporated into a second, or posttest, administration of the moral reasoning test booklet (some two weeks after pretesting) as follows: Students were told that two of the four dilemmas had been discussed by other people, and that the results of this discussion, along with the agreed-upon responses, were now included in the booklets. A two-paragraph "discussion summary," drawn from Kohlberg's scoring manual and presenting either $+1$ *or* -1 stage reasoning, preceded the dilemmas. Also, for all questions concerning the first two dilemmas, the $+1$ or -1 stage responses were circled and attributed to the people mentioned above. A second set of these questions was included to be answered by the students, and the remaining two dilemmas were presented as they had been at pretesting. A delayed posttest, identical to the pretest, was given two weeks after this exercise.

The results of the study were strikingly similar to our findings with map drawing, both the longitudinal and intervention studies, particularly with respect to changes in modal level. Modal stage change scores from pretest to posttest and from pretest to delayed posttest were examined in separate analyses of variance, using type of treatment, bias, and high- versus low-level mixture as contrasts. Results showed that the $+1$ treatment was superior to the -1, and the positive bias students advanced more than negative bias students. This was true both at posttest and, although the effect was somewhat weaker, at delayed posttest. The only students showing a mean reversion in modal level were those who were in the -1 treatment *and* who were negative bias when the study began. The only significant effect of level mixture in the entire study was an interaction with bias which revealed that students with negative bias and high mixture showed a negative mean change in modal level at the delayed posttest.

Perhaps more revealing than the formal analyses of the data were the simple percentages of subjects who advanced in modal level under the two experimental conditions. In the $+1$ treatment, positive bias students advanced in modal level more frequently than their negative bias peers—62% versus 50% at posttest, and 71% versus 19% at delayed posttest. In the -1 treatment, by contrast, negative bias students more often regressed in modal level—67% versus 28% at posttest and 44% versus 6% on the delayed posttest.

These results replicate quite closely our findings with map drawing. They are encouraging on at least two counts: They are based on work in a different domain, leading us to believe that our six-phase model may have wider utility than simply as a transition model for map drawing; and, the tests were not confounded by using the same data to construct and then evaluate a model, a major problem of the data reported in Chapter 3. In the present study, predictions were based on the existing six-phase model and extended into the domain of moral judgment and reasoning. The fact that the results were so consistent with previous findings in a quite different realm of reasoning was encouraging. But not everyone was so convinced that our model was well formed; as we shall see, the model was put to demanding test by other researchers. As we shall also see, it has survived the endeavor rather well.

FURTHER STUDIES OF THE TRANSITIONS MODEL

Studies of Positive Justice, Parental Authority, and Self-Understanding

Using data from studies of social cognition, specifically of positive justice, parental authority, and self-understanding, William Damon and Daniel Hart have explored the relative utility of our transitions model verus their own model in predicting change, especially modal level change in these domains. In a study published the same year as the first edition of *Beyond Universals in Cognitive Development,* Damon (1980) reported that spread (or mixture) above a subject's modal level was a good predictor of a transition from level to level in both the positive justice and parental authority domains, thus validating our claim that a positive bias index signals progressive potential in the gradual process of stage-to-stage change.

Damon had cast this work in the context of comparing three models of how stage mixture might relate to developmental advance, specifically to a change in modal level. Based on the significant relation of positive spread to mode change, he concluded that total spread in general and particulary low spread around the mode (i.e., a characteristic of consolidation) were less powerful predictors of stage-to-stage change. Although Damon's results were consistent with our model, we were concerned that total mixture and low mixture did not receive the attention they deserved as indications of important aspects of developmental change.

In order to examine in greater detail the interaction among

mixture, bias, and mode change, Snyder and Feldman (1984) re-analyzed data from the 1977 map-drawing study in a manner identical to that used by Damon (1980) in his study of social reasoning. When analyzed in a parallel manner the mapping data replicated very nicely the pattern of effects reported by Damon. For example, Damon found correlations of .43 (for Positive Justice) and .44 (for Parental Authority) between positive spread and mode advance; our parallel correlation was .54. The principal contribution of our reanalysis, however, was in showing that positive bias and negative bias subjects produced very different patterns of effect. These differences were not revealed in Damon's (1980) research because he analyzed his data without regard to the bias index. For example, consistent with the six-phase model, we found that positive mixture predicted mode advance only among the positive bias children ($r = .50$, $p < .01$). No such relationship was found among those children who had a negative bias index ($r = .003$, N.S.). Positive mixture, therefore, did predict mode advance, as Damon suggested; but, as we predicted, this was true only for those children having more positive than negative mixture (i.e., only when the bias index was positive).

In addition, a number of other analyses of variabilities that Damon reported were replicated in our whole-sample analyses and extended in those analyses done separately for positive and negative bias children. Finally, correlations calculated without regard to bias on measures of total mixture taken at successive times of testing were consistently negative, thus suggesting that periods of low mixture or consolidation alternated with periods of higher mixture or transition between modal levels.

In similar fashion, Snyder and Norcini (1982b) analyzed data from a training study (Norcini & Snyder, 1983) examining moral reasoning among adolescents. Once again, correlations calculated between various measures of mixture and modal level advance replicated Damon's (1980) results. However, as was the case in Snyder and Feldman (1984), when the sample was separated by bias index and the correlations recalculated, Snyder and Norcini (1982b) found more detailed results in good agreement with the six-phase model. Specifically, seven of the nine predictions received significant support, and an eighth was supported at the $p = 0.08$ level.

To summarize, based on the reanalyses of our mapping data and the analysis of newer data, the phase model held up quite well. More than that, it has gained credibility for its ability to account for data in three different realms: spatial representation, social-cognitive development, and moral reasoning.

Not willing to concede that the six-phase model should guide future efforts to describe transition states, Hart and Damon (1984) reported findings and analyses intended to counter some of our arguments. These findings were on the topic of self-understanding and were gathered over a three-year period, with 18 months separating each of three interviews. Self-understanding was assessed in interviews with boys and girls of elementary school age using questions such as "Can you tell me what kind of person you are?" (Damon & Hart, 1984, p. 4).

Damon and Hart attempted to test the utility of using positive and negative bias in addition to their own positive and negative mixture indices. They reported that, contrary to our results, mixture above the mode was a good predictor of modal level advance for all subjects, not just those with positive bias. They also reported weaker negative correlations between total spread (i.e., 90% of responses not at the modal stage) at different points in time (a measure of consolidation) than the six-phase model would predict. On the basis of these sorts of interpretations, they recommended the earlier model proposed by Damon (1980) which did not include distinct phases in the transition process, but rather argued for continuous change toward more advanced modal levels. The "consolidation phases" of Snyder and Feldman were singled out as particularly unnecessary.

Although Hart and Damon consider some of the methodological differences between their technique and ours, and although they recognized that these differences might help explain why their results differed somewhat from ours, they focused instead on elaborating domain differences between self-understanding and map drawing as the more likely source of differences found in the data. Of course, in the absence of studies holding constant one or the other set of possible sources of differences, it is unlikely that we will find a clear answer to the question of why one or the other model is shown to better fit a particular data set.

Perhaps more important than proving one or the other model's superiority is to note that, in fact, both models are strikingly similar in their fundamental approaches to transitions. Our model places greater emphasis on distinct phases of elaboration and consolidation than Damon's, but both models are continuous partial transformation of structure approaches in the tradition of Turiel (1966, 1969, 1983) and of Vygotsky (1978; Zender & Zender, 1974). These are in contrast to the structures-as-a-whole models of Piaget and Kohlberg.

A recent volley in this friendly war was fired from yet another research group studying yet another domain: the development of reasoning about friendship using Selman's (1980) work as a framework (Berkowitz & Keller, in press). Based on a six-year longitudinal study of 97 children between their 9th and 15th years, Berkowitz and

Keller analyzed their findings in relation to the issues raised in the studies just summarized. After reviewing the findings of our group and of Damon's, they make two points: the first is that the results in Hart and Damon rarely reach statistical significance, making it difficult to know how much confidence to place in their findings; and, they point out that the *interval* between testings is a critical variable in prediction how the data should fall. Differences in the pace of change characteristic of the particular domains under study will interact with the testing interval to determine predicted changes in mode, mixture, and bias. If, for example, map drawing is a domain where stage advance takes on the average three years, then the prediction for a three-year interval represents a complete transition cycle. The same kind of reasoning applies to other intervals.

This makes it crucial to know how long an interval there tends to be between stages or levels in a particular domain, and to match the predicted changes to: (a) where in a transition cycle a subject starts, and (b) how much progress in the domain can be expected during the between test interval. Hart and Damon (1986) tend to ignore these constraints in their interpretation of our model and the predictions following therefrom. Even if their report produced nothing else (which is not the case), Berkowitz and Keller have made a positive contribution to the understanding of transitions in cognitive development by showing that domains differ in the length of their transition cycles.

They go on to cite evidence from other studies, including another study by Hart and Damon (1986), as well as studies on moral reasoning (Colby, Kohlberg, Gibbs, & Lieberman, 1983; Walker & Taylor, 1991), logical reasoning (Piaget, 1970), friendship (Selman, 1980), and all three of the above (Edelstein, Keller, & Schroder, in press). The weight of the evidence suggests that four to six years is a reasonable interval for stage changes in the above domains. Based on this evidence, Berkowitz and Keller argue that transitions might be studied fruitfully by examining shifts of less than a full stage, particularly when looking at relatively microlevel processes. This is the line they pursue in their research on friendship reasoning.

The subjects in the study were 97 schoolchildren between their 9th and 15th years. Their interviews were scored using Selman's five-stage sequence of friendship reasoning, but with as many as 13 steps for the entire sequence of 1/3-stage intervals. Results were reported in terms of the same sorts of variables used in the studies of map drawing, justice, and authority (i.e., positive and negative spread, total spread, modal stage, and bias).

Although a number of detailed findings were reported, we will mention only those that bear directly on the six-phase model. It was found, for example that Total Spread was unrelated to shift in modal level of reasoning, that Positive Spread was positively correlated with modal level advance for the entire sample ($r = .42$, $p < .01$), and for the negative bias subjects ($r = .27$, $p < .02$), but not for the positive bias subjects. Negative Spread was negatively correlated with modal level shifts for the entire sample only ($r = .43$, $p < .01$). Negative and positive bias groups had mean modal stage changes of, respectively, 0.49 and 1.92 levels (measured in 1/3 stage increments). The difference between these groups was statistically significant ($t(158) = 7.22$, $p < .01$).

Relationships between positive and negative spread and mode advance replicated those reported in both our own and the Damon studies. The results for bias, however, were not altogether consistent with previous findings. Berkowitz and Keller explain plausibly the inconsistencies by recalling the length of interval for the domain issue and bringing in as well the fact that some of our findings were based on *interventions*. The nature and type of interventions involved makes it quite likely that the "natural" course of transition, whatever that might be, was disrupted to some degree.

In addition, a question was raised about how much reasoning in advance of the mode is required to energize the transition process. Their own point of view (and their data seem to support it) is that *any* amount of reasoning above the mode is sufficient to energize the system and to begin a transition process that leads, in due course, to a shift in modal level. Without going into the details of the argument, Berkowitz and Keller found that relationships among mode and mixture were consistent with previous findings when differences in modal level advance rates were considered, and that these relationships held up for shifts of one-third of a stage or level in reasoning about friendships over the six-year span of the longitudinal study.

When bias is brought into the picture, the results are more complicated and seemed, at first, to be inconsistent with our findings in map drawing. By invoking the fact that interventions were used in some of our earlier work, and by arguing that any amount of development beyond a mode is functionally equivalent, the discrepancies among our findings, those of Damon (1980; Hart & Damon, 1984, 1966), and Berkowitz and Keller were accounted for plausibly. With respect to mode shift differences, for example, Berkowitz and Keller (in press) say:

> The question still remains as to why the present data are in part discrepant from the data reported by Snyder and Feldman (1984), by Walker and Taylor (1991), and by Hart and Damon (1984). Extrapolating from Damon and Hart's (1986) more complete report of their data, 35% of their subjects evidenced mode shift compared to 61% of the present

subjects. Walker and Taylor (1991) report that nearly 40% of positive bias, but only 5% of negative bias, subjects advanced in modal stage. This lower frequency of change, in contrast to the present data set, is likely due to both the shorter time frame and the use of whole stage mode shift rather than substage shift as is the case here. Snyder and Feldman do not report amounts of change. They base their analyses on the data from a prior intervention study (Snyder & Feldman, 1977) in which they report mean stage change scores. Extrapolated from that report, 33% of the subjects changed in mode on a delayed posttest. These differences in the amount of change observed in the four studies may help explain the differences in the results reported. It may not be the case that the differences reported indicate the lack of validity of the bias/spread microprocess model. Rather, it may simply be that the differences in the designs of the four studies generate different outcome situations. The present study finds the most change and hence little variation in change scores and no significant relations for the highest change group, positive bias subjects. Snyder and Feldman, using a short-term intervention strategy, and Walker and Taylor, find change variation only in the positive bias group, the group most likely to change (17 of 20 of Snyder and Feldman's subjects and 43 of 49 of Walker and Taylor's subjects with modal change were positive bias subjects). In this case, one should find no variation in the negative bias group and therefore no significant correlations, and strong variation in the positive bias group (about half of those subjects experienced mode shift) and consequently significant correlations. This is precisely what they report. (pp. 30–31)

Similar arguments are proposed for other seemingly problematic findings. These authors conclude:

The findings of this investigation bear on stage theory in general and equilibration in particular in three ways. First, they strongly confirm the Snyder and Feldman (1977) model, based explicitly on the Piagetian equilibration model, in three ways: (a) the results are generally quite consistent with the consolidation/transition mechanisms of bias and spread; (b) the results lead to a methodological reevaluation of the prior literature which explains apparently contradictory findings and demonstrates them to be consistent with the Snyder and Feldman model; (c) the data reported here tend to support a structural model of stage transition by demonstrating that the miscroprocesses described by Snyder and Feldman are operative both for an alternative analysis of subcontent issues and their standing relative to the modal reasoning used by an individual and for a molecular measure of stage, that is, one-third stage steps. (pp. 33–34)

More Moral Judgment and Reasoning Evidence. An even more recent study specifically designed to test the phase sequence model, and more specifically to pit this model against its close relative, the

model of Damon and Hart, was research reported by Walker and Taylor
(1991). Having reviewed the literature somewhat as we have done
here, Walker and Taylor wanted to determine if the consolida-
tion/elaboration phases and the bias index so central to our account of
transitions would hold up in the realm of moral judgment and
reasoning as assessed by Kohlberg's well-known moral dilemmas
(Colby & Kohlberg, 1987).

Although their results were complex, on the whole they tended to
support our model, and specifically, they supported our model over the
continuous change model of Damon and Hart. Before turning to the
results themselves, let us briefly summarize the design and methods
of the study.

A sample of 227 children, adolescents, and adults were interviewed
twice over a two-year interval. The children came from grades 1, 4,
and 10, and were part of family triads gathered for other purposes.
Each subject was given a score based on the number of times various
moral judgment levels were present in his or her protocol. Based on
these scores, modal level, mixture, and bias were calculated for each
subject at each of two points in time, as well as two measures used in
the continuous change model: positive mixture and negative mixture.

Results were in some ways very similar to map drawing: most
subjects (more than 70%) remained stable over two years, forward
movements in modal stage were more than three times more frequent
than backward movements, bias predicted stage transition more
powerfully than other variables, and the combination of bias and
mixture gave greater power to the prediction than either variable
alone.

A more complex set of findings was reported bearing on our earlier
finding that consolidation/elaboration goes through recursive or cycli-
cal phases between stages. On the whole, the results tended to support
this finding (158 of 227 subjects' patterns of change were consistent
with our model). A number of other subjects' patterns might have also
been consistent with the model, but the data were sufficiently ambig-
uous to lead to caution in interpreting them. Walker and Taylor
interpret 61 patterns as "inconsistent" with our model.

Even these 61 patterns may not all be inconsistent with our model if
the notion of reversion is included, as it was at least informally in our
earlier research. As mentioned earlier in this chapter, the problem
with our analyses of reversion is that they have not been put to
statistical test. But if we assume that backward movement is a
systematic part of the transition process, as we believe it is, then all
but 19 of Walker and Taylor's patterns seem to us potentially consistent with our transitions model. Granted that we cannot make a strong
claim for such dramatic confirmation of the model (it would be 206 of

227 subjects at its most optimistic). But even at the most conservative estimate, the results are impressive. Somewhere between two-thirds and 90% of the movements are consistent with our model.

Their results led Walker and Taylor (1991) to the following conclusion:

> The findings of this study were, in general, consistent with [the Snyder & Feldman] model. High total mixture was predictive of stage transitions, as was positive bias. Indeed, direction of bias was a powerful predictor—seven times as many positive bias subjects (who are in a period of consolidation)....The present findings do not support [the Damon–Hart model]. Analyses of the changes in modal stage, bias, and mixture over the longitudinal interval indicated that most were consistent with the notion of alternating periods of elaboration and consolidation. (p. 336)

One methodological point might be added. Because the map-drawing scoring and the moral judgment and reasoning scoring differed in several ways, it would not have been surprising if there had been greater discrepancies in results that were in fact found. For example, in map drawing, all scores are based on a single drawing, whereas in moral judgment, several dilemmas are used as the basis for scoring.

Once again it appears that, although not without its problems, the model we proposed in 1980 seems to have fared well, particularly given the fact that widely varying techniques have been used to test it.

CONCLUSIONS

On the whole, the six-phase model of Chapter 3 has stood up fairly well in subsequent research trials. We regret that the number of studies using the model has been relatively small, but take heart in the fact that for the most part the data seem to support a model along the lines that we originally constructed to account for changes in map drawing. That these data come from such widely disparate realms as moral judgment and reasoning, self-understanding, positive justice, parental authority, and reasoning about friendship, suggests that the model is surprisingly robust. That the studies summarized have in addition used somewhat different research techniques and employed research designs that vary in significant ways adds further weight to the utility of the six-phase model of transitions. We can only hope that more studies will add precision to our current understanding of the stage change process and lead to suggestions of where the model should be revised. We certainly never expected it to stand without modification.

5

Studies in the Development of Expertise

As Charles Brainerd (1981), one of the early (and more critical) reviewers of *Beyond Universals*, wrote:

> I would maintain that this book has little of substance to offer either the general developmental reader or investigators working in the areas where most contemporary research on cognitive development is concentrated (e.g., memory development, mental retardation, language development, development of reading, concept development).... Given that one of their principal aims was to modify unacceptable assumptions of the theory, it is curious that Feldman et al.'s [1980] modifications focused on assumptions that only dyed-in-the-wool Piaget orthodoxers believe anyway (e.g., universalism, spontaneous development). In the absence of a forthright attempt to deal with more central criticisms, it seems unlikely that readers who do not already have strong Piagetian leanings will be inclined to accept the authors' views. (p. 79)

Although we found these words difficult to have to confront in 1981 and tried to reduce their force in a reply (Feldman, 1981), there was more than a grain of truth in the charge that our work tended to appeal to and generate interest mostly from those already committed to Piagetian, or more generally, cognitive-developmental, ways of approaching progressions in thinking.

The research reviewed in the previous chapter, our own and that of other investigators, was for the most part carried out by members of the same tribe, a tendency not uncommon in the field but nonetheless a serious concern (Kessen, 1984). At the time we thought that most of the problem was with the task (map drawing) and the technique (tedious, labor intensive, and requiring extensive training). We thought that the wider research community would respond to our work better if the domain were an intrinsically more interesting one (map drawing continues to fascinate us, but...) and the research techniques used were more readily transportable.

These concerns were probably well placed, but should have been broadened to reflect what our critics were trying to tell us, namely, that there were other lines of ongoing work that might enrich, and in turn be enriched by, our efforts to study transitions in cognitive development. Indeed, a major example of the widespread recognition that the study of transitions should be a central concern of the field was the appearance of Robert Sternberg's small edited volume *Mechanisms of Cognitive Development* (Sternberg, 1984). Taking an avowedly information processing orientation to the problem, work on a wide variety of topics by several major investigators was summarized. And nowhere was our work mentioned. It was impossible to ignore the fact that, whatever our feelings might be about the importance of our work or the contributions it might make to the field, we would have no chance to participate in the dialogue if our work was not read, cited, extended, or even criticized by other researchers.

In order to show that our work is relevant to the wider field, we began to describe it in terms of *expertise* and to carry out studies informed by and influenced by work done during the past 20 years on novice/expert contrasts. Having gotten a kick start through the highly visible work on chess done by Simon and Chase during the early 1970s (Chase & Simon, 1974; Simon & Chase, 1973), and with increased attention to artificial intelligence possibilities and other computer applications (Pea & Kurland, 1984), expertise research in mainstream cognitive psychology (later to be included in the emerging field of cognitive science) has proceeded at a brisk pace. Inasmuch as one of us had been using a novice-to-expert progression to describe levels of development within specific domains since the mid-1970s (Feldman, 1976, 1977), it did not require much of a stretch to couch the work in these terms.

Coming up with appropriate domains to study and techniques less laborious and more transportable was harder, much harder. To date we have begun empirical studies in three new domains, and colleagues elsewhere have embarked on studies of a fourth domain, computer programming, all within the context of efforts to understand the development of expertise. What distinguishes our approach from that of other investigators interested in expertise is our focus on *development* or learning (i.e., on how and under what conditions a novice moves) in measured strides, toward becoming an expert—or even a master—in a highly challenging developmental domain.

In an essay called "The Child as Craftsman" (first published in 1976 and also Chapter 6 of the first edition of this book), Feldman argued for craftsmanship as a goal for education. Arguing that experts in various fields be made available as mentors for school children, he wrote:

> What I have in mind is not, strictly speaking, an apprentice relationship between novice and master. This relationship implies too much power on the part of the master. Still, there is an apprentice-like quality to the educational relationship I have in mind, and such a relationship should be available early. (p. 149)

In another article, this one a discussion of Mihalyi Csikszentmihalyi's ideas about artistic reasoning and artistic development (Csikszentmihalyi, 1977), Feldman proposed a series of stages or levels of expertise to chart the path between the individual just beginning to prepare for a career in the arts and the great master:

> A person becomes creative in the arts and elsewhere by learning how to do something well and wanting to do it better still. This ingredient is what seems missing from the set of needs or motives [described by Csikszentmihalyi]. I would suggest that what I call movement through a domain is the missing ingredient, and that it is what occurs when a person who becomes interested in a field—it may be art, it may be something else—traverses the levels of mastery and pushes on toward higher ones. Let me suggest these steps through a domain: *novice*, a person who has just begun to try to do something; *apprentice*, somebody who decides to do it seriously enough to study with a master, somebody more advanced than he or she; *journeyman*; *craftsman*; *master*; and perhaps in the extreme, *pre-eminent contributor*. (Feldman, 1977, p. 311)

These ideas were certainly part of the context in which we did our theorizing and research, but they did not explicitly frame our work until much later. And of course the fields of cognitive and educational psychology, as well as the growth of artificial intelligence, contributed to our awareness that expertise makes sense as a way to describe our work.

The distinguishing feature of our approach to expertise is that it is *developmental* in the sense that we see movement from novice to expert as proceeding through a sequence of levels. This is in contrast to the typical cognitive science literature where novices are contrasted with experts without attempts to capture movements through developmental levels that are central to our approach. There are encouraging signs that the cognitive science community is beginning to take the problem of progression through levels of skill more seriously. In a work intended to show the limits of artificial intelligence, Dreyfus and Dreyfus (1986) proposed a series of five general stages or levels of expertise that bear a substantial resemblance to our novice-to-master sequence (Table 5.1). Computers, they argue, can only be programmed to achieve the first two levels, while the more advanced levels require human experience. The important point from our perspective is that, within the cognitive science community, the idea of developmental levels or stages has begun to have currency.

Relatedly, we realized that the domain we had chosen to study, map drawing, was not the best choice for studying the development of expertise. The levels that we established for map drawing were ones that encompass the range of expertise expected by the culture for all children (although, as we pointed out, not an expectation that was a very high priority). The further reaches of the domain, those of the professional cartographer, were beyond the measurement capabilities of our instruments. With these thoughts in mind, we began to search for nonuniversal developmental domains further along the universal to unique continuum for research purposes (see Chapter 1). Development of expertise in the regions of discipline-based and/or idiosyncratic developmental domains seemed likely to meet our requirements.

Table 5.1. Five Stages of Skill Acquisition

Skill Level	Components	Perspective	Decision	Commitment
1. Novice	Context-free	None	Analytical	Detached
2. Advanced beginner	Context-free and situational	None	Analytical	Detached
3. Competent	Context-free and situational	Chosen	Analytical	Detached understanding and deciding. Involved in outcome
4. Proficient	Context-free and situational	Experienced	Analytical	Involved understanding. Detached deciding
5. Expert	Context-free and situational	Experienced	Intuitive	Involved

From: Dreyfus, H., & Dreyfus, S. (1986). *Mind over machine*. New York, NY: The Free Press. Reprinted by permission.

The availability of an avid amateur juggler in our research group made it easy to decide which among the many interesting disciplines and idiosyncratic domains would be the first to be studied.

THE JUGGLING STUDY

In the Spring semester of 1987, 21 undergraduates from a course in intellectual development at Tufts participated in an updated version of a Metahobby Project (see Chapter 3). Instead of being able to choose their semester-long project from among numerous metahobby possibilities, as is typically the case, students were offered the option of participating in a 10-week juggling course with Ronald Walton, a Ph.D. student who had been working on becoming better at three-ball juggling for several years. The project also represented a follow-up of Mr. Walton's MA thesis on metahobby, done the prior year (Walton, 1987), although that thesis was not on juggling.

The study aimed to examine transition phases in juggling along lines similar to our map-drawing research, but it also had an additional purpose: to study some of the emotions that are involved as students move from level to level within a nonuniversal developmental domain. We had noticed that the metahobby journals, which all students submitted at the end of the semester along with their formal papers, seemed to reveal systematic patterns of emotions that accompanied changes in thinking about their domains. In fact, as early as 1983–1984, we had begun to ask students to record their emotions as well as their analyses of learning and development as part of the metahobby assignment, hoping to eventually do some research on how systematic the patterns of emotions might be.

In order to be able to gather the data we needed, some work had to be done to analyze the various levels and elements of the domain of juggling; we now call the set of techniques for doing this "developmental domain analysis." Our first task was to try to determine the developmental levels of the domain; for this purpose, we consulted an expert, something we now strongly recommend as an early step in the domain analysis process.

Our expert, Martin Berliner, had several years' practice as a professional street juggler, earning a living by entertaining the crowds of visitors and tourists who flock to Boston's popular waterfront attraction, the Fanueil Hall Market. Mr. Berliner was happy to collaborate with us, particularly since the pay, if not better than on the street, was at least more steady. Mr. Berliner served as a consultant to the project throughout the experiment, and occasionally thereafter.

The first job to tackle was an initial "mapping of the domain" (we never seem to get very far away from our map-drawing roots). Without imposing our framework on him, we asked Mr. Berliner for a description of the differences between people who were just starting out as jugglers and those who had achieved a measure of mastery in the domain. It became clear very quickly that the domain is quite readily organized into developmental levels, and that this way of thinking about it was natural and unforced on our consultant. Within a few meetings, we were able to describe in rough detail provisional stages or levels of juggling (see Table 5.2).

Subsequent discussions produced a set of elements, analogous but not conceptually identical to the map-drawing elements of Chapter 3. The major difference between the two sets was that the juggling domain did not seem to allow as elegant and symmetrical a solution to the elements problem. For example, some elements appeared at and moved through only a subset of the eight developmental levels identified for the domain. In other words, the elements did not permit a straightforward concepts-applied-to-features framework as was the case with map drawing. Still, we were able to come up with a set of 12 elements which could vary among the eight developmental levels (see Table 5.3).

Subjects in the study were 21 undergraduates who elected the juggling option as their project for the Intellectual Development course at Tufts. Dividing the total number of students into two sections made the size of each group more manageable. Results from the two groups were comparable. Students took part in weekly sessions of about an hour each over a 10-week period. The lessons consisted primarily of teacher demonstration and explanation, group practice, and some individualized instructions.

Aside from its intrinsic interest to the students, juggling is also a relatively inexpensive metahobby choice (three juggling balls are the only equipment needed). More important for our purposes is the fact that movement through the initial levels of juggling tends to occur relatively quickly, making it likely that we would be able to observe transitions in most of our subjects during the course of the project. For the most part, the students enjoyed the experience of learning to juggle and were able to see clear improvement by the end of the term.

Before the lessons began, subjects completed a questionnaire requesting guesses about their initial juggling ability and their expectations for progress over the course of the lessons. After each session, subjects evaluated their performance during the lesson by rating themselves on the following 12 component juggling skills: Timing, Accuracy, Height, Stability, Pattern Width, Plane, Exchanges, Right

Table 5.2.   Proposed Levels of Juggling Performance

1. Raw Beginner—No sense of timing or pattern whatsoever. Cannot throw 1 ball from hand to hand with any consistency. NO PATTERN

2. Beginner—Can throw 2 balls from hand to hand with some consistency of accuracy and timing. Grasps physically and cognitively the idea of exchanging 2 balls. Height, width, stability, maintaining a plane uncontrolled. Dominant hand much better than nondominant hand. Rigid posture with hands held too high and/or too far in front of body. Cannot maintain exchanges without moving entire body. EXCHANGE

3. Novice I—Can put 2 exchanges back to back (1 cycle). Beginning to understand the idea of "juggling." Cannot maintain more than 10 cycles. Accuracy and timing sufficient to juggle but are inconsistent, and pattern falls apart. Typically balls are thrown too high and stability of height is lacking. Sometimes balls are thrown very low in an effort to maintain control. Pattern width is too narrow and maintaining a plane is erratic. Nondominant hand has improved but there is still imbalance between hands. Hands inch up too high. Body control sufficient but variable; there is still rigidity and chasing of pattern. JUGGLING

4. Novice II—Can maintain between 10 and 20 cycles. Accuracy, timing, and plane consistent but deteriorate over juggling span. Can keep height and stability of balls for a time but these too deteriorate as juggling continues. Pattern width generally is still too narrow. Imbalance between hands is not as noticeable. Posture more relaxed and not much running after balls. Is comfortable with juggling. Can begin to do variations with 3 balls (e.g., 2 in 1 patterns, circle juggling, reverse patterns, etc.) and some partnership juggling (e.g., passing, take-aways, etc.).

5. Intermediate I—Accuracy, timing, pattern width, and plane fairly consistent over juggling span. Can vary height of throw at will and has steady stability of height. Can begin to vary timing and width. Nondominant hand almost as proficient as dominant hand. Can put two 3 ball variations together. Can juggle items of slightly different weights and sizes. Beginning partnership juggling with more than 3 balls. Can maintain more than 20 cycles. Body is relaxed, only chases patterns on new variations. VARIATIONS

6. Intermediate II—Does variations with 3 balls smoothly. Can maintain cycles for extended periods of time while mixing patterns. Can juggle 5 balls. Can vary patterns in idiosyncratic ways. Hands of essentially equal adeptness. All basic elements are secure enough to be varied at will without loss of pattern and only begin to deteriorate as pattern gets more complex. STABILITY

7. Craftsman—Levels 1 through 6 are rock steady, all basic elements are completely automatized. Objects of different types can be juggled together with no difficulty. Difficult patterns can be maintained alone and in concert with other jugglers. AUTOMATIZATION

8. Expert—Can perform the most difficult routines. Juggles at highest degree of technical proficiency with style and creativity. Recognized by other jugglers as being in top echelon. Can juggle 7 balls, 5 clubs. HIGHEST SKILL + HIGHEST STYLE

From: Walton et al. (1987). *A study of the relation between thought and emotion in the development of expertise*. Reprinted by permission.

and Left Hands, Hand Position, and Body Stability. Ratings were done using 9-point Likert scales with the following five labels at alternating points: Very Poorly (0), Not Too Well (2), Average (4), Good (6), and Very Well (8).

Table 5.3. Levels of Expertise in Early Childhood Teaching as Indicated by Selection of Educational Materials

Level	Brief Description	Basis for Materials Selection
Novice	Entertains children	Children's enjoyment
Apprentice	Keeps children occupied and safe	Time tested value
Journeyman	Teaches according to objectives	Educational objectives
Craftsman	Teaches according to theory and/or ideology	Educational philosophy
Expert	Teaches according to context	Teaching situation

From: Benjamin, A. (1989). *Levels of expertise in early childhood teaching: An initial diagnostic field test of a diagnostic instrument.* Republished by permission.

TRANSITION PHASES IN JUGGLING

Transition phases were computed in the manner of the map-drawing work, using the instructor's skill ratings as basic elements. Levels were computed from the subject skill ratings by summing and averaging the scores of the elements at each time period. This was done because subjects' ratings of themselves were extremely labile, and provided no clear patterns amenable to a transition cycle interpretation. More will be given on this later.

The two experimenter/instructors also made 9-point ratings of each student's performance on the 12 individual juggling components during each lesson. Experimenter rating levels were based on Walton and Berliner's (1987) analysis of the quantitative and qualitative differences in level of performance by juggling practitioners. The intraclass correlation obtained for instructor reliability on the 12 elements was .85; the Pearson correlation on modal level was $r = .89$.

Experimenter ratings of subjects' performance yielded scatter consistent with the idea that level mixture is the rule. Subjects' performance on the component skill elements showed at least some scatter nearly 80% of the time. As with map drawing, there was evidence of both forward and backward movement among elements. The ratio of forward to backward movement was strikingly similar to that found in map drawing (about 2:1). Every subject but one had moved forward at least one developmental level by the end of the term, and no subject had reverted at that point. Average advance was 2.2 levels in the domain of juggling.

A special feature of the juggling study was its attempt to track students' emotional responses to their juggling experience as well as their progress in learning how to juggle. Scales similar to those for rating performance were used to rate feelings about that performance in terms of 18 affect adjectives. The scales were labeled with: Not At All (0), Somewhat (2), Moderate Amount (4), Very much (6), and Extremely Much (8). The affect adjectives used in the juggling study are listed in Table 5.4. We hoped to be able to determine if certain emotions were associated with one or another of the transition phases, a goal we were not really able to achieve. Using discriminant function analysis, we tried to predict the six transition phases using emotions. Results showed that less than 40% of the time were we able to accurately predict transition phase. Still, some promising leads did occur. For example, the adjective "frustrated" received highest intensity ratings during phases marked by high-level mixture. Similarly, ratings of "unsure" were highest in phases associated with the breakdown of the old mode and the reformulation of a new mode. We hope to sharpen up the technique used in this study so that emotions might be incorporated into the transition phases model more systematically (Walton, Adams, Goldsmith, & Feldman, 1987).

EXPERIMENTER VERSUS STUDENT RATINGS

When experimenter and subject ratings of performance were compared, significant differences were found between subjects' perceived progress and experimenter ratings. Subjects typically made higher assessments of their abilities than did the experimenters. Subjects ratings on the average placed themselves at Level 4.41, whereas instructor ratings averaged 2.93. Correlations between student and instructor ratings were not statistically significant both for overall performance and individual element performance. These correlations did not improve over time. Subjects' ratings were also more labile; the range of difference between ratings from one week to the next was 74 points. For instructor ratings the range was 14. Subjects saw themselves as remaining at the same level for consecutive sessions only 3.3% of the time, as contrasted with the instructors' 25.4%.

The differences between "novice" jugglers' ratings and the ratings of their more advanced instructor were striking. Although not part of the original design of the juggling study, the findings seem to open up a line of investigation that should be further pursued. What are the reasons for novices' inflated ratings of their performance and weekly progress? Would their ratings more closely approximate those of their instructors as they became more skilled in the domain? Would the discrepancy between student and instructor differ with different instructors? These questions may help reveal how direct instruction affects progress within nonuniversal developmental domains, an issue of growing concern in the field as Vygotsky's work becomes more widely known (Rogoff & Wertsch, 1984).

The juggling research showed that, on the whole, the six phase transition model held up quite well in this domain. Phases matched those of the map-drawing work closely, as did movement among elements and from level to level. The extent of congruence is especially satisfying considering that juggling, unlike any of the domains studied before, is largely a psychomotor skill. The developmental model, then, has applicability across cognitive, social cognitive, and psychomotor domains. Because juggling is relatively easy to study and less cumbersome to analyze, we hope that other researchers might be attracted to the study of development using this nonuniversal developmental domain.

AESTHETIC JUDGMENT AND REASONING

In a recent MA thesis, Carol Mockros (Mockros, 1989) applied some of our ideas about levels and transitions to aesthetic judgment and reasoning, a domain which has had two recent attempts to map its developmental stages (Housen, 1984; Parsons, 1987). Mockros wanted to see if a questionnaire-based technique could yield results comparable to those obtained more laboriously through open-ended or structured interviews as used in previous studies of the domain. If it is possible to "map" a domain-like aesthetic judgment and reasoning using a relatively straightforward procedure such as was used in our study, it would open another line of possible research on transitions. In this instance, much of the initial mapping had been done by others; we tried to develop a more efficient technique for assessing levels.

As in earlier studies, subjects were asked to respond to various works of art, but Mockros used a fixed set of questions and standard response criteria designed to tap and reflect the levels proposed by Housen (1984) and by Parsons (1987). Subjects were asked to respond to three reproductions of modern works: Renoir's *Luncheon of the Boating Party*, Magritte's *The Steps of Summer*, and Chagall's *Noah Under the Rainbow*; these works were chosen from among those used by Housen and by Parsons.

Rather than study individual subjects over time or do open-ended interviewing, Mockros selected subjects who varied in the amount of background and experience they had in art, making predictions about developmental levels of aesthetic judgment based on a set of assumptions about the progression from novice to expert.

Subjects were 72 adults ranging in age from 18 to 52. Fifty-one subjects were women and 20 were men. Subjects were divided into groups based on amount of formal training in art; in addition, age was included as a variable because pilot work showed that age seemed to influence results. Five groups of subjects were formed based on the criteria below:

- *Group 1* ($n = 18$) consisted of undergraduates with no expressed interest in art.
- *Group 2* ($n = 13$) were graduate students and professional adults with no specified interest in art.
- *Group 3* ($n = 13$) were undergraduates who had declared themselves either art history or art theory majors.
- *Group 4* ($n = 10$) were graduate students in either art theory or art history.
- *Group 5* ($n = 18$) were professionals in the arts, including graphic artists, fine artists, art historians, and art critics.

Previous work by Housen and by Parsons had yielded two five-stage sequences of developmental levels with similar, but not identical, qualities. Both sequences were utilized in Mockros's study, and results will be reported using both stage descriptions. On the whole, the two schemes proved to be fairly comparable and compatible, at least using these techniques. Responses were coded separately according to each stage scheme, with every "thought unit" (a single coherent statement) receiving a rating of 1 through 5. Ratings were then multiplied by the number of times they were present, and divided by the total number of thought units, to yield a developmental level average similar to the map-drawing average of Chapter 3. Two coders did the ratings independently, and acceptable levels of reliability were achieved in all instances (between 75% and 85% initially, well over 90% after discussion of discrepant ratings).

RESULTS

Two, one-way analyses of variance showed that there were significant differences among groups in each of the sequences, while contrast tests (using Scheffe's procedure) showed a pattern of between groups differences consistent with predictions. The results are also well illustrated in Figure 5.1, which shows how each group performed, on the average, in terms of the two sequences of developmental levels. On the whole the two developmental schemes proved quite similar, although not identical. The fact that both schemes produced similar overall results suggests that there is concurrent validity between them. For our purposes, either would be appropriate for studying developmental levels and transitions.

Our effort to more efficiently "map" the developmental levels of a domain was for the most part successful. Particularly encouraging were the findings that our procedure allows data gathering in about an hour (as contrasted with much longer periods of time in previous work) and produced reliable scoring that is also relatively easily achieved. We were not able to break down the domain into elements at this point, making detailed analyses of transitions a goal for future research. But the domain of aesthetic judgment and reasoning does seem to conform quite well to theoretical predictions about developmental levels and sequences, leading us to conclude that further research in this domain is justified.

Figure 5.1.   Aesthetic Judgments

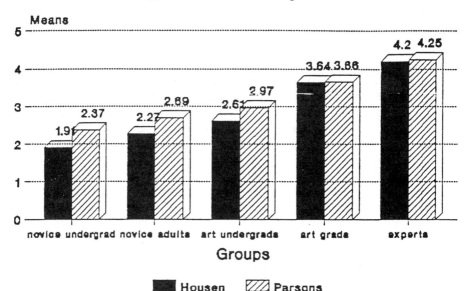

From: Mockros, C. (1990). *Aesthetic judgement: An empirical comparison of two- stage developmental theories.* Reprinted by permission.

RESEARCH ON COMPUTER PROGRAMMING

For the past several years, a group under the leadership of Robert Campbell then of IBM Research and now at Clemson University, has been studying the development of expertise in computer programming, specifically programming in a language called Smalltalk (Campbell, 1989, 1990; Campbell, Brown, & DiBello, 1992).

Based on theoretical work done with Mark Bickhard (Campbell & Bickhard, 1986, 1987, 1992) as well as on our framework, Campbell has argued that developmental analysis is critical for understanding the improvement of expertise in programming. The arguments take a form quite similar to those we make about expertise in general, namely, that simple novice/expert contrasts provide only crude and insufficient descriptions of a task domain. Moreover, they are unlikely to lead to adequate techniques for facilitating the development of expertise. Campbell (1992) wrote:

> The cognitive science work on expertise is nondevelopmental. It typically makes a binary contrast between novice and expert, examining no interesting points between the beginning and the endpoint of development. This violates the principle that the more steps that can be identified in a developmental sequence, the better it is understood. The cognitive science research also fails to illuminate the process of development; [cognitive science approaches cannot]...specify developmental processes powerful enough to produce the changes they report. (p. 1)

Campbell and his associates have gathered interview data from a total of ten programmers varying in amount of experience in learning to use Smalltalk, a highly challenging programming language. Based on a mixture of structured interviews and audiotape diaries, a sequence of seven developmental levels of Smalltalk programming has been provisionally established. "Scenarios" characteristic of each level have been established as well, making diagnosis of levels feasible. Scenarios were devised for the specific purpose of research on human/computer interaction (Carroll, 1989; Carroll & Campbell, 1989), and "represent actual or possible task accomplishments or errors" (Campbell, 1992, p. 2). An example of a scenario for the first level of Smalltalk is as follows:

> While exploring the Smalltalk/visual interface, you try to resize a window. You do this by clicking on the resize icon at the right hand of the title bar. You then drag with the mouse on the rubber band window outline that appears, and release the mouse button when you achieve the window size you want. Unfortunately, the rubber band window outline always starts at a small size which you must then enlarge, rather than

starting at the current size of the window. That means that if you click on the corner of the window by accident, you'll have to resize it, because it will automatically shrink down to a small size. (Campbell, 1992, p. 2)

Using data from scenarios such as these, Campbell has been able to map out a sequence of seven developmental levels of Smalltalk; they are summarized by these descriptions:

Developmental Levels of Smalltalk Programming

1. Interacting with the visual interface
2. Syntax rules and order of precedence
3. Locating classes and methods in the hierarchy
4. Class vs. instance distinction
5. Model-Pane-Dispatcher
6. Object-oriented design
7. Grandmaster level

A total of 14 scenarios have been identified, at least one for all but the most advanced level in the sequence; none of the interviewed programmers at IBM practiced Smalltalk programming at the most sophisticated level, although several recognized that such a level exists and could describe some qualities that would be characteristic of that level.

Although there have been no studies to date of transitions in Smalltalk programming, the domain seems particularly well suited to research. Anecdotal data gathered in the interviews suggest that the effort to identify specific emotional aspects of developmental transitions in this domain is also not without promise. Campbell (1992) reported that:

> programmers often spoke of their feelings about Smalltalk. For instance, PM [a subject], in transition to Level 5, spoke of his "manic-depressive" experiences; in the manic phase, he could borrow methods from the environment and get the results he wanted immediately; in the depressive phase, he had to modify existing methods in ways that required deep understanding, leading to days of arduous search and experimentation. (p. 7)

Study of transition phases, particularly emotional aspects of transitions, seems a promising next step in research on the development of expertise in computer programming. And the results for development levels seem to provide additional support for the viability and utility of the general approach we have been using in the study of expertise.

As Campbell (1992) pointed out, developmental levels may turn out to be too simple and not as clearly sequenced as initially mapped, but they do represent a reasonable and parsimonious first pass through highly complex bodies of knowledge and skill.

That such disparate domains as juggling, map drawing, aesthetic judgment, and computer programming seem to conform as well as they do to a theoretically required sequence of developmental levels suggests that our framework is one that has wide applicability. But it no doubt also has some limitations that will only be established as we continue to extend and refine our techniques for research in evermore far-flung domains. Indeed, the last study to be summarized has begun to show us one set of constraints on nonuniversal developmental theory when it is applied to a domain very close to home: teaching.

MAPPING THE DOMAINS OF TEACHING

As readers of the first edition remember, the impetus for the universal-to-unique continuum of developmental domains came largely from the author's experience in education. It seemed that Piaget's theory, however powerful it might be in other ways, was inadequate as a guide for educational theory and practice.

It has been our hope for some time to be able to begin the study of teaching as a nonuniversal developmental domain (Berliner, 1987). Were such studies to be done, it would move the theoretical and empirical work directly into the arena that motivated the broader effort in the first place. There have been formidable obstacles to overcome in launching developmental domain studies of teaching; we were not wrong to wait until now to tackle a domain so complex and difficult. And the work to date is little more than a beginning. But we now believe that it may be feasible to launch a program of research intended to map the levels and study the transitions in the domain or domains of teaching.

Our initial effort was a study of developmental levels in day care teaching; the study was carried out by Ann C. Benjamin as a PhD dissertation at Tufts (Benjamin, 1989). An instrument for diagnosing levels of expertise in early childhood teaching was created, pilot tested, and administered to 60-day care teachers who varied in background, experience, and formal preparation. The teachers' supervisors rated them on their level of competence in the classroom to provide validity data for the instrument. Finally, teachers completed Rest's (1986) Defining Issues Test (DIT) of moral judgment and reasoning in order to estimate the extent to which teaching requires capabilities distinctive to the domain. The literature had suggested that higher levels of moral judgment would lead to higher levels of teaching, and we wanted to explore this possibility (Sprinthall & Theis-Sprinthall, 1980).

The diagnostic instrument used in the study, in some respects technically similar to the DIT, required that teacher subjects judge six educational materials (dominoes, incentive chart, alphabet chart, flash cards, unifix cubes, and sand), and then consider pedagogical reasons for holding a particular opinion. Teachers either approved or disapproved of each material and then supported their judgment by indicating which of several reasons was "most important" in guiding their choice. Whether a teacher liked a material or not was expected to be much less indicative of developmental level than were her reasons for viewing a material favorably or unfavorably. That is, the teachers' choices of reasons were expected to show how their thinking might change over time and as they gained greater expertise. The reasons, which had been selected from pilot interviews with teachers and nonteachers, represented categories of reasoning that were provisionally assigned to the novice to expert sequence. The predicted levels of expertise in early childhood teaching are summarized in Table 5.4.

We expected our instrument to be able to discriminate among groups of teachers varying in training and experience (somewhat similar to our study of aesthetic judgment and reasoning in this respect), to be positively correlated with supervisors' ratings of classroom competence, and to show only moderate correlations with the OIT. This latter prediction was made with the idea that if teaching is a distinct set of developmental domains, which we believe it to be, then our test of teaching knowledge should be only loosely related to broader measures of cognitive development. Since Rest's DIT has been used (inappropriately, we believe) as a measure of teacher development (Sprinthall & Bernier, 1978; Sprinthal & Theis-Sprinthall, 1980), it seemed like a reasonable measure to (hopefully) contrast with the TOPS. A moderate correlation was expected.

Six groups of 10 teachers each were formed: those with less than a BA degree versus those with a BA or more, crossed with those with less than two years of experience, those with two to four years of experience, and those with five or more years of experience. When compared with each other, there were sufficient overall differences among the groups to produce significant main effects both for education and for experience independently, with no interaction between them, an unexpected result. Other results were for the most part consistent with predictions. Teachers with different amounts of experience and training did differ in the reasons they used to justify their

Table 5.4.   Affect Adjectives Used in the Juggling Studies

Affect Adjectives
AMBIVALENT
ANGRY
ANXIOUS/WORRIED
BORED
CHALLENGED
COMFORTABLE
COMPLIANT
CONFIDENT
CONFUSED
CONTENT
DEPRESSED
ENTHUSIASTIC
EXCITED
FRUSTRATED
HAPPY
INTERESTED
MOTIVATED
PLEASED
PROUD
RESISTANT
SAD
UNEASY
UNSURE

opinions of the various classroom materials, making it possible to identify a plausible sequence of teacher development. Specifically, evidence for ordering four of the five categories of pedagogical reasons was found, with the low to high order being: "Children's Enjoyment," "Education Objectives," "Educational Philosophy," and "Educational Context."

The data bearing on validity were similarly encouraging but modest in strength. The correlations among the various measures were on the whole as predicted; the sizes of the correlations, however, were modest. Correlations are summarized in Table 5.5.

Of the three pedagogically related measures that were used, the teachers' own identification of their level of expertise was the best predictor of TOPS performance; but this measure was based in part on the TOPS itself, making it more of an internal validity check than a

Table 5.5. Pearson Correlation Coefficients among Teacher and Supervisor Variables

	IP	SC	TC	SR	TS	PS
IP		.4173 (53) p = .001	.4494 (60) p = .000	.3651 (53) p = .004	.9422 (60) p = .000	.2983 (58) p = .011
SC			.2670 (53) p = .027	.6654 (53) p = .000	.3562 (53) p = .004	.3232 (51) p = .010
TC				.2129 (53) p = .063	.3631 (60) p = .002	.3369 (58) p = .005
SR					.3455 (53) p = .006	.2749 (51) p = .005
TS						.2496 (58) p = .029
PS						

IP = Individual Performance Score (TOPS)
SC = Supervisor Choice of Level of Expertise
TC = Teacher Choice of Level of Expertise
SR = Supervisor Rating
TS = Teaching Score (TOPS)
PS = Principled Score (DIT)

Note. Numbers in parentheses refer to number of subjects.

genuine predictor. Of the other measures, TOPS performance was moderately related to supervisors' ratings, indicating that the TOPS was measuring capabilities relevant to classroom performance.

Comparing the DIT and the TOPS produced a correlation of the predicted size and direction. The two measures were modestly related, but clearly do not measure the same qualities. This is consistent with our belief that teaching is a distinct and separate domain, one that cannot be captured by general developmental measures such as the DIT, Loevinger's Ego Development Scale (Loevinger, 1976), or general Piagetian measures.

Further support for this belief about the relative independence of DIT reasoning and pedagogical reasoning is found in the fact that, although both very high and very low scores on the DIT appeared in our sample, the high scorers were not necessarily the expert teachers, nor were the low scorers the novice teachers. The 16-year-old who achieved the *lowest* possible score on the TOPS (1.00), achieved a moral reasoning score on the DIT that fell close to the average for practicing physicians! (Benjamin, 1989, p. 98). Clearly, other measures of both teaching and cognitive development are called for if we are going to be able to describe adequately the distinct qualities of each of the relevant domains. But the results to date seem to point in the direction of considerable independence between domains, consistent with our theoretical predispositions.

TRANSITIONS AND LEVELS

As with all of our studies, the goal in studying teaching was to produce a sequence of levels for the domain so that it is possible to study movement from one to another. With respect to teaching (really early childhood/day care teaching), we have made a promising beginning, but further studies are needed before we are confident about the sequence of levels, even for the restricted domain of early childhood teaching. Once such data are at hand, we can begin to think about the conditions under which teachers move from one level of expertise to the next.

Having begun to establish broad-gauged levels of expertise in early childhood teaching, attention should now turn to more refined within-level analyses, perhaps using some form of "elements" approach, that would ultimately allow a consideration of processes of change and the effects of intervention on those processes.

One of the consequences of the work on teaching has been to raise questions about the viability of stages of expertise as descriptions of the domain. There is without question a place for levels of expertise as descriptions like teaching, but the assumption that it is always better to move to a more advanced level may have to be questioned. We found that it was not altogether straightforward matter to analyze the domain of teaching.

It may be that for a given teacher in a given situation, moving to a more advanced level of expertise would actually reduce his or her effectiveness. If a teacher is working in an environment where a particular philosophical position is pervasive, and where practice is guided closely by that philosophical position, the teacher may be better advised to enrich and extend practice within the prevailing framework than to try to transcend it. There are many ways to structure an educational environment, and levels of expertise may or may not complement the prevailing structure in which a teacher may be working.

To make a decision to continue an individual line of growth in spite of its disruptiveness to a well-functioning educational environment is something not to be done without careful reflection. At times it may be necessary to try to transform the context; at other times it may make more sense to move to a location or setting where the individual's developmental path may be encouraged, or at least tolerated; at still other times it may be the wisest course of action to try to improve practice *within* an existing setting. No formula or simple set of rules can make such a decision easy, but an understanding of the relationship between levels of expertise and contextual constraints might help in making such decisions.

Stimulated (and challenged) by feminist developmentalists, stage theories themselves have been questioned once again. Initially, the challenge was from researchers who saw stage notions as too broad to be of scientific merit (see Chapter 1); more recently stages are being criticized because they do not reflect the range of developmental realities of development, particularly in women (cf. Gilligan, 1982). The image of a "web" of evermore complex interrelationships has been proposed as an alternative to the "ladder" of ever greater mastery and increasingly individuated frameworks. Feminist thinkers have thus questioned the fundamental basis on which most major developmental theories have been built.

These are issues that will be occupying and preoccupying us for many years to come. It appears that there is merit in both frameworks when applied to realms like teaching (and very likely parenting and friendships and relationships as well). That there is a core of knowledge to master and a set of techniques to acquire seems to be true of teaching as it is of other developmental domains, but there are also contextual considerations that may determine the degree to which a particular ladder will be ascended, considerations that go well beyond those of talent, motivation, and opportunity.

In the end, we may have to ask whether we value "theoretical" expertise more highly than we value effective practice, even when the domain under consideration is surely one of the most unrelentingly "practical" areas of knowledge in our culture. The point of view that we take is that expertise in the domain of teaching should be seen as intrinsically valuable in its own right, not as a pale reflection of capabilities in other domains. And if it should turn out that moving to the most advanced level of the domain does not always make sense, so be it. If we are able to show that educational domains are distinct and valuable and independent of other fields, the original purposes for beginning this work will be directly addressed, even if in doing so we find that other sorts of theories will need to be constructed in order to comprehend them.

FINAL THOUGHTS ON EXPERTISE

The research summarized in this chapter shows both continuity and change in our research. Work on transition phases has continued and been extended into other domains. The topic has also been taken up by other research groups, challenged by some and supported by others. On the whole, the model seems to have weathered the research storms reasonably well, particularly given the variations in technique, sample, and content that have been brought into the arena. The notion of distinct phases of transition between developmental stages, while far from adequately demonstrated, seems well on its way toward becoming part of the established body of knowledge about transitions in cognitive development.

The work on specific "element movements" has fared less well. The main problems have been methodological; there are no workable statistical procedures we know of that use *elements* as units of analysis. Available statistical procedures use individual subject data, while we are primarily interested in movements within systems of related elements, some of which come from the same individuals, some of which do not. Although the results reported to date, based as they are on summary statistics and informal patterns, are quite compelling (at least to us), there is currently no way to tell just how robust these findings are, nor how much they differ from chance movement. They have certainly proven their value heuristically and will likely continue to do so. But the study of "novelties" in development, as Piaget knew better than anyone, will continue to pose formidable challenges to empirical science.

The work within our own group, which we now call the Developmental Science Group (Feldman, 1983), has moved quite briskly into the study of expertise. The family resemblance to our earlier research is certainly easy enough to see, but there have also been some clear shifts. The very use of the term expertise to describe the work represents an effort to bring it closer to the mainstream of theory and research, to describe it in terms that are meaningful to a wider segment of the community. And the extension into domains like juggling, aesthetic judgment, and teaching has made the work of potentially greater interest to various research and applied communities.

Still, the expertise research is just getting underway. To date, we have barely been able to "map" the levels of only a few new domains; each one requires techniques specially constructed for that domain. Theory has to be good enough to allow for variations in technique across domains, to be able to predict and guide research in seemingly unrelated bodies of knowledge. So far, theory seems to be adequate, and research has been guided and focused reasonably well. What would really improve the quality and yield of the research, however, would be for specific domains to be chosen for study for theoretically motivated reasons rather than for reasons of convenience, opportunity, or serendipity.

To date, our main reasons for choosing juggling, aesthetic judgment and reasoning, and teaching, as domains to study have been the availability of eager graduate students with backgrounds in these fields. Not to diminish the importance of motivation and interest in producing quality research, it would help the program if a plan of attack on certain domains were to follow more directly from questions posed or predictions made from theory. Because it is such a costly enterprise in human and material terms to map a developmental domain, the potential empirical yield should be as high as possible in order to justify the investment.

We also should acknowledge that the expertise research has been more successful at mapping levels of developmental domains than at studying transitions within them. Of course, within our framework establishing the levels of a developmental domain is prerequisite to studying movement from level to level. It is no small feat to carry out the initial mapping work; it requires a conceptual/task analysis of the domain, descriptions of the proposed levels (including guesses about how many levels to propose), studies of individuals with varying amounts and types of experience, a technique for determining at which level(s) a person functions, and validation studies of that technique. Transitions work is usually harder.

A domain that seems likely to yield highly detailed information about transitions, and which has already been mapped by the field itself, is *chess*. Chess is a domain that has interested cognitive psychologists for many years. With its long tradition of documentation and precise rating system, chess may yield the most important information of any available domain. It would be fitting for chess to be the arena in which some of the theoretical and empirical issues are played out. Chess was the original domain of novice/expert research begun by Chase and Simon in the early 1970s (Chase & Simon, 1974; Simon & Chase, 1973), and it has had an important place in discussions about the nature of knowledge and its development ever since (see, for example, articles by Keil, Sternberg, and Fischer/Pipp in Sternberg, 1984). Now if we can just find a highly motivated graduate student chess player.

It should come as no surprise that we believe our work on developmental domains has been productive and generative. But not everyone will likely see it that way. Charles Brainerd did after all write of *Beyond Universals* in 1981: "it is quite unlikely that anything in this book will lead to productive new lines of empirical research" (p. 64). In reply, David Feldman (1981a) said that the empirical work reported in 1980 itself contradicted Brainerd's prediction, and that "further work now in progress should further weigh against Brainerd's argument" (p. 89).

Whether the work now completed in our own research group and elsewhere qualifies as a "productive new line of empirical research" is for the field to judge. We think that the evidence speaks in the affirmative, and hope that in another 10 years it will do so with greater clarity and force. No one said it would be easy.

6

Creativity: Proof That Development Occurs*

We appear to be in the midst of a resurgence of radical nativism, a viewpoint that attributes much of human experience and activity to innate factors. This resurgence has gone so far as to raise questions about the viability of the concept of development itself (Chomsky, 1980b; Fodor, 1980, 1983; Liben, 1987b). Although there are now strong counterresponses in the literature to the claim that development is yet another human illusion, like self or God or progress, the need still remains to put the antidevelopmental claims to rest once and for all (Bickhard, 1979, 1980a, 1980b; Campbell & Bickhard, 1986, 1987; Feldman & Benjamin, 1986; Liben, 1987b). The purpose of this chapter is to provide another argument against the radical nativist position by showing that, because it is impossible to ignore the reality of human creativity, development must perforce exist.

There are, however, a number of preliminaries to be attended to before tackling the main points in the argument. First, it must be acknowledged that an argument for development does not require a denial that biological factors play a significant part in the process. As we shall see, natural human qualities are vital aspects of the overall

---

* This chapter is reprinted with permission from W. Damon, Ed., *Child development today and tomorrow*, 1989. San Francisco: Jossey-Bass.

account. Second, it is essential to be explicit about what is meant by creativity and development in the context of the present discussion. Finally, it must be recognized that the argument put forward here is substantially conceptual and theoretical in nature and, by virtue of this, must be taken as preliminary to the establishment of a firmer empirical base on which to make (and test) its claims.

DEFINITIONAL ISSUES

For the past 30 years, creativity has most often been taken to mean the ability to generate infrequent or unusual ideas, and it typically has been assessed by standardized tests (Guilford, 1950; Torrance, 1962). Unfortunately, there has been little evidence that these tests actually assess anything resembling the ability to make truly creative contributions, such as establishing a new theorem, producing a remarkable work of art, or discovering a new subatomic particle (Feldman, 1970; Gardner, 1988; Wallach, 1971, 1985).

I use the term *creativity* here to mean the purposeful transformation of a body of knowledge, where that transformation is so significant that the body of knowledge is irrevocably changed from the way it was before. This kind of transformation can be accomplished conceptually, as in the case of proposing a new theory, or by making new products or representations, developing new technologies, or proposing innovative practical techniques. This notion of creativity emphasizes high-level functioning brought to bear on specialized problems, in contrast to notions of creativity that argue for a generic life force (Maslow, 1972) or quality of mind (Guilford, 1950). There is a place for such notions in an overall account of creativity, but that is not the best place to start. As Gruber (1981) has argued, it is best to begin with unambiguous cases of creativity, such as Darwin's theory of biological evolution, Einstein's ideas about the physical universe, or Mozart's great operatic works. From there we can move, if we wish, toward establishing common qualities among more widespread transformational uses of mind.

Obviously, the definition proposed here assumes a quality of human purposefulness, an unusual set of talents and probably optimal circumstances for developing those talents in a distinctive direction. This point will be discussed further later in this chapter. For now, it is sufficient to note that, as used here, creativity refers to relatively rare events that are marked by their transforming effect on existing bodies of knowledge. When domains are reorganized in ways that can reasonably be described as qualitative and irreversible, then creativity of the sort defined here has occurred. It is itself a formidable problem to judge when a change is sufficiently powerful to be considered qualitative and irreversible, but criteria do exist and have been tested empirically with some success (Feldman, Marrinan, & Hartfeldt, 1972; Jackson & Messick, 1965).

The relationship between creativity and development, then, is based on the importance of transformations to both of these processes. The concept of development is of course the broader of the two, referring to any internal transformation of a body of knowledge that yields a qualitatively advanced (for that person) reorganization of knowledge. Developmental changes may be as common as the periodic systemwide reorganizations of each individual's intellectual structure, as described by Jean Piaget, or as idiosyncratic as the achievement of a more advanced level of mastery of an esoteric body of knowledge, such as chess or juggling (Feldman, 1980b; Walton, Adams, Goldsmith, & Feldman, 1987). Creativity is a particularly strong and powerful instance of development, in which a personal, internal reorganization also leads to a significant change in the external form of a domain. A given instance of development may or may not contain the possibility for creative reorganization, but it always sets the stage for such a possibility (see Feldman, 1980b, 1982a; Feldman & Benjamin, 1986, for discussions of the relation between creativity and development).

By emphasizing purposefulness in the creative process, I do not mean to deny the importance of natural biological factors, for they are vital in at least two senses. Some people are more naturally gifted and/or inclined toward representing experience through various domains than are others. Individuals also differ naturally in the personal, emotional, and social qualities that co-occur with their cognitive strengths and weaknesses (Gardner, 1982, 1988; Chapter 11, this volume; Wexler-Sherman, Gardner, & Feldman, 1988). The sources of such individual variations are numerous to be sure, but at least some of that variation is undoubtedly a direct function of biological processes.

The second sense in which biology is central to the account proposed here is Piagetian. Development is assumed to be a universal human process, which means that it must be strongly supported by a biological substrate (Bringuier, 1980; Piaget, 1971a). Creativity, being a special case of development, must also be based on biological processes, but less directly so. Understanding creativity therefore requires understanding development, including the biological aspects of development (Feldman, 1974, 1980b, 1982a; Gardner, 1982).

However, biological processes alone are not a sufficient source of explanation for creativity, let alone development. To argue that innate capabilities determine in every important detail all that an individual will ever accomplish is to legislate against the existence of a problem, but it fails to provide any better an explanation for the phenomenon than any other radically reductionist scheme. To "explain" that a fire attributable to arson started because of a reaction between flammable material and a heat source is to miss the point, even if (and this is closer to the mark) the nature of the material can be specified and the heat source can be identified.

That there are biologically programmed processes that are common across individuals is no reason to assume that such processes adequately explain why individuals differ from one another in what they accomplish, and it is certainly no warrant for denying the existence of such phenomena as development or creativity. Turning away from complex issues like creativity in favor of explaining other phenomena at other levels—even if those explanations turn out to be an important part of the story—is not a satisfactory response to the issue of development and the implications of assuming a nondeterministic view of human development and change.

The main purpose of this discussion is to begin to glimpse the form that an explanation of development and creativity must take. The best place to start is with what we already know about the process, and what we already know about development comes largely from the work of Piaget and his collaborators.

DEVELOPMENT AS CONSTRUCTION:
THE INFLUENCE OF PIAGET

The most important advance of this century for understanding development and, by virtue of this, for understanding creativity was Piaget's constructivist theory (Feldman, 1985a; Piaget, 1971a, 1971b, 1975, 1979, 1982a). Piaget knew that it was vital to the achievement of his epistemological goals to be able to account for creativity, although he was never able to do so to his own satisfaction (Bringuier, 1980; Feldman, 1982a, 1988; Feldman & Benjamin, 1986; Piaget, 1971b). What he was able to do was to provide the fundamental breakthrough in epistemology upon which an adequate explanation of creativity might be built.

The central problem in understanding creativity is understanding change—how it is experienced and how it is controlled: How much change is there in the real world of experience? How do changes occur? Can there be changes in knowledge or experience that go beyond what already exists? What is the relationship between the individual's experience of change and a decision to create changes that alter aspects of the world?

Piaget argued that, while change is inevitable, it has order and can be comprehended. He saw individuals during their life spans going through a series of lawful changes both large (the four stages of thought) and small (local accommodations). Bodies of knowledge also change, and even the physical world changes, although the principles upon which it does so change slowly, if at all. For Piaget, the goal of epistemology was to describe the various systems that people construct for describing and explaining changes in their world. This way of thinking about change places the human mind (Piaget's "Epistemic subject") at the center of the process, in control of the mental structures developed to bring stability and order to systems for understanding the world. In this respect, Piaget's developmental psychology was the first distinctly psychological theory of intellectual change.

Instead of being driven to explaining development on the basis of the external world alone, as behaviorist approaches had done, or to supporting nativist explanations of innate biological unfolding, Piaget held to a "constructivist" position. He argued that changes in experience and in the interpretation of experience are inevitable but that the source of such interpretation lies in individuals' building and revising theories based on their experiences with the world rather than in the individual alone or in the environment alone. Piaget posited that there were laws to be discovered and revised regarding how such cognitive changes take place, and establishing such laws was the central goal of his epistemology.

Piaget attempted to provide an explanation of change in knowledge structures through a process termed *equilibration*. His formulation was revolutionary in at least two respects. First, his change mechanism led to transformations not only in the individual's store of knowledge but in the very mental structures that are the sources of knowledge. Thus not only does knowledge change, but knowledge-gathering capabilities also change. Second, Piaget proposed that changes in knowledge come about not just from mental reflection but also from action, which he defined as the desire to understand the world through activity, exploration, and interpretation (Feldman, 1985a; Flavell, 1963; Piaget, 1975, 1979). What makes Piaget's epistemology so much more powerful than its predecessors' is this distinctly constructivist character.

Finally, since the principles of knowledge formation change as a function of the individual's own epistemological purposes, Piaget gave new substance and status to the self: "Free will" can exist as biological adaptation and psychological epistemic reality. The most remarkable examples of individually rendered changes in thought processes are often called "creative" because they not only change a person's understanding of a domain but lead to changes in the codified structures of knowledge in that domain as well—that is, they change existing bodies of knowledge (Feldman, 1974, 1980b, 1988; Feldman & Benjamin, 1986).

Despite these extraordinary advances, Piaget was unable to account for how creative changes come about. He did understand that his theory would be incomplete until he was able to explain adequately how truly new, qualitative changes can be achieved through the conscious, directed efforts of individuals. Near the end of his life, he reiterated a point he had made many times before: "The central problem of constructivist epistemology is the problem of the construction or creation of something that did not exist before" (Piaget & Voyat, 1979, p. 65). It was his failure to fully recognize the importance of differences between universal and nonuniversal domains that left him unable to posit a satisfying account of novel, creative thought (Piaget, 1982).

LIMITATIONS OF PIAGET'S THEORY

As concerned as Piaget was about the systems people create for understanding the world, he failed to see any theoretical importance in differences between universal reorganizations of knowing systems (the famous four "stages" of development) and nonuniversal reorganizations such as we are considering here (Feldman, 1980b). Nonuniversal reorganizations are those transformations in knowing systems that apply to a particular domain of knowledge but are not universally attained. Such changes are not guaranteed to occur in all individuals or for mastery of all bodies of knowledge, but they nonetheless are developmental in all other essential senses of the term (Feldman, 1980; Vygotsky, 1962).

In both universal and nonuniversal development, the individual struggles to interpret the world. But because development in nonuniversal domains is not guaranteed, there is more of a role for individual talent or inclination, on the one hand, and for specific, domain-related influences, on the other. While Piaget frequently used examples from mathematics and other nonuniversal domains to illustrate what he meant by qualitative shifts in knowing, he failed to exploit important differences between universal and nonuniversal shifts in knowing systems (Feldman, 1980b).

The key problem with Piaget's account of individual change, then, is that it does not deal systematically with the humanly crafted aspects of a changing world. The world that Piaget's system deals with best is a stable, natural, physical world, with durable underlying logical principles governing its functioning. The child's challenge is to discover these immutable principles. These discoveries lead to mental changes that are more than quantitative, as, for example, when a child "solves" the integration of number and order in a seriation problem. What does not change either qualitatively or quantitatively in such a situation is the domain, the body of knowledge itself. Even the term that Piaget uses to describe individual changes—*accommodation*—signifies that change is in the child's mind, not in the external world as represented by the body of knowledge. Creative changes that require the domain to "accommodate" along with the individual are simply not well integrated into Piaget's universalist framework.

Piaget believed that the same principles of change that account for universal knowledge development could also account for change in bodies of knowledge (Bringuier, 1980). This idea offered a productive point of departure, and it has led to efforts to describe creativity as a cognitive-developmental phenomenon governed by equilibration processes (Feldman, 1923/1974, 1980b, 1982a; Gruber, 1981). But it eventually led to an impasse, since it is not obvious where to look within the Piagetian framework for the reasons why some individuals and some reorganizations lead to changes in the domain whereas others do not. The universalist assumption virtually prevents serious consideration of other processes that might be called into play to help explain unique reorganizations as distinguished from universal ones (Feldman, 1980b).

It seems clear, despite these criticisms, that Piaget was moving toward considering nonuniversal bodies of knowledge and their role in development. Indeed, as early as around 1970, he began to wonder if his most mature stage of Formal Operations was truly as universal as he had originally thought (Piaget, 1972). He mused that perhaps individuals did not display Formal Operational thinking in all domains but rather manifested the tendency toward this form of thought only through a particular domain, with different domains accessible to different individuals. While never giving up his belief in the underlying unity of the development of mind, he began to consider the possibility that identifying universal processes in different minds might require accessing them through different, specific knowledge domains. This line of thought brought Piaget as close as he was to get to the crucial distinction between universal and nonuniversal bodies of knowledge (Feldman, 1974, 1980b, 1982a, 1988; Feldman & Gold-smith, 1986).

What is of central importance for understanding creativity is that the processes that govern such changes, while sharing much in common with the universals of Piaget's theory, are also different in certain important respects. For Piaget, the creation of Boolean algebra was a novelty in need of an explanation. For deep epistemological reasons, Piaget was tied to the centrality of universal qualities of mind, the application of which might lead to both universal and nonuniversal reorganizations of thought. When applied to particular bodies of knowledge, universal cognitive achievements might indeed lead to specific changes in nonuniversal domains such as Boolean algebra, but just *how* they might do so cannot be explained within Piaget's universalist framework. The phenomenology of change in the two situations—trying to better comprehend an existing body of knowledge versus trying to transform its deep structure—is a different sort of activity and requires a different epistemology.

Although Piaget's own epistemology prevented him from accounting for truly creative accomplishments, he was still extremely close to the mark. Piaget wrote that: "The whole of human history is a history of *inventions* and creations which do not stem simply from the potentialities of the human race as a whole" (Piaget, 1971b, p. 212; emphasis in original). Having come this close, Piaget characteristically fell back on biology, saying that the answer to how such inventions could arise would come from studies of the evolution of the nervous system. Yet he was very close to a plausible psychological explanation of novelties, including nonuniversal ones.

In spite of Piaget's monumental contributions to our understanding of mental development, and in spite of the truly revolutionary nature of his theory, he was unable to propose a plausible explanation for major examples of human creativity. This was no small piece of unfinished business. And Piaget was aware that he had failed to resolve a central issue: "[The] crux of my problem is to try to explain how novelties are possible and how they are formed" (Piaget, 1971b, p. 194).

THE CRAFTED WORLD:
SOURCE OF A DIFFERENT EPISTEMOLOGY

Piaget assumed that the same epistemological purposes that accounted for universal changes in thought would account for nonuniversal ones. It is no doubt true that the child's inherent curiosity about the world and efforts to comprehend it through equilibration processes are key factors in the desire to know. These qualities are necessary, to be sure, but are they sufficient? Beyond an inherent curiosity, individuals must come to believe that bodies of knowledge, disciplines, and fields of endeavor are not immutable but in fact can be changed. The distinctive feeling necessary for creativity in the larger sense in the belief that the knowledge structures existing in the world—its disciplines and technologies—have been changed by consciously directed human efforts and can continue to be changed when necessary. This is a vastly different epistemological position from the one Piaget explored, and it is essential to creativity (Bruner, Olver, & Greenfield, 1966).

Piaget's framework requires individual accommodation to an existing system for comprehending the world, a powerful but ultimately limiting source of new knowledge. Creativity, in the form of major new transformations of knowledge, occurs when a different stance is taken—a stance that questions the adequacy of existing domains for comprehending the world and that requires the world itself to accommodate. Although subtle, this shift in expectation and orientation is essential if creativity is to occur. Where does the feeling come from that the world must accommodate? It comes at least in part from the world itself—from clear evidence that other people have already made significant changes in the world and have forced it to accommodate. This kind of evidence, which is virtually everywhere, may not be obvious to the growing mind without assistance from those who have gone before. It also comes from culturally held beliefs that intentional changes are, at least some of the time, desirable and that those people who can facilitate valuable changes are given special recognition (Csikszentmihalyi & Robinson, 1986).

The world is therefore made up of fundamentally different sorts of things, those that are "natural" and those that are "humanly made." There is increasing evidence that children are inherently aware of certain distinctions among properties of objects, such as alive/not alive (Carey, 1985; Keil, 1986). These ontological distinctions are natural divisions of the young mind. Although the matter has not been empirically tested, it seems plausible to propose that children might also make a distinction at an early age between natural and humanly crafted aspects of the world: things that have "always been there or were put there by God" and things that are there because other people made them. Although it may take some time for children to refine this distinction, it is vital to the process of creative transformation that such a distinction be deeply appreciated by the developing mind.

When creativity occurs, it occurs in part because a person is motivated by the belief that, through his or her individual efforts, the world can be changed. Certain features of the world seem less changeable, and it is the understanding of these features that Piaget sought to capture in his universal stages: the logic underlying knowledge about space, time, causality, and morality. Most of the environment, however, particularly in urban, industrialized cultures, is in fact of human construction and human design. Awareness of this distinction is one of the most powerful sources for understanding that it is possible to transform the world—to make it a different place. The perception of this possibility is essential to all major forms of creativity.

This last point touches upon the crux of the nativist/constructivist debate (Piattelli-Palmarini, 1980): Is it possible to create something genuinely new with a mind that does not inherently already contain that new thing? Antidevelopmentalists argue that in principle it is impossible to create a more powerful mind from a less powerful one (Chomsky, 1980b; Fodor, 1980, 1983). Yet recognizing the importance of the crafted world allows us to show that the mind can indeed create something new without already possessing a preformed version of the new idea. The crafted world offers myriad examples of new ideas and products, as well as cultural prosthetics that encode the techniques and provide the tools for making other new things (Bruner, Olver, & Greenfield, 1966; Olson, 1970). The crafted world provided the opportunity for a developing mind to access the accumulated knowledge of a culture, perceive selected and preserved examples of human efforts at transformation, and learn about the techniques for bringing about such changes. It is upon the crafted world that the possibility of creativity depends, not the preexistence of new ideas in the mind.

The error of earlier analyses, including Piaget's, was the assumption that every new idea and product of importance had to be invented in its entirety by an individual. In fact, this is not true. Know-how, tradition, and example after example of the fruits of earlier creative activity are available to the growing mind. From these sources, in conjunction with the individual's own disposition toward novel activity, will emerge the makings of genuinely new things. Without accepting the strong form of the behaviorist argument, I would argue that new possibilities can be catalyzed in the developing mind from the outside, interacting with and influencing the individual's future course of understanding.

It is indeed possible for there to be something new under the sun. One need only consider how much of what is now under the sun would not be there if the humanly crafted world were to suddenly disappear

(Csikszentmihalyi & Robinson, 1986; Feldman, 1988; Gardner, 1988). The implications of this argument are that development and creativity do occur—indeed they must occur—since the evidence for their occurrence is all around us in the form of the crafted world of human cultures.

The antidevelopmentalist argument is false because its assumptions are false; development is from the outside in as well as from the inside out. The potential for using outside information must be inherent in the human mind, of course, but a more powerful non-universal mental structure can be constructed from a less powerful mental structure through the use of externally available information, prosthetics, and instruction (Bruner, Olver, & Greenfield, 1966; Olson, 1970). All that must be assumed is the potential to use such information, not its presence in some preformed state.

THE TRANSFORMATIONAL IMPERATIVE: A MECHANISM FOR CHANGE

Having just proposed that creativity (and, in fact, most nonuniversal development) depends upon the existence and availability of both humanly crafted environments and techniques for changing them, the question remains as to where the principles of change themselves come from. The crafted world provides numerous examples of significant, radical transformations in bodies of knowledge, as well as an appreciation for the fact that what is now "the state of the art" can be changed again. The actual capabilities for effecting such changes, however, must come from individual minds. I have called this tendency of mind to produce novel constructions "the transformational imperative" (Feldman, 1988).

The transformational imperative differs quite substantially from the equilibration mechanism proposed by Piaget, because it is intended to account for the tendency to transform away from stable knowledge states—in direct contrast to the Piagetian emphasis on transformation toward more logically mature structures and greater stability. In my own reflections on and speculations about transformation, I have found it helpful to distinguish between knowledge processes that seek to preserve reality and those that seek to change it. For the most part, the study of cognitive development has dealt with processes whose primary function is to construct a stable, coherent, internally consistent view of reality. The processes traditionally studied represent conscious, rational, logical, and categorical efforts to establish and preserve a stable and unchanging interpretation of experience. Piaget was of course a preeminent contributor to this line of thought.

Yet anecdotal accounts and self-reports from individuals who have made creative contributions strongly suggest that such rational thought processes are complimented by nonrational, noncategorical, fluid, and transformational thinking that often goes on outside of conscious awareness (Feldman, 1988; Freud, 1958; Gedo, 1983; Ghiselin, 1952). Creators themselves maintain that this sort of transformational thinking contributed in critical ways to the eventual form of their work—be it poems, mathematical equations, musical compositions, or scientific theories. When asked to reflect on the process of inspiration, Jean Cocteau wrote: "We indulge ourselves like invalids who try to prolong dream[ing] and dread resuming contact with reality; in short, when the work that makes itself in us and in spite of us demands to be born, we can believe that the work comes to us from beyond and is offered us by the gods" (Ghiselin, 1952, p. 82).

Piaget's preoccupation with the consciously directed aspects of transformation may have kept him from explicitly including within his system these more primitive tendencies to transform. Yet it is precisely these processes that are necessary to the appearance of the "novelties" that Piaget so earnestly wanted to explain. This has of course been clear to the psychoanalytic community for many years (Arieti, 1976; Freud, 1958; Gedo, 1983; Kris, 1952). Any explanation of creativity that does not include some kind of inherent nonrational tendency to take outrageous liberties with reality is likely to fall short of the mark (Feldman, 1988).

Granting, then, that a powerful tendency to change reality occurs naturally in human mental functioning, there remains the formidable challenge of specifying the principles upon which such a tendency might operate. Kurt Fischer (Fischer & Pipp, 1984) has proposed a set of transformation rules for rational thought; a complementary set for nonrational thought could prove useful to the further understanding of creative thought. Perhaps further studying transformations in a variety of other states of consciousness, such as dreaming, daydreaming, drug states, or meditation, will make it possible to build a plausible set of such principles (Hartmann, 1984; Wilber, Engler, & Brown, 1986).

At the very least, it makes sense to consider the very real tension between the competing tendencies to preserve a constructed reality and to change it (Arieti, 1976). It is almost certain that such tendencies vary in intensity from person to person and within persons across domains. So far as we know, Einstein lived a quiet and conservative life; it was only in his thoughts about the forces governing the physical universe that his ideas were radically transformational. It is virtually certain that individuals also vary in how readily or in what domains they are inclined to transform knowledge; understanding these differences should help account for why some individuals seem more prepared to change things in various realms than do others.

ESSENTIALS FOR CREATIVITY

Based on the previous discussion, an adequate explanation of creativity would seem to require a tripartite set of processes: (a) something like Piaget's equilibration process, which is a rational, conscious, intentional tendency to construct systems of order; (b) the perception of the external world of crafted objects and ideas as a changeable reality; and (c) a powerful innate tendency to change reality outside the bounds of stable, ordered experience. All three seem to be critical ingredients for an adequate account of change, particularly for changes that substantially transform the world.

The third ingredient, the transformational imperative, is intended to contrast with the conscious, rational preference for assimilation to an already known reality. Accommodation has always seemed awkward within Piaget's system, performed only reluctantly and grudgingly by the epistemic subject. I suspect that this is because accommodation runs counter to the purposes of a system dedicated to preserving itself, whereas the opposite is true of a system whose purpose is to transform itself. It would seem that a framework invoking assimilation, accommodation, *and* transformation as equal components in a balanced system would yield a better rendering of the equilibration process, all operating within the context of a world of both cultural and natural objects (Feldman, 1986b). Were such an expanded version of Piaget's change process adopted as a heuristic to guide inquiry, it would be better suited to the purpose of building a satisfying explanation of major reorganizations in thought.

ANTIDEVELOPMENTALISM RECONSIDERED

This chapter began with the observation that radical nativism has challenged the viability of the concept of development. I hope it is clear by this point that, while this challenge needs to be met head on, it need not discourage developmentalists interested in articulating major qualitative transformations in thinking. The basic premise of the nativist charge is false: It *is* possible for something more developed to emerge from something less developed without resorting to preformist explanations. The existence of the crafted world in all its manifestations, including techniques and technologies for making qualitatively different things from other things, ensures that development can and does occur.

The clearest examples of development are those changes in the crafted world that we identify as "creative." By so labeling the fruits of certain human efforts to transform, we give objective credibility to the existence of qualitative, irreversible transformations, both in various objects in the world and in our understanding of them (Jackson & Messick, 1965). In other words, we have demonstrated that development, in the sense that the term is usually meant, exists. By interacting with domains that are available in the world of humanly created culture, individuals are able to transcend constraints and extend systems. When such interactions lead to significant changes in the domains themselves, then the individuals who created these external reorganizations have concurrently created internal changes in their own systems for understanding and interpretation.

Not all significant reorganizations in thought can be considered creative in the sense of leading to transformations in a body of codified knowledge. Strictly speaking, we have only proven that development occurs in those instances in which the label "creative" can be conferred on the outcome of an effort to transform. It is much more difficult to support a claim that qualitative reorganization has taken place in a person's mind when that person is only able to do what others have done before. This is why Piaget's theory was so vulnerable to the nativist attack, a vulnerability that is avoided in the present discussion.

TOMORROW

To have shown—at least in the extreme situation of creative accomplishment—that development exists is surely a step forward. But it leaves a great deal to be done. If development *only* occurs in extreme situations such as those we have called creative, then the argument for development still lacks sufficient force to refute the nativist logic entirely; the strong form of the present argument rests on an unproven assumption that all qualitative reorganizations in thought—creative and noncreative alike—rest on similar principles. What must be done is to show in what senses more common forms of reorganizations in thought also transcend constraints and establish qualitative advances in thought. But note how far we have come toward constructing a positive framework for guiding efforts to comprehend developmental change and how little this framework depends on innate structures.

That events occur that are genuinely developmental should now be clear; that they can be achieved by processes that do not require preexisting structures or innate knowledge should also be clear. The question now is to understand *how* development works and, in particular, how development works when it changes the world in ways that become part of the crafted human culture (Feldman, 1988). However sufficient or insufficient the processes proposed in the present account turn out to be for explaining development, they do not describe *how* such processes might be used in the construction of a qualitatively new thought or idea. This seems to be the next step in understanding development, and a giant step it will be.

7

Cultural Organisms[1]

The burden in this chapter will be to say as clearly as possible what has been learned from studying extreme cases of talent development that might shed light on how environmental influences release, shape, and refine great potential.

I will begin with an idiosyncratic review of what some others have said about how to conceptualize environments, move somewhat autobiographically to my own previous (if unsystematic) efforts to do so, and then try to offer some observations and ideas that might be of use in extending our understanding of how environment and individual interact over extended periods of time toward the realization of great potential (cf. Gruber, 1982; Wallace & Gruber, 1989).

Environments Conceptualized

As early as 1970 or so I was aware of attempts to make sense of environments in more interesting ways than as sources of reinforcement histories or contingency relationships. I knew about Urie Bron-

[1] The material on which this chapter was based was first presented at the Annual Meeting of the Jean Piaget Society in Philadelphia in June 1989. I am grateful to the society and its President Kurt Fischer for permission to use this material, and to Professor Robbie Case for a set of stimulating and instructive comments on the original presentation. A substantially similar version of this chapter will appear in the Society's publication: R. Wozniak & K. Fischer (Eds.). *The effects of specific environments on cognitive development.* Hillsdale, NJ: Erlbaum, 1993.

fenbrenner's efforts to conceive of ecological issues in child development, and for the need to analyze environments in terms of system, pattern, and organization (Bronfenbrenner, 1974). Although these efforts made sense to me, they unfortunately did not make much impact, as I was still very much tied up with the individual notion of development à la Piaget.

I knew a bit about the work on classroom environments being done at Stanford, by Rudolf Moos and others, and appreciated the value of this approach in the work of my colleague at Yale, Ed Trickett. But this work was about community psychology and making a difference in the lives of students being pulverized by schooling, a much more practical goal than anything I was working on at the time. I could see how this kind of analysis could be of real value, but again, no sale (Moos, 1973).

My preoccupation in earlier days (and still today) was with issues of *qualitative shifts in reasoning*, in particular questions of how one moves through the levels of developmental domains, particularly domains of the sort I have come to call nonuniversal (Feldman, 1974). Probably the most potent influences on my thinking at the time were several developmentalists whose ideas continue to hold important places in my mental landscape. First were Jerome Bruner and David Olson (Olson & Bruner, 1974), whose work on cultural "prosthetics" stunned me into realizing that everything does not necessarily spring from the inside, spontaneously, as a diehard Piagetian would tend to believe. Their book (Bruner, Olver, & Greenfield, 1966), which reported work done in other cultures, was especially moving. Bruner laid out the theoretical and conceptual basis for arguing that pedagogy, prosthetics, and culturally evolved forms of assisting the young to learn were powerful ingredients of development, a lesson I eventually learned.

Somewhere along the way Vygotsky's *Thought and Language* (1934/1962) was put under my nose, I expect by Joe Glick, who taught me a great deal while we walked together through Minnesota winters on the way to work in 1969 and 1970. Although I apparently repressed the powerful influence Vygotsky had on me for several years, the striking resonance between my own formulations and those of Vygotsky are evermore apparent to me (cf. the Preface to this volume). Knowing now that Bruner was himself greatly influenced by Vygotsky makes it only more apparent that I was on a collision course with "environment" long before I was aware of it.

The distinction between "spontaneous" and "scientific" concepts in Chapter 6 of *Thought and Language* (Vygotsky, 1934/1962) bears testimony to its place in my own central theoretical distinction between "universal" and "nonuniversal" developmental domains. The achievement of all nonuniversal, nonspontaneous advances in under-standing requires active, systematic, and sustained intentional efforts on the part of those who would teach the child. Although I tried to be more detailed than Vygotsky had been in my presentation of environ-ment in the earliest published version of "universal to unique" (Feldman, 1974), my notion of "crystallizing conditions" in the environ-ment that catalyze cognitive structures was, to put it mildly, sketchy (although see Walters & Gardner, 1986).

I should also point out that by the early 1970s I was becoming increasingly uneasy with the relatively minor role environment plays in Piaget's theory. Having read Beilin's critique of Piaget (Beilin, 1971) which claimed Piaget was more of a maturationist than he admitted, and having read Kessen's, Bruner's, and Flavell's (cf. Flavell, 1971; Kessen, 1962; Olson & Bruner, 1974) general critiques of stage theories, I was impressed with the need to articulate a position that included systematic roles for agents of the culture in cognitive develop-ment. Writing in 1971, Flavell put it in this way:

> Beilin argues that Piaget's view of cognitive development is actually more maturationistic and preformationistic than Piaget himself admits it to be. I believe that Beilin is correct in so arguing....It is obvious, however, that consideration of environmental effects must continue to figure very prominently in any such genetically determined, matura-tionistic, conception of how development proceeds, if that view is to be taken seriously, and I would submit that there is at present no good theory about these environmental effects. (Flavell, in Mischel, 1971, pp. 121–122)

Recognizing how difficult a task it would be to specify how environment works in development, Flavell (1971) continued:

> I personally take as a major objective for our field the search for possible *universal* outcomes of human cognitive development....The point I am making is that the role of environment within a more matura-tionistically oriented view of development is subtle and hard to con-ceptualize, but its conceptualization is a necessary task. (p. 122; emphasis in original)

The other work that most influenced my thinking during that period was the 1971 book by Cole, Gay, Glick, and Sharp, *The Cultural Context of Learning and Thinking*. The importance of sensitivity to cultural context in assessing cognitive capabilities was driven home with full force in this elegant and compelling work in which the Kpelle of Liberia were found to be subtle and high-level thinkers when given an appropriate context for revealing their capabilities. Again, however, the message was that all individuals in all cultures can be expected to reach high levels of reasoning ability (i.e., the emphasis was on universals).

Nonuniversal Development: Crystallizing Conditions

Given the consensus that a theory of cognitive development must include systematic accounts of how environment contributes to advances in reasoning, and, given the preoccupation with universals in thought structures as the target of theory and research, I did the only honorable thing. I sidestepped the issue and turned my attention to other matters, and until very recently most of the rest of the field has sidestepped it as well.

John Flavell, William Kessen, Jerome Bruner, and Michael Cole, the people who might reasonably be expected to chart the way, headed for the high ground of the experimental laboratory, the computer network, the policy arena, or other safer places. There have of course been exceptions, including an ambitious effort by Frances Horowitz (1987) to integrate environment and maturation, behavioral and cognitive developmental frameworks, and universal and nonuniversal developmental changes. Some important work has become available on apprenticeship, another promising line of theory and research (cf. Rogoff, 1990, for a summary). But remarkably little progress in conceptualizing context on cognitive development has been made since the early to mid-1970s.

For my part, as the 1970s opened, there was a practical problem to be confronted. *Child Development* rejected the article I wrote based on my dissertation on map understanding, and I needed to find a way to get the work into print. I came up with the idea of a set of hypothetical conditions I called "crystallizers of cognitive structures" as an ex post facto rationale for the research I had done on stage and skill sequences in map drawing. The ruse worked, and the study was published (Feldman, 1971). But there was now this idea that I found myself intrigued by, the idea of "crystallizers of cognitive structures." What was a crystallizer and how did it work?

A crystallizer was originally conceptualized as an existing part of the environment that played a critical, catalytic role in the formation of new cognitive structures. It was a set of conditions that had been crafted to provide just the right kind of stimulation during the proper time to precipitate a transition in cognitive development. In its earliest form, there was no distinction made between a crystallizer of universal structures and any other kind of crystallizer. Here is how I introduced the idea:

The rationale for the present study follows from the premise that there may be tasks which function as "crystallizers" in the development of cognitive structures; that is, tasks which are significantly related to cognitive development but which are also influenced in important ways by patterns and sequences of planned experience provided by the environment. It would follow that if such tasks exist, they would merit the attention of the educational researcher because of their possible long-range importance for later learning. (Feldman, 1971, p. 486)

When the map-drawing work was published in 1971, it had not occurred to me (yet) that map drawing might be seen as a *cultural* activity as much as a manifestation of the development of universal spatial reasoning capabilities in children, which was how Piaget and Inhelder (1956) viewed the task. It was in working with my student at Yale, Sam Snyder (cf. Chapters 1, 3, 4), that the importance of cultural knowledge became clear, or at least clearer.

I had seen maps as perhaps having qualities that gave them special status when universal spatial reasoning structures were ready to become transformed to more advanced developmental levels. If it could be demonstrated that such activities were at least in part teachable, it would indeed follow that they would merit the attention of educational researchers. Crystallizer tasks, as the argument went, would have the potential to transfer, to generalize more than most other parts of the curriculum. A crystallizer would provide more "bang for the buck."

Although I never did follow this line of research very far, I went so far as to think about two further sets of issues. I tried to imagine what *other* kinds of things might be nominated as crystallizing activities, and came up with a few possibilities like writing paragraphs and stories, playing and composing songs, or starting and running a small business (Feldman, 1981). I also extended the general formulation of crystallizers into realms of development beyond those of the typical universal sort; I did this in an essay on creativity published in 1974 in which I introduced the idea of "nonuniversal" developmental change (Feldman, 1974).

In that essay I proposed four sets of crystallizing conditions: universal, cultural, idiosyncratic, and creative. I tried to outline what kinds of environmental events and experiences might fall under each of these broad rubrics. Rereading the proposed crystallizers with hindsight is a humbling experience. Yet, what is clear from these early efforts is that I was trying to conceptualize environment in a systematic way that would relate to the conditions under which progressive change in mastery of knowledge domains might take place. This was my first tendency to divide environment into broad conceptual categories ranging from universal to unique, a tendency that persists into, and very likely beyond, the present effort.

I had in mind that stored in a culture's bag of tricks were a few preorganized and widely available knowledge domains, ready to engage the energies of individuals prepared to acquire them. Rather than informally passed from elders to youngsters in culturewide activities, these more specialized opportunities are always present but not actively imparted, at least not actively imparted to all youngsters. Some domains, if introduced properly, permit even young children to comprehend the nature of their abilities and find life direction through them (the "crystallizing experience" of Walters & Gardner, 1986).

Prodigies. All cultures maintain domains of expertise in which early prodigious achievement occurs, although the domains vary from culture to culture. I thought that the study of such situations might reveal how talent is crystallized. The more extreme the talent under investigation, I reasoned, the clearer would be the processes through which that talent revealed itself and was developed (Feldman, 1979a, 1979b).

Sensing that the most promising place to learn about the interplay of specific environmental conditions and individual development might be with child prodigies, I embarked on a study of six prodigies that was to span more than a decade (Feldman, 1976, 1979a, 1979b, 1982a, 1982c, 1982d, 1986b; Feldman & Goldsmith, 1989). I saw the main purpose of that work to tease apart the environmental influences, especially family and teachers, that went into the developing of the prodigy's natural talents.

I also believed that a vital set of crystallizing conditions resided in the body of knowledge that the prodigy was mastering, and that it was therefore necessary to understand the structure of the knowledge domain which the child was trying to master. Broader contextual matters such as the place of the domain in the value system of a society, current economic and institutional conditions, etc. were also addressed. Some of these conditions are now referred to as having to do with the "field" rather than the domain itself, following the important conceptual distinction made by Mihalyi Csikszentmihalyi (cf. Csikszentmihalyi, 1988b; Csikszentmihalyi & Robinson, 1986).

Cultural Organisms

It was not until I began work on this chapter that I started to conceptualize entities that might organize domain and field into purposeful entities for the purpose of developing and giving expression to great potential. I will focus on three sorts of environmental entities that were particularly crucial in the development of my own six subjects from the prodigy study, particularly the three who turned toward music: these are of course the "cultural organisms" referred to in the title of this chapter.

Before turning to the specific features of the cultural organisms that gave form to the talents of the prodigies, however, I should acknowledge the conceptual debt I owe to Lewis Thomas, the author of *The Lives of a Cell* (Thomas, 1974), who has elegantly described qualities of the natural world that are models for most of what I will present; indeed, the label "cultural organism" is based on the title of one of his essays: "On Societies as Organisms." Much of what I will describe does indeed exist in one form or another in other parts of nature, among other organisms—much, but crucially, not all.

Perhaps because he is such a keen student of nature, Thomas in fact missed seeing the "cultural organism" that is most vital to my story, perhaps because what I observed were in some respects uniquely *human* forms of organization. As Vygotsky before me, I see an adequate explanation of development, of both the humble and the more exalted sort, as requiring an appreciation of the distinct qualities that set human experience apart from the rest of the organic world (Vygotsky, 1934/1962, 1978).

Still, one cannot help but be impressed, even humbled, by the realization that creatures we typically think of as beneath us have evolved social organizations that rival our own. Consider what Thomas (1974) says about the termite society:

> Two or three termites in a chamber will begin to pick up pellets and move them from place to place, but nothing comes of it; nothing is built. As more join in, they seem to reach a critical mass, a quorum, and the thinking begins. They place pellets atop pellets, then throw up columns and beautiful curving symmetrical arches, and the crystalline architecture of valued chambers is created. It is not known how they communicate with each other, how the chains of termites building one column know when to turn toward the crew on the adjacent column, or how, when the time comes, they manage the flawless joining of the arches. The stimuli that set them off at the outset, building collectively instead of shifting things about, may be pheremones released when they reach committee size. They react as if alarmed. They become agitated, excited, and then they begin working like artists. (pp. 13–14)

Since the data on prodigies were not gathered with the current way of organizing things in mind, what is reported here are largely impressionistic, descriptive, and unsystematic observations. These observations are buttressed to some degree by complimentary findings from other investigators of extreme cases, particularly those of Bloom and his associates (Bloom, 1985).

In an example that I will discuss in more detail later on, Thomas likens the system through which scientific knowledge is organized and cumulated to the social activity of termites; not the building of termite hills as in the above quote, but in the transmission of information. Thomas opines that one of the most significant kinds of social structures created by humans is an *information structure*, and we are as unconscious of these as the termites seem to be of their architecture.

The initial, more solitary aspects of scientific work Thomas likens to the aimless activity of the termite alone or in small groups. It is when there is effort to let others know what is going on that a larger and vastly more important part of the enterprise is engaged.

> Perhaps, however, we are linked in circuits for the storage, processing, and retrieval of information, since this appears to be the most basic and universal of all human enterprises. It may be our biological function to build a certain kind of hill. We have access to all the information of the biosphere, arriving as elementary units in the stream of solar photons. When we have learned how these are rearranged against randomness, to make, say, springtails, quantum mechanics, and the late quartets, we may have a clearer notion of how to proceed. (Thomas, 1974, p. 15)

My own preoccupation for many years has been with what is suggested in the last part of this quote, the part about how things are arranged into patterns of exquisite form from time to time. Although prodigies generally are not the ones who rearrange things, they may reveal some of the processes that make such rearrangements possible.

My concern is thus with the conditions that make it *possible* for major new works to be achieved, the broader structures within which potential is harnessed and organized and directed toward mastery and expression. These are not themselves the conditions that directly lead to the creation of a grand new citadel from which new vistas are glimpsed for the first time. They are rather the more humble entities that, in turn, make possible those rare ascents toward the heavens that mark human life as unique in the universe, a sort of base camp for scaling a mountain of our own creation.

As I think of them, cultural organisms are specialized social structures designed to carry out ambitious human goals; in the current context their special purpose is to nurture and direct the expression of extreme talent. They evolve and change according to their utility (as contrasted with those of termites which are essentially stable). Such structures are designed to be stable enough to develop exceptional talent, a process that takes a decade at the very least, yet supple enough to allow for periodic changes that may make them better suited to the task (Bruner & Haste, 1987; Vygotsky, 1978).

A cultural organism is therefore defined in the present context as *a cooperative structure that is formed and reformed in order to enhance the possibilities for discovery, development, and (occasionally) optimal expression of human talents in various domains.* They also serve as repositories for knowledge and wisdom about how to select, preserve, and enhance the qualities of the domain itself.

Cultural organisms are constructed with humanly crafted tools, techniques, technologies, symbol systems, traditions, rules, customs, and beliefs, organized around a particular human collective enterprise. That enterprise may be more or less explicit, more or less conscious, more or less shared, more or less sanctioned by larger cultural organisms, more or less common, or more or less rare.

A nuclear family may be thought of as a relatively small cultural organism when it focuses its resources on the development of talent of one or more of its members (Deakin, 1972). An extended family or a family with several generations of sustained activity focused on activity aimed toward a specific domain might provide a somewhat larger vehicle for preserving, transmitting, and protecting a tradition of expertise in a particular field. The Zildjian family, for example, has been making what are arguably the world's best percussion cymbals for several centuries. This sustained use of family resources is a phenomenon we have called "transgenerational influences" and have explored in the case of violinist Yehudi Menuhin and his family (Feldman & Goldsmith, 1986).

The question may be asked whether it adds anything to our knowledge about human development to propose yet another term for entities that are for the most part already known. If there is value to doing so, it lies in directing attention to certain distinctive features of these entities that may not have been highlighted before. It also may serve the purpose of revealing commonalities and patterns that may help us better comprehend how human environments function.

As Vygotsky emphasized in his cultural psychology, the central purpose of introducing a notion like cultural organisms is to try to highlight some of the uniquely human qualities that are reflected in them. This does not mean that the astonishing analogy to human social life found in Lewis Thomas's descriptions of termite hills, ant nests, and bee hives should not give us pause and remind us of our kinship with other living creatures. At the same time, though, no other living thing *sets out* to build a particular sort of social structure,

then tinkers with that structure constantly, devises and tests variations, and chooses significant changes that affect the environments of
others (including sometimes the termites) by virtue of this process. As
Karl Marx wrote in *Capital*:

> The spider carries out operations reminiscent of a weaver and the boxes
> which bees build in the sky could disgrace the work of many architects.
> But even the worst architect differs from the most able bee from the very
> outset in that before he builds a box out of boards he has already
> constructed it in his head. At the end of the work process he obtains a
> result which already existed in his mind before he began to build. The
> architect not only changes the form given to him by nature, within the
> constraints imposed by nature, he also carries out a purpose of his own
> which defines the means and the character of the activity to which he
> must subordinate his will (in Vygotsky, 1978, p. xiv)

And Friedrich Engels, in *Dialectics of Nature*, wrote this about human
activity: "It is precisely *the alteration of nature by men*, not nature as
such, which is the most essential and immediate basis of human
thought" (in Vygotsky, 1978, p. xiv; emphasis in original).

It seems clear that Lewis Thomas, the inveterate biologist, ran wide
of the mark in drawing such a close parallel between human and
nonhuman social structures. Not seeing the distinct kinds of social
structures that human beings construct as essential either to survival
or (and more to the point), to the nature of human cultural life, he
suggested that the cathedral at Chartres, computers and lasers,
synthetic proteins, and the like, do not hold the keys to human
survival and well being, that they are but byproducts of the elemental
essential *biological* processes.

In Thomas's view it is *language*, only language, that ties human
beings together, because language is programmed into the genes of
people in a biologically prepared language acquisition device
(Thomas, 1974, pp. 104–106). In those places where Marx and Engels
and Vygotsky (and humanistic psychology too) have endeavored to
make their case, Thomas finds ephemeral, fleeting, byproducts of
human wanderlust and tinkering, however beautiful the result. The
argument is not that the great cathedral does not possess surpassing
beauty (as does the termite hill); it is that its importance in the sense
of biological survival is minimal.

And yet, a few pages later in *The Lives of a Cell* (1974), Thomas
recognizes that there is something quite unique about human language, and this is its ability to entertain *ambiguity* and deviate from
the precise point, indeed its *inability* to do otherwise. "The great thing
about human language," he wrote, "is that it prevents us from sticking

to the matter at hand" (pp. 111–112). Without this quality, he says, it is "unlikely that we would have been able to evolve from words to Bach" (pp. 111–112). And it is precisely the possibility of evolving from "words to Bach" that is the issue. Thomas seems to sense this, but not to know what to do with it. He nonetheless writes with real feeling about the majesty of human creativity, such as in the following passage:

> The real surprises, which set us back on our heels when they occur, will always be the mutants...They have slightly different receptors for the information cascading from other minds, and slightly different machinery for processing it, so that what comes out to rejoin the flow is novel, and filled with new sorts of meaning...In this sense, the Art of the Fugue and the St. Matthew Passion were, for the evolving organism of human thought, feathered wings, opposing thumbs, new layers of frontal cortex. (pp. 168–169)

Somehow, appreciating the significance of great works of creativity as major shifts in the evolution of thought is not enough to get Mr. Thomas to connect his earlier ideas about social insect behavior with his later thoughts about language and invention.

This is the connection that underlies my interest in cultural organisms, because what is at issue is precisely the relationship of social behavior of the sort that I am trying to describe and creativity of the sort that Lewis Thomas sees as major turning points in the evolution of thought. I believe that cultural entities such as particular kinds of family structures, structures for preparing and nurturing neophytes in various fields, technologies for storing and transmitting information, and larger entities, are (perhaps unconsciously) designed to set conditions that will increase the likelihood that "mutations" of the Bach and Einstein sort will occur.

Thomas seems to think that we should not try to analyze such things, but rather to trust that the good stuff will simply emerge from the random and undirected flow of information around the species. Or perhaps because we know so little about how to form productive structures to carry out the essential mission of organizing and directing information, it is better to leave well enough alone. By describing what I have noticed in studying extreme cases of talent development, the essential link between culturally formed social structures and powerful mental mutations, will, it is hoped, become more apparent. It is clear that, language notwithstanding, there is more to the process than ambiguity, random reorganization, and slight variations in information receptors.

Humans, uniquely among living things, create environmental

structures specifically designed to enhance talent development. The most powerful feature of these environments is that they can be modified and refined, fine-tuned as it were, to accomplish their purposes. My own interest in these uniquely human tendencies is somewhat different from that of Marx and Engels; for me the most interesting quality about such human constructions is that they serve both collective *as well as* individual purposes. With the prodigies, what is striking is how a large, collective enterprise serves the purpose of providing the precise conditions under which the individual prodigy's talents will be enabled to develop fully.

In fact, I have come to see the prodigy as dramatic testimony to a kind of reciprocity between nature and culture. The natural talents of prodigies have apparently been available for millenia (Gould, 1981). What has changed with time are the critical cultural conditions for detecting, developing, and refining such talents, the cultural organisms of the current discussion.

I have often thought about what it would be like for a musical talent of the quality of Mozart or a chess talent of the quality of Bobby Fischer to have appeared in a time and place that provided little specific opportunity for the expression of those talents. The Indian boy of poverty Ramanujan is perhaps the best example in recent decades of a mismatch of time and circumstances (Gardner, 1981; NOVA, 1988). Consensus within the mathematics community seems to be that Ramanujan was as naturally gifted a mathematician as any during this century, perhaps ever. But opportunities for learning mathematics as well as for finding appropriate mentors, books, and colleagues were very limited in the slums of Ramanujan's native Madras.

A chance visit to his town by an English mathematician led to Ramanujan's opportunity to connect with modern mathematics. Encouraged by this visitor, Ramanujan wrote to Professor Hardy of Cambridge University in England asking for advice on his work. Hardy knew at once that he was dealing with a mathematical mind of the first rank and invited the young man to Cambridge. By the time Ramanujan found his way to Cambridge at age 26, he had reinvented much of Western mathematics and mastered many of its most challenging problems, although in idiosyncratic ways.

Ramanujan's methods here highly intuitive, unconventional, and in some instances defied rational analysis. Indeed, the profoundly religious Ramanujan attributed the source of his mathematical insights to the goddess Namagiri. His methods of proof were completely unconventional; even mathematicians trained in the specific field in which his work was done are baffled by his techniques (NOVA, 1988). Ramanujan's creativity and flashing insights and intuitions may in fact have been crystallized by the very environmental conditions that also limited his ability to achieve conventional technical skill.

In fact, the shock of moving to a completely different culture eventually proved too much for Ramanujan, and after many illnesses he died at the age of 32; not, however before he and Hardy created a formula for calculating the number of primes of any number, a stunning solution that stands as one of mathematics' greatest achievements of the 20th century.

Hardy knew, however, that by the time he reached Cambridge, Ramanujan's gifts were too crystallized to be much affected by instruction. Hardy, the Cambridge don, perhaps the most highly respected mathematician of his day, wrote that the opportunity to know Ramanujan was the highlight of his life as well as its greatest frustration.

Therefore, when we see a prodigy, a child who has mastered the fundamentals of a highly challenging field in a fraction of the time it takes even a talented adult to do so, we are witnessing a triumph of humanity's patient construction of a receptacle and medium for expression of some of nature's most powerful gifts. When opportunity, timing, and environmental response are optimal, a prodigy is able to find full expression of his or her natural talents and gifts through guided mastery of a culturally preserved nonuniversal developmental domain. Were Ramanujan to have been born in England and not India, were his gifts recognized earlier so that he could be better withstood the shock of relocation, the world might have had greater benefit from his enormous talent.

On the other hand, the possibility must be recognized as well that the striking originality and unwillingness to accept constraints that characterized Ramanujan's approach to mathematical problems may have developed *because* his early experience was so unusual (Gardner, 1988). A distinction must therefore be made between mastery of a domain as it exists, which is the province of the prodigy, and transforming it, which is the mark of creative accomplishment (Feldman, 1988, 1989a).

Glimpses of Three "Cultural Organisms" Stimulated by the Study of Prodigies

What began in 1975 as an informal study of two 8-year-old chess players and a 9-year-old composer (see Feldman, 1979a, 1980a, 1980c) evolved into a 10-year longitudinal study of six prodigies and their families (reported in Feldman, with Goldsmith, 1986). One of the conclusions reached from that work was that the appearance and development of a prodigy depends as much on the state of a body of knowledge at a particular period in its own development as it does on a child with extreme talent. When both child and domain seem opportune for prodigy development, whether or not it happens depends on the availability of culturally preserved and protected intermediaries, which become the crystallizers and developers of the prodigy's talents.

Once initial engagement has occurred, a prodigy becomes a prodigy through sustained, systematic, specific, and appropriate experiences under the guidance of attentive and devoted mentors, who use techniques and technologies passed down from generation to generation, and who operate through structures such as guilds, unions, schools, and the like. If it happens that a talent is developed fully, it happens because of the availability and support of such "cultural organisms" accessed and used in appropriate ways by families, teachers, mentors, and others associated with a field of expertise.

Of the many social structures that struck me during the prodigy research, three stand out. These I have labeled "cocoons," "gatekeepers and barriers," and the "grand edifice." Although there was evidence of such entities in all of the fields where I studied prodigies (writing, chess, science, and music), their presence seemed more coherent and better organized in music. With one exception drawn more from my own experience (mentioned earlier) in an academic field, I will focus on cultural organisms that develop talent in music.

Cocoons

I have noticed two cocoonlike cultural organisms that play important roles in the preparation of prodigies in music, particularly instrumental music. The first of these is simply a more extreme version of the nuclear family that is a waning ideal in this society. I recall being struck with how old-fashioned the families in the study seemed to be: traditional, deeply held values on the primacy of family and the importance of committed parenting, particularly mothering.

All of the mothers in my study gave the major portion of their time to caretaking; in the one partial exception to this, mother and father constructed an elaborate scheme for pursuing their jobs with minimum intrusion into their primary mission, which was to provide continuous, complete, and unlimited attention to the needs of their offspring. Such dedication to childrearing may not be uncommon for six months or a year or so, but to sustain it for well over a decade, as was the case in these families, is rare, especially in Western households.

The cocoon type of family arrangement seems to work best when there are only three members: parents and one child. Where there were other children, the effect was diluted, with some reduction in the sense of protective isolation that was created. To carry off the isolation and keep the sense of distance from the outside world with more than one child is much more difficult. The only documented case I know of was not in my study, but was a family with four children reported in the fascinating work *The Children on the Hill* (Deakin, 1972).

The three children (out of six) in my study who pursued music were all reared in cocoonlike families. Two were only children; the third contained two boys five years apart. In the latter case, my subject's parents acknowledged that they put vastly more energy into the preparation of their first-born for a career in music than was expended on their second, perhaps equally musically talented, son. Later on, when I read about violinist Yehudi Menuhin, whose family has produced prodigies for centuries, I could not help but be struck by similarities between descriptions of the Menuhins in biographical and autobiographical material and what I had been observing (Feldman & Goldsmith, 1986; Menuhin, 1977; Rolfe, 1978).

It is not clear the degree to which cocoonlike families might be found in other cultures, but in this culture at this moment, the need to form thick boundaries between what exists within the family unit and what exists outside seems clear, at least when it comes to the development of exceptional talent. Japanese and Chinese families are often described in terms like the ones we have used to describe our prodigy families (Gardner, 1989). Perhaps in another cultural setting the need to form cocoonlike structures would not be as necessary.

Were the families in my study to have been themselves highly musical (which they were not), or to have been located within more musically oriented communities (which they were not), the situation might also have been different. At least when it comes to the development of exceptional talent, the pervasive presence of music and the necessary devotion to pursuing it has to be actively supported. If a passion for music is not supported by an entity like the community or the state, a cocoonlike family can serve such a purpose in the earliest and perhaps most crucial phases of the process.

The second sort of cocoonlike social organism I observed was within the field of music itself. It was most evident in the "middle period" of preparation of the prodigy, coming after the inwardly protective family, after the warm, accepting initial teacher, but before the masters who bring the student to final readiness for entry into the professional field, usually by the late teens in the case of a prodigy (Bloom, 1985).

How common such entities are is difficult to say, but the one I saw was so interesting and peculiar that its existence must be noted.

Furthermore, it was of real importance in providing one of my subjects with certain fundamentals of musical knowledge and skill, fundamentals that served him in good stead as he moved to the next level of preparation in music (which in his case was the collegiate division of the Juilliard School and study with Dorothy Delay, a leading teacher of young violinists).

What was striking about this structure for musical preparation was its tendency toward total control over the process. It could be described as a school except that it had no formal status. It was a collection of individuals under the direction of a charismatic older leader, located in various spots around Boston, but with each node in close coordination with the center. My subject's musical education with this group during the time I observed him included piano, composition, and violin lessons, as well as solfège at a local university where the group had contacts.

The hallmarks of this peculiar cultural organism were its isolation from other groups and its self consciously "superior" understanding of how to achieve the best preparation for a career in music. The group achieved its intensity partly in reaction to its peripheral place in the established musical community. Indeed, as my subject became involved in more established schools and programs elsewhere, the response of his mentors within the "Jovanovich Group" (as it was called in *Nature's Gambit*) was to become disturbed, suspicious, and ultimately self-destructive, at least in the sense of losing a prized, perhaps uniquely talented student.

One of the problems that this particular cultural organism displayed was that it did not seem to perceive its limitations, had not accepted its place in the larger context. From the perspective of our longitudinal work, as well as from Bloom's (1985) retrospective work on world-class performers in several fields, a transition to another level of preparation may have been inevitable in the case of my subject Nils Kirkendahl (a pseudonym). But the Jovanovich group (as I called it) did not recognize itself as a "middle level" preparation experience and did not gracefully accept the loss of its most prized student.

Two other features of the musical preparation cocoon I observed were that it was held together by a set of beliefs about reincarnation and spirituality that all members were expected to embrace completely, including sexual abstinence. The leader of the group not only had remarkable musical capabilities but charismatic and intuitive powers as well. She was also exempt from the strictures on other members' behavior.

The group had an unmistakable cultlike quality about it, although for the most part was harmless enough. Which does raise the question of the possible significance of cults or cultlike entities for the develop-ment of extreme talent. Perhaps extreme cultural organisms exist at least in part to bring out extreme potential. For something remark-able to occur, in some instances it may be necessary to construct a social entity that stands outside established boundaries, isolated and inwardly directed, self-consciously "superior" in its beliefs about the domain in question.

At the age of 12, my subject chose to leave the Jovanovich group and pursue a more conventional course of preparation, a decision he does not regret. Yet he acknowledges that the experience with Jovanovich group gave him a great deal and may have been crucial to his later successful entry into the ranks of concert violinists.

Within the context of "middle level" entities, it may be that the cocoon is but one of several social constructions, and the key to successful preparation lies in the *match* of a specific form of cultural organism to specific possibilities of the aspiring musician, a process I have in a broader context called coincidence (Feldman, 1979, 1979b, 1980; Feldman & Goldsmith, 1989; Hunt, 1961).

Cocoons of two types, then, small nuclear families and highly centralized musical collectives, were found when extreme potential in music was developed in three of my subjects. The former were apparent in all cases studied, while the latter was evident in only one case. The database is meager in any event, and we will not know if the observations reported here will prove durable until more studies have been done.

Gatekeepers and Barriers

Moving to the second type of cultural organism, the example to be discussed has nothing directly to do with music. It is again based on Lewis Thomas' *The Lives of a Cell* (1974); there Thomas describes scientific journals and the crucial role they have played in the creation of modern science. The analogue in music would probably be the various juries, contests, panels, and prizes that stand between the promising young composer or performer and the recognition and rewards that come from winning such contests. In composition the analogue might be the process through which a composition becomes part of the repertoire.

I am in no position to discuss how music organizes these purposes, having never experienced them directly nor observed them sys-tematically (although I have certainly witnessed them as part of the prodigies research). I will confine my discussion to a kind of quality control and standards setting that is closer to my own experience, the academic journal. I am interested in human social constructions that serve the purposes of organizing into larger units contributions to knowledge by individuals. *The main point I wish to make is that human constructions have a different epistemological status from natural ones, making them subject to conscious transformations.*

As for the creation of journals and systems for judging quality and scientific merit, Thomas (1974) quotes Ziman, who in (the scientific journal) *Nature* wrote: "the invention of a mechanism for the systematic publication of *fragments* of scientific work may have been the key event in the history of modern science" (pp. 16–17). Thomas (1974) continues with a longer quotation, of which the following is an excerpt:

> *This technique, of soliciting many modest contributions to the story of human knowledge, has been the secret of Western science since the seventeenth century, for it achieves a corporate, collective power that is far greater than one individual can exert.* (pp. 16–17; emphasis in original)

As mentioned earlier, this enterprise is likened to the building of a termite nest, a brilliant if somewhat misleading observation, as I hope to show.

It is true enough that there is often an unreflective and unselfconscious tendency among humans to construct entities, including conceptual and social entities, without a clear guiding plan or purpose. Some seem pure whimsy, others appear to grow like topsy. Thomas's emphasis on the similarity between people and termites is in this sense well taken.

Even with an entity as seemingly purposeful as an academic journal, few who are involved in the business of starting and maintaining journals, let alone those who have to deal with them as potential contributors, think a lot about why they exist or what their larger purposes might be. And yet a reflective scholar (like Ziman) was able to perceive some of the more profound purposes of such an enterprise, making it possible to understand this particular human creation more fully. By virtue of these *reflections* made public, the likelihood of *conscious* decisions to change also increases, so that entity may carry out its now more clearly understood purposes more effectively. Termites don't do this.

It is the ability to reflect, to take an "intentional stance" to use Dennett's (1978, 1991) term, that distinguishes human behavior from all other. It is what makes real thought possible. Language is the vehicle of human thought par excellence (Piaget's work showing thought before language notwithstanding) because language more than any other medium permits humans to reflect on their own behavior, the behavior of others, and the effects of intentional changes on cultural entities, a conclusion which gives Piaget his due but not more (Feldman, 1988, 1989a).

Language, however, is not the only human creation that encourages reflection and awareness of purposeful change; all human symbol systems have this feature (Gardner, 1983). Lewis Thomas therefore puts too great an emphasis on language as the only real difference between humans and other animals, and by virtue of this overlooks the unique ontological status of crafted objects, systems, technologies, and yes, scientific societies and journals, that are put into the world by people with a purpose, however aware of it or not they may be at the time (Chen, Goldsmith, & Feldman, 1989; Vygotsky, 1978).

For Vygotsky the greatest moment in a human being's life, according to a passage in *Mind in Society* (1978), is that moment when speech and tool use begin to engage and influence each other. Vygotsky (and Marx and Engels before him) recognized that human culture is itself an everchanging, evolving set of shapers and formers of thought. Although they tended to overemphasize the power of these things, what exist in the world as crafted objects, symbols, systems, and myths, made by human beings, are epistemologically different from what exist as a consequence of nonhuman natural forces, *and humans uniquely recognize this difference*. The Marxists, including even Vygotsky probably, overestimated the power of human history and culture to determine the form and content of thought, but their great virtue was to make explicit how and why such forces are as influential as they are. It is because, to a degree, they offer the possibility of control and direction of the course of cultural evolution.

The impression one gets from Lewis Thomas, on the other hand, is of a collection of organisms basically bewildered about what they do and why they do it, as are the termites. The extent of human un-self-consciousness must not be exaggerated, however. Often the purposes of human activity are anything but dim, as Gruber's brilliant work on Darwin's quite conscious desire to construct a theory of evolution makes clear (Gruber, 1981). Indeed, the most likely reason for Darwin's decades-long delay in publishing his theory of evolution through natural selection is that he understood all too well what he was doing, why he was doing it, and what its likely ramifications and implications would be. Not all instances of intentional behavior have such explicitly comprehended purposes, of course, but they all share the essential quality that they are done by people with a purpose.

Now what does all of this have to do with the realization of great potential? Are there cultural organisms that contribute to the process of placing novel variations into the world, variations that come about through the intentional efforts of reflective human enterprise? This, as Bruner has pointed out in a valuable essay on Vygotsky, was the most problematic aspect of Marxist thought, and even Vygotsky didn't get all that far with it. As Bruner (1986) wrote:

> Marxism has always had difficulty with its Principle of Spontaneity, a principle to account for generativeness and creativity in human affairs beyond historical determinism. Vygotsky strived mightily...to provide a means of bridging the gap between historical determinism and the play of consciousness. (p. 78)

Perhaps if we think about scientific journals as cultural organisms, a glimmer of an explanation moves into view concerning a relationship between "historical determinism" and "the play of consciousness": thought of not so much as a gap to be bridged as a boundary to be transcended (cf. Perkins, 1988).

I bring up again my experience from almost two decades ago, when I was confronted with having my work rejected by a well-established scientific journal. Although I did not see it this way at the time, the challenge of having to find a way of getting my work out to the scientific community, or at least into print, was a crucial stimulus in forcing me to come up with the idea of crystallizing experiences, catalysts of cognitive structures, and a "middle level" theory to link learning and development (Feldman, 1971, 1980c, 1987b; Strauss, 1987). Had that rejection not occurred, it is possible I would not have thought of these things at all. Without evaluating the significance of my own "innovations," the point is that their very existence may have crucially depended upon being confronted with a stubborn gatekeeper.

Therefore, it seems plausible that human constructions such as scientific societies, journals, and the like serve a vital, if in a sense, negative function. They make it difficult for something brought into the world by a single person or small group to be shared with and connected with that of others, their scientific status certified and thereby sanctioned. The sheer bulk of established knowledge, received wisdom, and ingrained prejudice comprise the weight against which the intrepid innovator's lever must be applied.

Were such cultural organisms not to exist, or be impossible to intentionally change, then the possibility of novelty, creativity, trans-formation, revolution, in short, of significant change understood as significant change, would hardly exist at all. However, the evidence of significant changes brought about through intentional human effort, recognized as such by others, is overwhelming; in fact it is virtually beyond argument (cf. Chapter 6).

It can be said, then, that cultural organisms that organize, distill, select, and communicate knowledge are constructed to guard against frivolous innovation, to resist insignificant transformation, and ultimately to mark as clearly as possible the landmarks and boundaries that must be transcended when something new is to become part of culture (Perkins, 1988).

Whether or not these thoughts give comfort to the many who have suffered rejection of their work from a valued journal, it is vital to acknowledge the tension between this kind of cultural organism and the achievement of human potential. This tension is a plausible source of the relationship between "determinism" and "spontaneity." One can only hope that a deeper awareness of the function of journals as providing necessary resistance, and thereby serving as catalysts for innovation, might lead their editors to be somewhat more receptive to new ideas—but of course not *too* receptive or their vital purpose would be compromised.

As for the individual aspiring to establish a place, the existence of the sort of cultural organism we have been discussing can be a source of challenge or discouragement. The extent to which a given person's capabilities are well understood and appreciated by current gatekeepers will predict a great deal about the fate of that person's chances for the development of his or her potential within the field, and more importantly, for the chance to have one's work placed permanently among the selected works that make up the knowledge structures of a domain.

The Grand Edifice

I now turn to the third form of cultural organism I have observed in the development of great potential, that of the "grand edifice." It was in the summer of 1988 at the Aspen Music Festival that the idea occurred to me of a much larger entity than anything I had considered before. I was invited to give a talk on musical prodigies to a meeting of physicians who specialized in medical problems of performers. Among the materials I received prior to the meeting was a flier about the Festival.

What struck me on first reading was that the list of guest musical faculty ran well over 150 people. Then I glanced at the schedule of events and was impressed by their variety and number. The magnitude, the grandeur of the Festival overwhelmed me. I reflected on the numbers of people, working in concert, who had to have collaborated to make the Festival run, from the teenagers who picked up trash around the major event tent to the guest conductor who arrived by chartered flight for a last minute substitute performance. The level and degree of organization and cooperation required to pull off the Festival was remarkable.

This is, of course, not a novel response. Many have been impressed with the coordination, organization, management, and interpersonal skills required to make a major festival like the Aspen Festival work. What my experience with extreme cases may have added to the usual reaction was the realization that the primary purpose of such a cultural enterprise may be to provide precisely the conditions under which great potential in music could be extruded from the collective talents of all the participants, including (and perhaps most specifically) from those whose talents transcend the technical, musical, and aesthetic boundaries lovingly (and sometimes not so lovingly) provided by the musical community. When a truly wonderful performance occurs, as sometimes happens at Aspen, there is a collective affirmation of the rightness, the worthiness, and the importance of the whole enterprise.

I then found myself thinking somewhat differently about the lady in the neighborhood who gives piano lessons. People like her provide children with their initial exposure to the world of music. I also saw greater nobility in the little music store on Massachusetts Avenue in nearby Cambridge that provides an anchoring point and support network for aspiring performers and composers. It exists as a vital element in the large base upon which the social structures of music are meticulously (if unconsciously) built, level by level.

After leaving the Festival, I began talking with musician friends about the idea of a large scale, loosely organized structure that is constructed to serve the purpose of bringing forth the best music that all the participants, individually and collectively, might be able to produce. The idea seemed to make sense to people who participate in music, and even provide some comfort to those who toil in obscurity many levels down from the rarified heights of musical expression in evidence at such festivals as the Aspen.

To recall an earlier quote from Lewis Thomas (1974), humans seem to have access to, as he says, all the bits of information in the biosphere, but do not know yet what to do with them. "When we have learned how these are rearranged against randomness, to make, say, springtails, quantum mechanics, and the late quartets, we may have a clearer notion of how to proceed" (p. 15).

I began to see the social structures of music as perhaps the most advanced prototype of a system for knowing what to do to rearrange nonsense into wonder, to take the bits and make them into functional cultural entities. To see the musical community in this way makes it important for what it directly contributes to culture through music itself, but of perhaps greater importance as a source of understanding about how human cultural organisms are formed, sustained, transformed, and refined to fulfill their purposes. In this case, the purpose seems to be to give large numbers of people a worthy, overarching goal to pursue, with each having an important place and important part to play.

Without necessarily being aware of it (Thomas's point of course), people willingly devote their lives (or a portion of them) to making the Aspen Music Festival, the Philadelphia Music Festival, and Asbury Park Music Festival, and so on, the very best they can be. And when a prodigy appears, is prepared well, and in time plays superbly, the entire cultural organism rejoices.

The grandest edifice among the cultural organisms I have seen, then, is also the most humble. It seems to allow virtually everyone who wishes to participate to do so at some level, and it organizes and channels talent from the most modest to the most exalted. It is not the Aspen Music Festival alone that must be understood, since that event is for a selected few, but the much larger "organism" of which Aspen is a part. The Aspen festival exists as one of the most demanding and most extreme tests of talent, where the gatekeepers are formidable and the hurdles to overcome are raised almost impossibly high, so that the fruits of the other parts of the musical hill (or hive) can be gathered, for all to rejoice.

CONCLUSION

I have tried to do three sorts of things in this chapter. The first has been to recapitulate some of my own previous efforts to conceptualize specific environmental influences on the development of human potential. From this effort I realized that I have been working on various ways of reckoning humanly crafted environments for quite awhile, from crystallizing conditions to nonuniversal developmental domains. The opportunity to reflect on these matters has made me realize that even as I doggedly held to my individualist training and bias, I was in fact reaching for some way to bring systematic, specific environmental constructs into a way of looking at development.

The second theme has been to describe certain forms of what I have called "cultural organisms," or humanly constructed systems for detecting, developing, protecting, promoting, and rejoicing when great potential within certain selected domains is fulfilled. For the most part, the cultural organisms that struck me as the most effective and most refined have been in music, although a comparative study of such entities in other domains recommends itself forcefully. Cocoonlike families and teaching groups, organizers and boundary setters described as institutionalized gatekeepers, and a grand edifice with many layers of contributing units, including high-level major events like the Aspen Music Festival, were presented as vital elements in the development of talent, particularly great talent.

To mount an ascent of one of the great mountains of civilization (which, paradoxically, may reveal peaks that were previously unknown) requires monumental effort, superb organization, sustained application, substantial resources, and probably luck as well (Simonton, 1984). No less than the coordinated efforts of the entire domain-related community will make that ascent possible. This means that when a truly great performance occurs, it reflects the combined efforts of countless individuals working in voluntary harness over long periods of time. By virtue of their natural gifts, prodigies are especially well equipped with the talent and energy to carry forward the aspirations of the community that gives them nurture and support. When all goes well, prodigies fully justify the enormous resources that are invested in their preparation, both before they arrive on the scene and during their preparation.

I have also hinted at the limits of the pure prodigy, since for the most part she or he produces epiphany through a perfect match with an already existing domain. The boundaries and landmarks and hurdles all appear to be set just right for the prodigy; indeed, prodigies are perhaps most useful for showing how far along various domains are toward coherence and organization of purpose (Gardner, 1988).

Citing the example of my own experience with rejection as the catalyst for generating new ideas, I tried to suggest that cultural organisms may serve a purpose beyond collecting and organizing fragments of knowledge. They help establish the gap that has to be transcended in order for a new idea to be integrated into that evolving body of knowledge we call a developmental domain. I was motivated through rejection of a manuscript to come up with the idea of "crystallizing conditions," an idea that has had a profound role in the work I have done for the past 20 years.

The purposes of orderly transformation are thus served by the marking of boundaries and by transcending them. An interesting line of research would be to try to measure how well marked and how permeable the boundaries of various fields are at a given moment, and how large a gap can be bridged while still maintaining the orderly movement of the knowledge base of the domain. Genius, in this context, would represent a resetting of boundaries based on altered principles of organization governing the accumulation of knowledge in that domain (Feldman, 1982; Feldman & Goldsmith, 1986).

It seems to me that a goal of developmental science should be to try to understand better how cultural organisms are formed, how they function, and how they organize themselves around certain shared purposes. The observations reported here are of course anecdotal and unsystematic, lacking in many of the virtues of good empirical work. As a self-appointed explorer and scout, I have merely pointed out what a small number of "cultural organisms" look like at first glance, or more accurately, have recast things which we perfectly well know exist into a framework where they are intended to take on new meaning.

In particular, the role of cultural organisms (as I have called them) in the discovery, development, refinement, and expression of extreme potential is a necessary compliment to an understanding of the nature of potential itself. To comprehend one requires comprehension of the other. I have simply extended the target of inquiry and tried to give it form.

Indeed, a fruitful way to think about the development of human potential may be as a set of possibilities ranging from universal to unique that may or may not emerge through the ministrations of the available sets of cultural organisms and cultural catalysts. To know the specific conditions under which human potential—humble or great—is realized, and the much more common conditions under which it is not, may be as good a way as any to describe the cultural organism we call the field of cognitive development.

References

Alexander, P.A., & Judy, J.E. (1988). The interaction of domain-specific and strategic knowledge in academic performance. *Review of Educational Research, 58*(4), 375–404

Arbuthnot, J. (1975). Modification of moral judgment through role playing. *Developmental Psychology, 11*, 319–324.

Aries, P. (1962). *Centuries of childhood: A social history of family life.* New York: Knopf.

Arieti, S. (1976). *Creativity: The magic synthesis.* New York: Basic Books.

Bart, W., & Airasian, P. (1974). Determination of ordering among seven Piagetian tasks by an ordering-theoretic method. *Journal of Educational Psychology, 66*, 277–284.

Beilin, H. (1971). Developmental stages and developmental processes. In D. Green, M. Ford, & G. Flamer (Eds.), *Measurement and Piaget* (pp. 172–188). New York: McGraw-Hill.

Benjamin, A. (1989). *Levels of expertise in early childhood teaching: An initial field test of a diagnostic instrument.* Unpublished doctoral dissertation, Tufts University, Medford, MA.

Bereiter, C. (1982). Structures, doctrines, and polemical ghosts: A response to Feldman. *Educational Researcher, 11*(5), 22–25.

Bereiter, C. (1985). Toward a solution of the learning paradox. *Review of Educational Research, 55*(2), 201–226.

Berkowitz, M., & Keller, M. (in press). Transitional processes in social-cognitive development: A longitudinal study. *International Journal of Behavioral Development.*

Berliner, D. (1987). Ways of thinking about students and classrooms by more and less experienced teachers. In J. Calderhead (Ed.), *Exploring teachers' thinking* (pp. 60–83). London: Cassell.

Bickhard, M. (1980a). On necessary and specific capabilities in evolution and development. *Human Development, 22*, 217–224.

Bickhard, M. (1980b). A model of developmental and psychological processes. *Genetic Psychology Monographs, 102*, 61–116.

Blatt, S., & Kohlberg, L. (1973). Effects of classroom discussion upon children's level of moral judgment. In L. Kohlberg & E. Turiel (Eds.), *Recent research in moral development*. New York: Holt, Rinehart & Winston.

Bloom, B. (Ed.). (1985). *Developing talent in young people*. New York: Ballantine Books.

Bornstein, M.H., & Krasnegor, N.A. (Eds.). (1989). *Stability and continuity in mental development: Behavioral and biological perspectives*. Hillsdale, NJ: Erlbaum.

Brainerd, C. (1977). Cognitive development and concept learning: An interpretive review. *Psychological Bulletin, 84*, 919–939.

Brainerd, C.J. (1978). The stage question in cognitive-developmental theory. *The Behavioral and Brain Sciences, 1*, 173–182.

Brainerd, C.J. (1981). Stages II: A review of "Beyond universals in cognitive development." *Developmental Review, 1*, 63–81.

Brainerd, C., & Allen, T. (1971). Experimental inductions of the conversation of 'first order' quantitative invariants. *Psychological Bulletin, 75*, 128–144.

Bringuier, J.C. (1980). *Conversations with Jean Piaget*. Chicago: University of Chicago Press.

Bronfenbrenner, U. (1974). Developmental research, public policy, and the ecology of childhood. *Child Development, 45*, 1–5.

Broughton, J.M., & Freeman-Moir, D.J. (Eds.). (1982). *The cognitive developmental psychology of James Mark Baldwin: Current theory and research in genetic epistemology*. Norwood, NJ: Ablex.

Brown, A.L. (1982). Learning and development: The problem of compatibility, access, and induction. *Human Development, 25*, 89–115.

Brown, A.L., & Ferrara, R.A. (1985). Diagnosing zones of proximate development. In J.V. Wertsch (Ed.), *Culture, communication & cognition: Vygotskian perspectives* (pp. 273–305). New York: Cambridge University Press.

Brown, J.S., Collins, A., & Duguid, P. (1989). Situated cognition and the culture of learning. *Educational Researcher, 18*(1), 32–42.

Brown, R. (1973). *A first language*. Cambridge, MA: Harvard University Press.

Bruner, J.S. (1962). The conditions of creativity. In H. Gruber, G. Terrell, & M. Wertheimer (Eds.), *Contemporary approaches to creative thinking* (pp. 1–30). New York: Atherton Press.

Bruner, J.S. (1971). The nature and uses of immaturity. *American Psychologist, 27*, 1–22.

Bruner, J.S. (1986). *Actual minds, possible worlds*. Cambridge, MA: Harvard University Press.

Bruner, J.S., & Haste, H. (Eds.). (1987). *Making sense: The child's construction of the world*. New York: Methuen.

Bruner, J.S., Olver, R., & Greenfield, P. (1966). *Studies in cognitive growth*. New York: Wiley.

Campbell, D. (1974). Evolutionary epistemology. In P. Schilpp (Ed.), *The philosophy of Karl Popper* (Vol. 14, I, pp. 413–463). La Salle, IL: Open Court.

Campbell, D. (1975). On the conflicts between biological and social evolution and between psychology and moral tradition. *American Psychologist, 30*, 1103–1126.

Campbell, R.L. (1989). *Developmental levels and scenarios for Smalltalk learning* (IBM Research Report). Yorktown Heights, NY: IBM T.J. Watson Research Center.

Campbell, R.L. (1990). Developmental scenario analysis of Smalltalk programming. In J. Chew & J. Whiteside (Eds.), *Human factors in computing systems: CHI'90 Conference Proceedings* (pp. 269–276). New York: ACM.

Campbell, R.L., & Bickhard, M. (1986). *Knowing levels and developmental stages*. Basel, Switzerland: Karger.

Campbell, R.L., & Bickhard, M. (1987). A deconstruction of Fodor's anti-constructivism. *Human Development, 30*, 48–59.

Campbell, R.L., & Bickhard, M. (1992). Types of constraints on development: An interactivist approach. *Developmental Review, 12*, 311–338.

Campbell, R.L., Brown, N.R., & DiBello, A. (1992). The programmer's burden: Developing expertise in computer programming. In J.R. Hoffman (Ed.), *The psychology of expertise: Cognitive research and empirical AI* (pp. 269–294). New York: Springer-Verlag.

Carey, S. (1985). *Conceptual change in childhood*. Cambridge, MA: MIT Press.

Carroll, J.M., & Campbell, R.L. (1989). Artifacts as psychological theories: The case of human-computer interaction. *Behavior and Information Technology, 8*, 247–256.

Case, R. (1978). Intellectual development from birth to adulthood: A neo-Piagetian interpretation. In R.S. Siegler (Ed.), *Children's thinking: What develops?* (pp. 37–72). Hillsdale, NJ: Erlbaum.

Case, R. (1984). The process of stage transition: A neo-Piagetian view. In R.J. Sternberg (Ed.), *Mechanisms of cognitive development* (pp. 19–44). New York: W.H. Freeman.

Cavalli-Sforza, L., & Feldman, M. (1973). Cultural versus biological inheritance: Phenotypic transmission from parents to children. *American Journal of Human Genetics, 25*, 618–637.

Cavalli-Sforza, L., & Feldman, M. (1973). Models for cultural inheritance I: Group mean and within in group variation. *Theoretical Population Biology, 4*, 42–55.

Chase, W., & Simon, H. (1974). Perception in chess. *Cognitive Psychology, 4*, 55–81.

Chen, J.W., Goldsmith, L.T., & Feldman, D.H. (1989, June). *The crafted world: Children's understanding of the distinction between natural objects and artifacts.* Paper presented at the 19th Annual Symposium of the Jean Piaget Society, Philadelphia, PA.

Chomsky, N. (1980a). *Rules and representations.* New York: Columbia University Press.

Chomsky, N. (1980b). On cognitive structures and their development: A reply to Piaget. In M. Piattelli-Palmarini (Ed.), *Language & learning: The debate between Piaget and Chomsky* (pp. 35–52). Cambridge, MA: Harvard University Press.

Clark, G., & Zimmerman, E. (1986). A framework for educating artistically talented students based on Feldman, Clark and Zimmerman's models. *Studies in Art Education, 27,* 115–122.

Clarke, B. (1975). The causes of biological diversity. *Scientific American, 233,* 50–60.

Clark-Stewart, K.A. (1989). Infant day care: Maligned or malignant? *American Psychologist, 44*(2), 266–273.

Colby, A., & Kohlberg, L. (1987). *The measurement of moral judgment: Theoretical foundations and research validation* (Vol. I). New York: Cambridge University Press.

Colby, A., Kohlberg, L., Gibbs, J.C., & Lieberman, M. (1983). A longitudinal study of moral judgment. *Monographs of the Society for Research in Child Development, 48* (1,2, Serial No. 200).

Cole, M., Gay, J., Glick, J., & Sharp, D. (1971). *The cultural context of learning and thinking.* New York: Basic Books.

Commons, M.L., & Morse, S.J. (1988). How do we know? (A review of *Knowing levels and developmental stages). Contemporary Psychology, 33,* 699–700.

Cowan, P. (1978). *Piaget with feeling.* New York: Holt, Rinehart, & Winston.

Csikszentmihalyi, M. (1977). Phylogenetic and ontogenetic functions of artistic cognition. In S. Madeja (Ed.), *The arts, cognition, and basic skills* (pp. 114–117). St. Louis: Cemrel.

Csikszentmihalyi, M. (1988a). Motivation and creativity: Toward a synthesis of structural and energistic approaches to cognition. *New Ideas in Psychology, 6*(2), 159–176.

Csikszentmihalyi, M. (1988b). Society, culture, and person: A systems view of creativity. In R.J. Sternberg (Ed.), *The nature of creativity* (pp. 325–339). Cambridge: Cambridge University Press.

Csikszentmihalyi, M. (1990). The domain of creativity. In M.A. Runco & R.S. Albert (Eds.), *Theories of creativity* (pp. 190–212). Newbury Park, CA: Sage.

Csikszentmihalyi, M., & Robinson, R.E. (1986). Culture, time and the development of talent. In R.J. Sternberg & J.E. Davidson (Eds.), *Conceptions of giftedness* (pp. 264–284). New York: Cambridge University Press.

Damon, W. (1980). Patterns of change in children's social reasoning. *Child Development, 51,* 101–1017.

Deci, E. (1975). *Intrinsic motivation.* New York: Plenum.

Dennett, D.C. (1978). *Brainstorms: Philosophical essays on mind and psychology*. Montgomery, VT: Bradford Books.

Dennett, D.C. (1987). *The intentional stance*. Cambridge, MA: MIT Press.

Dennett, D.C. (1991). *Consciousness explained*. Boston: Little-Brown.

Dobzhansky, T. (1962). *Mankind evolving: The evolution of the human species*. New Haven, CT: Yale University Press.

Dobzhansky, T. (1970). *Genetics of the evolutionary process*. New York: Columbia University Press.

Dobzhansky, T. (1973). *Genetic diversity and human equality*. New York: Basic Books.

Dreyfus, H.L., & Dreyfus, S.E. (1986). *Mind over machine: The power of human intuition and expertise in the era of the computer*. New York: Free Press.

Eiseley, L. (1957). *The immense journey*. New York: Vintage. (Original work published 1946)

Ennis, R.H. (1989). The extent to which critical thinking is subject-specific: Further clarification. *Educational Researcher, 19*(4), 13–16.

Feldman, D.H. (1970). Faulty construction: A review of Wallach and Wing's "The talented student." *Contemporary Psychology. 15*, 3–4.

Feldman, D.H. (1971). Map understanding as a possible crystallizer of cognitive structures. *American Educational Research Journal, 8*, 485–501.

Feldman, D.H. (1973). Problems in the analysis of patterns of abilities. *Child Development, 44*, 12–18.

Feldman, D.H. (1974). Universal to unique: A developmental view of creativity and education. In S. Rosner & L. Abt. (Eds), *Essays in creativity* (pp. 45–85). Croton-on-Hudson: North River Press.

Feldman, D.H. (1976). The child as craftsman. *Phi Delta Kappan, 58*, 143–149.

Feldman, D.H. (1977). Review of W. Dennis' and M. Dennis' "The intellectually gifted: An overview." *Harvard Educational Review, 47*, 576–581.

Feldman, D.H. (1979a). The mysterious case of extreme giftedness. In H. Passow (Ed.), *The gifted and the talented: A yearbook of the National Society for the Study of Education* (pp. 335–351). Chicago: University of Chicago Press.

Feldman, D.H. (1979b). Toward a nonelitist conception of giftedness. *Phi Delta Kappan, 60*, 660–663.

Feldman, D.H. (1980a). Stage and sequence: Getting to the next level. *The Genetic Epistemologist, 9*, 1–6.

Feldman, D.H. (1980b). *Beyond universals in cognitive development*. Norwood, NJ: Ablex.

Feldman, D.H. (1980c). Stage and transition in cognitive-developmental research: Getting to the next level. *Genetic Epistemologist, 9*, 1–6.

Feldman, D.H. (1981a). The role of theory in cognitive developmental research: A reply to Brainerd. *Developmental Review, 1*, 82–89.

Feldman, D.H. (1981b). Beyond universals: Toward a developmental psychology of education. *Educational Researcher, 11*, 21–31.

Feldman, D.H. (Ed.). (1982a). *Developmental approaches to giftedness and creativity*. San Francisco: Jossey-Bass.

Feldman, D.H. (1982b, March). *Developmental science: An alternative to cognitive science.* Paper presented at MIT Division for Study and Research in Education, Cambridge, MA.

Feldman, D.H. (1982c). Transcending IQ in the definition of giftedness. *Early Childhood Review, 23,* 15–18.

Feldman, D.H. (1982d). A developmental framework for research with gifted children. In D.H. Feldman (Ed.), *Developmental approaches to giftedness & creativity* (pp. 31–45). San Francisco: Jossey-Bass.

Feldman, D.H. (1982e). A rejoinder to Bereiter. *Educational Researcher, 11*(5), 26–27.

Feldman, D.H. (1983). Developmental psychology and art education. *Art Education, 36*(2), 19–21.

Feldman, D.H. (1984). A follow-up of subjects scoring above 180 IQ in Terman's "Genetic Studies of Genius." *Exceptional Children, 50,* 518–523.

Feldman, D.H. (1985a). The end of a revolution or the beginning? (A review of Christine Atkinson's *Making sense of Piaget: The philosophical roots*). *Contemporary Psychology, 30,* 604–605.

Feldman, D.H. (1985b). The concept of nonuniversal developmental domains: Implications for artistic development. *Visual Arts Research, 11,* 82–89.

Feldman, D.H. (1986a). How development works. In I. Levin (Ed.), *Stage and structure: Reopening the debate* (pp. 284–306). Norwood, NJ: Ablex.

Feldman, D.H. (1986b). Giftedness as a developmentalist sees it. In R.J. Sternberg & J.E. Davidson (Eds.), *Conceptions of giftedness* (pp. 285–305). New York: Cambridge University Press (with A.C. Benjamin).

Feldman, D.H. (1987a). Developmental psychology and art education: Two fields at the crossroads. *Journal of Aesthetic Education, 21,* 243–259.

Feldman, D.H. (1987b). Going for the middle ground: A promising place for educational psychology. In L. Liben (Ed.), *Development and learning: Conflict or congruence?* (pp. 159–172). Hillsdale, NJ: Erlbaum.

Feldman, D.H. (1988). Creativity: Dreams, insights, and transformations. In R. Sternberg (Ed.), *The nature of creativity* (pp. 271–297). New York: Cambridge University Press.

Feldman, D.H. (1989a). Creativity: Proof that development occurs. In W. Damon (Ed.), *Child development today and tomorrow* (pp. 240–260). San Francisco: Jossey-Bass.

Feldman, D.H. (1986b). Universal to unique: Toward a cultural genetic epistemology. *Archives de Psychologie, 56,* 271 –279.

Feldman, D.H. (1991). *Nature's gambit: child prodigies and the development of human potential.* New York: Teachers College Press (with L.T. Goldsmith). (Original work published in 1986).

Feldman, D.H., & Goldsmith, L.T. (1986). Transgenerational influences on the development of early prodigious behavior: A case study approach. In W. Fowler (Ed.), *Early experience and the development of competence* (pp. 67–85). San Francisco: Jossey-Bass.

Feldman, D.H., & Goldsmith, L.T. (1989). Child prodigies: Children straddling two worlds. *Encyclopedia Britannica Annual Science and Health Supplement* (pp. 32–51). Chicago: Encyclopedia Britannica.

Feldman, D.H., & Markwalder, W. (1971). Systematic scoring of ranked distractors for the assessment of Piagetian reasoning levels. *Educational and Psychological Measurement, 31*, 347–362.

Feldman, D.H., Marrinan, B., & Hartfeldt, S. (1972). Transformational power as a possible index of creativity. *Psychological Reports, 30*, 335–338.

Fischer, K.W. (1980). A theory of cognitive development: The control and construction of hierarchies of skills. *Psychological Review, 87*, 477–531.

Fischer, K.W. (1981). The last straw for Piagetian stages? A review of "Beyond universals in cognitive development." *Contemporary Psychology, 26*, 338–339.

Fischer, K., & Pipp, S. (1984). Processes of cognitive development. In R. J. Sternberg (Ed.), *Mechanisms of cognitive development* (pp. 45–80). New York: W.H. Freeman.

Flavell, J.H. (1963). *The developmental psychology of Jean Piaget.* New York: Van Nostrand.

Flavell, J.H. (1970). Concept development. In P. Mussen (Ed.), *Carmichael's manual of child psychology* (pp. 983–1060). New York: Wiley.

Flavell, J.H. (1971a). Comments on Beilin's "The development of physical concepts." In T. Mischel (Ed.), *Cognitive psychology and epistemology* (pp. 189–191). New York: Academic Press.

Flavell, J.H. (1971b). Stage related properties of cognitive development. *Cognitive Psychology, 2*, 421–453.

Flavell, J.H. (1977). *Cognitive development.* Englewood Cliffs, NJ: Prentice-Hall.

Flavell, J.H., & Wohlwill, J. (1969). Formal and functional aspects of cognitive development. In D. Elkind & J. Flavell (Eds.), *Studies in cognitive development* (pp. 67–120). New York: Oxford University Press.

Fodor, J. (1980). Fixation of belief and concept acquisition. In M. Piattelli-Palmarini (Ed.), *Language & learning: The debate between Piaget and Chomsky* (pp. 14–162). Cambridge, MA: Harvard University Press.

Fodor, J. (1983). *The modularity of mind.* Cambridge, MA: MIT Press.

Freud, S. (1958). *On creativity and the unconscious.* New York: Harper & Row.

Gagne, R. (1968). Contributions of learning to human development. *Psychological Review, 75*, 177–191.

Gallagher, J.J. (1989). A new policy initiative: Infants and toddlers with handicapping conditions. *American Psychologist, 44*(2), 387–391.

Gardner, H. (1973). *The arts and human development.* New York: Wiley.

Gardner, H. (1981, May). Prodigies progress. *Psychology Today,* pp. 75–79.

Gardner, H. (1982). Giftedness: Speculations from a biological perspective. In D.H. Feldman (Ed.), *Developmental approaches to giftedness and creativity* (pp. 47–60). San Francisco: Jossey-Bass.

Gardner, H. (1983). *Frames of mind: The theory of multiple intelligences.* New York: Basic Books.

Gardner, H. (1988). Creative lives and creative works: A synthetic scientific approach. In R. Sternberg (Ed.), *The nature of creativity* (pp. 298–324). New York: Cambridge University Press.

Gardner, H. (1989). Creativity: An interdisciplinary perspective. *Creativity Research Journal, 1,* 8–26.

Gardner, H. (1991). *The unschooled mind.* New York: Basic Books.

Gardner, H., Howard, V., & Perkins, D. (1974). Symbol systems: A philosophical, psychological and educational investigation. In D.R. Olson (Ed.), *Media and symbols* (pp. 27–55). Chicago: University of Chicago Press.

Gardner, J. (1978). *Readings in developmental psychology.* Boston: Little-Brown.

Garwood, S.G., Phillips, D., Hartman, A., & Zigler, E.F. (1989). As the pendulum swings: Federal agency programs for children. *American Psychologist, 44*(2), 434–440.

Gedo, J.E. (1983). *Portraits of the artist: Psychoanalysis of creativity and its vicissitudes.* New York: Guilford Press.

Geertz, C. (1973). *The interpretation of cultures.* New York: Basic Books.

Gelman, R., & Gallistel, C.R. (1978). *The child's understanding of number.* Cambridge, MA: Harvard University Press.

Gerard, R.W. (1952). The biological basis of imagination. In B. Ghiselin (Ed.), *The creative process: A symposium* (pp. 226–251). New York: Mentor. (Original work published 1946)

Getzels, J., & Csikszentmihalyi, M. (1976). *The creative vision: A longitudinal study of problem finding in art.* New York: Wiley.

Ghiselin, B. (Ed.). (1952). *The creative process: A symposium.* New York: Mentor.

Gilligan, C. (1982). *In a different voice.* Cambridge, MA: Harvard University Press.

Ginsburg, H., & Opper, S. (1979). *Piaget's theory of intellectual development* (2nd ed.). Englewood Cliffs, NJ: Prentice-Hall.

Glick, J.A. (1983). Piaget, Vygotsky, and Werner. In S. Wapner & B. Kaplan (Eds.), *Toward a holistic developmental psychology* (pp. 35–52). Hillsdale, NJ: Erlbaum.

Goldsmith, L.T., & Feldman, D.H. (1989). Wang Yani: Gifts well given. In W. Ho (Ed.), *Yani: The brush of innocence* (pp. 51–62). New York: Hudson Hills Press.

Gould, S.J. (1981). *The mismeasure of man.* New York: Norton.

Greeno, J. (1989). A perspective on thinking. *American Psychologist, 44,* 134–141.

Gruber, H. (1981). *Darwin on man: A psychological study of scientific creativity* (2nd ed.). Chicago: University of Chicago Press.

Gruber, H. (1982). On the hypothesized relation between giftedness and creativity. In D.H. Feldman (Ed.), *Developmental approaches to giftedness and creativity* (pp. 7–29). San Francisco: Jossey-Bass.

Gruber, H., & Voneche, J. (1978). *The essential Piaget.* New York: Basic Books.

Guilford, J.P. (1950). Creativity. *American Psychologist, 5,* 444–454.

Hart, D., & Damon, W. (1984). Models of social cognitive development. *The Genetic Epistemologist, 14,* 1–8.

Hart, D., & Damon, W. (1986). Developmental trends in self-understanding. *Social Cognition, 4,* 338–407.

Hartman, E. (1984). *The nightmare: The psychology and biology of terrifying dreams.* New York: Basic Books.

Hatano, G., Yoshio, M., & Binks, M. (1977). Performance of expert abacus users. *Cognition, 5,* 47–55.

Henle, M. (1975). Fishing for ideas. *American Psychologist, 30,* 795–799.

Horowitz, F.D. (1987). *Exploring developmental theories: Toward a structural/behavioral model of development.* Hillsdale, NJ: Erlbaum.

Horowitz, F.D., & O'Brien, M. (Eds.). (1985). *The gifted and talented: Developmental perspectives.* Washington, DC: American Psychological Association.

Horowitz, F.D., & O'Brien, M. (1989). *American Psychologist* [Special issue: Children and Their Development: Knowledge Base, Research Agenda, and Social Policy Application], *44* (whole issue).

Housen, A. (1984). The eye of the beholder: measuring aesthetic development (Doctoral dissertation, Harvard University, 1983). *Dissertation Abstracts International, 44,* 1945B.

Hunt, J.McV. (1961). *Intelligence and experience.* New York: Ronald Press.

Inhelder, B., & Chipman, H. (Eds.). (1976). *Piaget and his school.* New York: Springer-Verlag.

Jackson, P., & Messick, S. (1965). The person, the product and the response: Conceptual problems in the assessment of creativity. *Journal of Personality, 33,* 309–329.

John-Steiner, V. (1985). *Notebooks of the mind: Explorations of thinking.* New York: Harper & Row.

Karmiloff-Smith, A. (1986). Stage/structure versus phase/process in modeling linguistic and cognitive development. In I. Levin (Ed.), *Stage and structure: Reopening the debate* (pp. 164–190). Norwood, NJ: Ablex.

Keil, F.C. (1984). Mechanisms in cognitive development and the structure of knowledge. In R. Sternberg (Ed.), *Mechanisms of cognitive development* (pp. 81–100). San Francisco: W.H. Freeman.

Keil, F.C. (1986). On the structure-dependent nature of stages in cognitive development. In I. Levin (Ed.), *Stage and structure* (pp. 144–163). Norwood, NJ: Ablex.

Kessen, W. (1962). "Stage" and "structure" in the study of children. *Monographs of the Society for Research in Child Development, 27,* 53–70.

Kessen, W. (1984). Introduction: The end of the age of development. In R. Sternberg (Ed.), *Mechanisms of cognitive development* (pp. 1–18). New York: Freeman.

Kohlberg, L. (1969). Stage and sequence: The cognitive-developmental approach to socialization. In D. Goslin (Ed.), *Handbook of socialization theory and research* (pp. 347–480). New York: Rand McNally.

Kohlberg, L. (1971). From is to ought: How to commit the naturalistic fallacy and get away with it in the study of moral development. In T. Mischel (Ed.), *Cognitive development and epistemology* (pp. 151–235). New York: Academic Press.

Kohlberg, L. (1973). The claim to moral adequacy of a highest stage of moral development. *Journal of Philosophy, 70*, 630–646.

Kohlberg, L., & Gilligan, C. (1974). The adolescent as philosopher: The discovery of the self in a postconventional world. In H. Kraemer (Ed.), *Youth and culture: A human-development approach* (pp. 598–630). Monterey, CA: Brooks/Cole.

Kris, E. (1952). *Psychoanalytic explorations in art.* New York: International Universities Press.

Kris, E. (1958). *The neurotic distortion of the creative process.* Lawrence, KS: University of Kansas Press.

Kuhn, D. (1972). Mechanisms of change in the development of cognitive structures. *Child Development, 43*, 833–844.

Kuhn, D. (1989). Making cognitive development research relevant to education. In W. Damon (Ed.), *Child development today and tomorrow* (pp. 262–287). San Francisco: Jossey-Bass.

Kuhn, T. (1962). *The structure of scientific revolutions.* Chicago: University of Chicago Press.

Langer, J. (1969a). Disequilibrium as a source of development. In P. Mussen, J. Langer, & M. Covington (Eds.), *Trends and issues in developmental psychology* (pp. 22–37). New York: Holt, Rinehart, & Winston.

Langer, J. (1969b). *Theories of development.* New York: Holt, Rinehart, & Winston.

Langer, J. (1974). Interactional aspects of cognitive organization. *Cognition, 3*, 9–28.

Levin, D. (1978). *Peer interaction as a source of cognitive developmental change.* Unpublished doctoral dissertation, Tufts University, Medford, MA.

Levin, I. (Ed.). (1986). *Stage and structure: Reopening the debate.* Norwood, NJ: Ablex.

Liben, L. (Ed.). (1987a). *Development and learning: Conflict or congruence?* Hillsdale, NJ: Erlbaum.

Liben, L.S. (1987b). Information processing and Piagetian theory: Conflict or congruence? In L.S. Liben (Ed.), *Development learning: Conflict or congruence?* (pp. 109–132). Hillsdale, NJ: Erlbaum.

Loevinger, J. (1976). *Measuring ego development.* New York: Jossey-Bass.

Markwalder, W. (1972). Stage mixture and cognitive development. *The Southern Journal of Educational Research, 6*, 219–225.

Maslow, A. (1972). A holistic approach to creativity. In C.W. Taylor (Ed.), *Climate for creativity* (pp. 287–294). Elmsford, NY: Pergamon Press.

Mayr, E. (1970). *Populations, species and evolution.* Cambridge, MA: Harvard University Press.

McClearn, G. (1972). Genetic determination of behavior (animal). In L. Ehrman, G. Omenn, & E. Caspari (Eds.), *Genetics, environment and behavior: Implications for education* (pp. 55–67). New York: Academic Press.

McLuhan, M. (1964). *Understanding media: The extensions of man.* New York: McGraw-Hill.

Menuhin, Y. (1967). *Unfinished journey.* New York: Knopf.

Mischel, T. (Ed.). (1971). *Cognitive development and epistemology*. New York: Academic Press.

Mockros, C.A. (1989). *Aesthetic judgment: An empirical comparison of two stage developmental theories*. Unpublished Master's thesis, Tufts University, Medford, MA.

Moos, R.H. (1973). Conceptualization of human environments. *American Psychologist, 28*, 652–665.

Murray, F. (1972). The acquisition of conservation through social interaction. *Developmental Psychology, 6*, 1–6.

Murray, F.B., & Ames, G.J. (1982). When two wrongs make a right: Promoting cognitive change by social conflict. *Developmental Psychology, 18*, 894–897.

Norcini, J.J., & Snyder, S.S. (1983). The effects of modeling and cognitive induction on moral reasoning of adolescents. *Journal of Youth and Adolescence, 12*, 101–115.

Norcini, J.J., & Snyder, S.S. (1986). Effects of modeling and cognitive induction on moral reasoning. In G.L. Sapp (Ed.), *Handbook of moral development* (pp. 249–259). Birmingham, AL: Religious Education Press.

NOVA. (1988). "Ramanujan." A Video Shown on Public Television on Public Television Stations (First aired in March).

Olson, D.R. (1970). *Cognitive development: The child's acquisition of diagonality*. New York: Academic Press.

Olson, D.R. (1972). On a theory of instruction: Why different forms of instruction result in similar knowledge. *Interchange, 3*, 9–24.

Olson, D.R. (Ed.). (1974). *Media and symbols: The forms of expression, communication and education*. Chicago: University of Chicago Press.

Olson, D.R., & Bruner, J.S. (1974). Learning through experience and learning through media. In D.R. Olson (Ed.), *Media and symbols* (pp. 125–150). Chicago: University of Chicago Press.

Parsons, M.J. (1987). *How we understand art: A cognitive developmental account of aesthetic experience*. Cambridge: Cambridge University Press.

Pea, R., & Kurland, D.M. (1984). On the cognitive effects of learning computer programming. *New Ideas in Psychology, 2*, 137–168.

Perkins, D. (1988). The possibility of invention. In R.J. Sternberg (Ed.), *The nature of creativity* (pp. 362–385). New York: Cambridge University Press.

Piaget, J. (1954). *The construction of reality in the child*. New York: Basic Books.

Piaget, J. (1960). *Logic and psychology*. New York: Basic Books.

Piaget, J. (1963). *The origins of intelligence in children*. New York: Norton. (Original work published 1952).

Piaget, J. (1968). *Structuralism*. New York: Basic Books.

Piaget, J. (1970). Piaget's theory. In P. Mussen (Ed.), *Carmichael's manual of child psychology* (Vol. 1, pp. 703–732). New York: Wiley.

Piaget, J. (1971a). *Biology and knowledge*. Chicago: University of Chicago Press.

Piaget, J. (1971b). The theory of stages in cognitive development. In D. Green,

M. Ford, & G. Flamer (Eds.), *Measurement and Piaget* (pp. 1–11). New York: McGraw-Hill.

Piaget, J. (1972). Intellectual evolution from adolescence to adulthood. *Human Development, 15*, 1–12.

Piaget, J. (1974). *The language and thought of the child.* New York: New American Library. (Original work published 1923)

Piaget, J. (1975). *The development of thought: Equilibration of cognitive structures.* New York: Viking Penguin.

Piaget, J. (1979). Correspondences and transformations. In F. Murray (Ed.), *The impact of Piagetian theory on education, philosophy, psychology* (pp. 17–28). Baltimore, MD: University Park Press.

Piaget, J. (1982a). Creativity. In J.M. Gallagher & D.K. Reid (Eds.), *The learning theory of Piaget and Inhelder* (pp. 221–229). Monterey, CA: Brooks/Cole.

Piaget, J. (1982b). Reflections on Baldwin. In J.M. Broughton & D.J. Freeman-Moir (Eds.), *The cognitive developmental psychology of James Mark Baldwin* (pp. 80–86). Norwood, NJ: Ablex.

Piaget, J., & Inhelder, B. (1967). *The child's conception of space.* New York: Norton. (Original work published 1948)

Piaget, J., & Voyat, G. (1979). The possible, the impossible and the necessary. In F. Murray (Ed.), *The impact of Piagetian theory* (pp. 65–85). Baltimore, MD: University Park Press.

Piattelli-Palmarini, M. (Ed.). (1980). *Language and learning: The debate between Jean Piaget and Noam Chomsky.* Cambridge, MA: Harvard University Press.

Piirto, J. (1992). *Understanding those who create.* Dayton, OH: Ohio Psychology Press.

Popper, K. (1959). *The logic of scientific discovery.* New York: Basic Books.

Reis, S.M. (1989). Reflections on policy affecting the education of gifted and talented students: Past and future perspectives. *American Psychologist, 44*(2), 399–408.

Rest, J. (1986). *Revised manual for the defining issues test.* Minneapolis, MN: Moral Research Projects, University of Minnesota.

Rieber, R.W., & Carton, A.S. (Eds.). (1987). *The collected works of L.S. Vygotsky: Problems of general psychology.* New York: Plenum.

Rogoff, B. (1982). Integrating context and cognitive development. In M.E. Lamb & A.L. Brown (Eds.), *Advances in developmental psychology* (Vol. 2). Hillsdale, NJ: Erlbaum.

Rogoff, B. (1990). *Apprenticeship in thinking: Cognitive development in social context.* New York: Oxford University Press.

Rogoff, B., & Wertsch, J.V. (Eds.). (1984). *Children's learning in the "zone of proximal development."* San Francisco: Jossey-Bass.

Rolfe, L. (1978). *The Menuhins: A family odyssey.* San Francisco: Panjandrum/Aris Books.

Salomon, G. (1974). What is learned and how it is taught?: The interaction between media, message, task and learner. In D.R. Olson (Ed.), *Media and symbols* (pp. 383–406). Chicago: University of Chicago Press.

Salomon, G. (1979). *The interaction of media, cognition and learning.* San Francisco: Jossey-Bass.

Schaie, K., & Strother, C. (1968). A cross-sequential study of age changes in cognitive behavior. *Psychological Bulletin, 70,* 67–680.

Scribner, S., & Cole, M. (1973). Cognitive consequences of formal and informal instruction. *Science, 182,* 553–559.

Selman, R.L. (1980). *The growth of interpersonal understanding: Developmental and clinical analysis.* New York: Academic Press.

Siegler, R. (1981). Developmental sequences within and between concepts. *Monographs of the Society for Research in Child Development, 96*(2, whole issue).

Silverman, I.W., & Geiringer, E. (1973). Dyadic interaction and conservation induction: A test of Piaget's equilibration model. *Child Development, 44,* 815–820.

Simon, H., & Chase, W. (1973). Skill in chess. *American Scientist, 61,* 364–403.

Simonton, D.K. (1984). *Genius, creativity, and leadership: Historiometric inquiries.* Cambridge, MA: Harvard University Press.

Snyder, S.S., & Feldman, D.H. (1977). Internal and external influences on cognitive developmental change. *Child Development, 48,* 937–943.

Snyder, S.S., Feldman, D.H., & LaRossa, C. (1976). A manual for the administration and scoring off a Piaget-based map drawing exercise. In O. Johnson (Ed.), *Tests and measurements in child development: A handbook (II)* (Abstract). San Francisco: Jossey-Bass.

Sprinthall, N.A., & Bernier, J. (1978). Moral and cognitive development of teachers. *New Catholic World, 221,* 179–184.

Sprinthall, N.A., & Thies-Sprinthall, L. (1980). Educating for teacher growth: A cognitive developmental perspective. *Theory into Practice, 19,* 278–286.

Sternberg, R.J. (1984a). Testing intelligence without I.Q. tests. *Phi Delta Kappan, 65,* 694–698.

Sternberg, R.J. (Ed.). (1984b). *Mechanisms of cognitive development.* New York: W.H. Freeman.

Sternberg, R.J. (1986a). *Intelligence applied: Understanding and increasing your intellectual skills.* San Diego: Harcourt Brace Jovanovich.

Sternberg, R.J. (1986b). A triarchic theory of intellectual giftedness. In R.J. Sternberg & J. Davidson (Ed.), *Conceptions of giftedness* (pp. 223–243). New York: Cambridge University Press.

Sternberg, R.J. (1988). A three-facet model of creativity. In R.J. Sternberg (Ed.), *The nature of creativity* (pp. 125–147). New York: Cambridge University Press.

Sternberg, R.J., & Davidson, J.E. (Eds.). (1986). *Conceptions of giftedness.* New York: Cambridge University Press.

Strauss, S. (1972). Inducing cognitive development and learning: A review of short-term training experiments I: The organismic developmental approach. *Cognition, 4,* 329–357.

Strauss, S. (1987). Educational-developmental psychology and school learning. In L. Liben (Ed.), *Development and learning: Conflict or congruence?* (pp. 133–158). Hillsdale, NJ: Erlbaum.

Strauss, S., & Rimalt, I. (1974). Effects of organizational disequilibrium training on structural elaboration. *Developmental Psychology, 10,* 526–533.

Sullivan, E. (1970). The issue of readiness in the design and organization of the curriculum: A historical perspective. *Educational Technology, 1,* 439–448.

Thomas, L. (1974). *The lives of a cell: Notes of a biology watcher.* New York: Bantam Books.

Thrower, N. (1972). *Maps and man.* Englewood Cliffs, NJ: Prentice-Hall.

Torrance, E.P. (1962). *Guiding creative talent.* Englewood Cliffs, NJ: Prentice-Hall.

Turiel, E. (1966). An experimental test of the sequentiality of developmental stages in the child's moral judgments. *Journal of Personality and Social Psychology, 3,* 611–618.

Turiel, E. (1969). Developmental processes in the child's moral thinking. In P.H. Mussen, J. Langer, & M. Covington (Eds.), *Trends and issues in developmental psychology* (92–133). New York: Holt, Rinehart and Winston.

Turiel, E. (1974). Conflict and transition in adolescent moral development. *Child Development, 45,* 14–29.

Turiel, E. (1979). Distinct conceptual and developmental domains: Social convention and morality. In H.E. Howe & C.B. Keasey (Eds.), *Nebraska symposium on motivation, 1977* (pp. 77–116). Lincoln, NE: University of Nebraska Press.

Turiel, E. (1983). *The development of social knowledge.* New York: Cambridge University Press.

Tyler, L. (1978). *Individuality.* San Francisco: Jossey-Bass.

Vygotsky, L. (1962). *Thought and language.* Cambridge, MA: MIT Press. (Original work published 1934)

Vygotsky, L.S. (1978). *Mind in society: The development of higher psychological processes* (Ed. by M. Cole, V. John-Steiner, S. Scribner, & E. Souberman). Cambridge, MA: Harvard University Press.

Waddington, C. (1953). Genetic assimilation of an acquired character. *Evolution, 7,* 118–126.

Waddington, C. (1957). *The strategy of the genes.* London: Allen & Unwin.

Walker, J.J., & Taylor, J.H. (1991). Stage transitions in moral reasoning: A longitudinal study of developmental processes. *Developmental Psychology, 27,* 330–337.

Wallace, D., & Gruber, H. (1989). *Creative people at work.* New York: Cambridge University Press.

Wallach, M.A. (1971). *The intelligence/creativity distinction.* New York: General Learning Press.

Wallach, M.A. (1985). Creativity testing and giftedness. In F.D. Horowitz & M. O'Brien (Eds.), *The gifted and talented: Developmental perspectives* (pp. 99–132). Washington, DC: American Psychological Association.

Walters, J., & Gardner, H. (1986). The crystallizing experience: Discovering an intellectual gift. In R.J. Sternberg & J.E. Davidson (Eds.), *Conceptions of giftedness* (pp. 306–331). New York: Cambridge University Press.

Walton, R. (1987). *Emotional concomitants of developmental transition: A study of "metahobby."* Unpublished Master's thesis, Tufts University, Medford, MA.

Walton, R., Adams, M.L., Goldsmith, L.T., & Feldman, D.H. (1987, April). *A study of the relation between thought and emotion in the development of expertise.* Paper presented at the Biennial Meeting of the Society for Research in Child Development, Baltimore, MD.

Walton, R., & Berliner, M. (1987). *Levels of expertise in juggling.* Unpublished manuscript, Tufts University, Medford, MA.

Werner, J. (1957). The concept of development from a comparative and organismic point of view. In D.B. Harris (Ed.), *The concept of development: An issue in the study of human behavior* (pp. 125–148). Minneapolis: University of Minnesota Press.

Wertsch, J. (Ed.). (1985). *Culture, communication and cognition: Vygotskian perspectives.* Cambridge: Cambridge University Press.

Wexler-Sherman, C., Gardner, H., & Feldman, D.H. (1988). A pluralistic view of early assessment: The Project Spectrum approach. *Theory into Practice, 27,* 77–83.

Wilber, K., Engler, J., & Brown, D.P. (1986). *Transformations of consciousness: Conventional and contemplative perspectives on development.* Boston: New Science Library.

Wilson, E.O. (1975). *Sociobiology.* Cambridge, MA: Harvard University Press.

Wohlwill, J. (1970). The place of structured experience in early cognitive development. *Interchange, 1,* 13–27.

Wohlwill, J. (1973). *The study of behavioral development.* New York: Academic Press.

Zender, M.A., & Zender, B.F. (1974). Vygotsky's view about the age periodization of child development. *Human Development, 17,* 24–40.

Author Index

A

Adams, M.L., 127, 129, 147, *201*
Airasian, P., 21, *187*
Alexander, P.A., 4, *187*
Allen, T., 62, *188*
Arbuthnot, J., 78, *187*
Aries, P., 17, *187*
Arieti, S., 156, *187*

B

Bart, W., 21, *187*
Beilin, H., 163, *187*
Benjamin, A., 128, 135, 139, 145, 147, 148, 150, *187*
Bereiter, C., 5, 10, *187*
Berkowitz, M., 106, 114, 116, *187*
Berliner, D., 11, 135, *188*
Bernier, J., 136, *199*
Bickhard, M., 6, 133, 145, *188, 189*
Binks, M., 31, *195*
Blatt, S., 27, *188*
Bloom, B., 168, 175, 176, *188*
Bornstein, M.H., 2, *188*
Brainerd, C.J., 18, 62, 121, 142, *188*
Bringuier, J.C., 147, 148, 151, *188*
Brown, A.L., 5, *188*
Brown, D.P., 156, *201*
Brown, J.S., 4, *188*
Brown, N.R., 133, *189*

Bruner, J.S., 3, 28, 29, 153, 154, 155, 162, 163, 169, 180, *188, 197*

C

Campbell, D., 44, 45, 133, 134, *189*
Campbell, R.L., 6, 133, 134, 135, 145, *189*
Carey, S., 153, *189*
Carroll, J.M., 133, *189*
Case, R., 6, *189*
Cavalli-Sforza, L., 46, *189*
Chase, W., 122, 142, 189, *199*
Chen, J.W., 179, *190*
Chipman, H., 64, *195*
Chomsky, N., 145, 154, *190*
Clark, G., *190*
Clarke, B., 55, *190*
Clark-Stewart, K.A., 2, *190*
Colby, A., 115, 118, *190*
Cole, M., 29, *190, 199*
Collins, A., 4, *188*
Commons, M.L., 6, *190*
Cowan, P., 59, *190*
Csikszentmihalyi, M., 31, 123, 153, 155, 166, *190, 194*

D

Damon, W., 112, 113, 114, 115, 116, 145n, *190, 194, 195*
Davidson, J.E., 8, *199*
Deci, E., 63, *190*

Dennett, D.C., 178, *191*
DiBello, A., 133, 134, 135, *189*
Dobzhansky, T., 46, 50, 54, 55, *191*
Dreyfus, H.L., 4, 124, *191*
Dreyfus, S.E., 4, 124, *191*
Duguid, P., 4, *188*

E
Engler, J., 156, *201*
Ennis, R.H., 4, *191*

F
Feldman, D.H., 3, 5, 7, 10, 12, 54, 63, 75,
    94, 95, 98, 108, 121, 122, 123, 127,
    129, 141, 143, 145, 146, 147, 148,
    149, 150, 151, 152, 155, 156, 157,
    162, 163, 164, 165, 166, 169, 173,
    175, 177, 179, 180, 185, *190, 191,
    192, 193, 194, 199, 201*
Feldman, M., 46, *189*
Fischer, K.W., 5, 6, 142, 156, *193*
Flavell, J.H., 16, 17, 26, 36, 57, 59, 62, 81,
    92, 99, 149, 163, *193*
Fodor, J., 145, 154, *193*
Freud, S., 156, *193*

G
Gagné, R., 18, *193*
Gallagher, J.J., 2, *193*
Gallistel, C.R., 43, *194*
Gardner, H., 5, 12, 28, 31, 37, 146, 147,
    155, 163, 166, 172, 173, 175, 179,
    193, 194, 200, 201
Gardner, J., 59, *194*
Garwood, S.G., 2, *194*
Gedo, J.E., 156, *194*
Geertz, C., 24, *194*
Geiringer, E., 27, *199*
Gelman, R., 43, *194*
Gerard, R.W., 45, *194*
Getzels, J., 31, *194*
Ghiselin, B., 32, 156, *194*
Gilligan, C., 27, 140, *194, 196*
Ginsburg, H., 59, *194*
Glick, J., 4, *190, 194*
Goldsmith, L.T., 7, 12, 127, 129, 147, 152,
    166, 169, 173, 175, 177, 179, 185,
    190, 192, 194, 201
Gould, S.J., 172, *194*
Greenfield, P., 29, 153, 154, 155, 162, *189*
Gruber, H., 44, 53, 55, 59, 99, 146, 151,
    161, 179, *194, 200*
Guilford, J.P., 146, *194*

H
Hart, D., 114, 115, 116, *194, 195*
Hartfeldt, S., 147, *193*
Hartman, A., 2, *194*
Haste, H., 169, *189*
Hatano, G., 31, *195*
Henle, M., 54, *195*
Horowitz, F.D., 2, 4, 8, 164, *195*
Housen, A., 130, *195*
Howard, V., 28, *194*
Hunt, J.McV., 63, 177, *195*

I
Inhelder, B., 27, 63, 64, 165, *195*

J
Jackson, P., 147, 158, *195*
John-Steiner, V., 9, *195*
Judy, J.E., 4, *187*

K
Karmiloff-Smith, A., 6, *195*
Keil, F.C., 6, 142, 153, *195*
Keller, M., 106, 114, 115, 116, *187*
Kessen, W., 56, 122, 163, *195*
Kohlberg, L., 27, 37, 110, 140, *188, 190,
    195, 196*
Krasnegor, N.A., 2, *188*
Kris, E., 99, 156, *196*
Kuhn, D., 2, 78, 79, *196*
Kuhn, T., 32, *196*
Kurland, D.M., 122, *197*

L
Langer, J., 57, 61, 63, 81, *196*
Levin, D., 27, 80, *196*
Levin, I., 5, *196*
Liben, L., 5, 6, 145, *196*
Loevinger, J., 138, *196*

M
Markwalder, W., 63, 79, *193, 196*
Marrinan, B., 147, *193*
Maslow, A., 146, *196*
Mayr, E., 55, *196*
McClearn, G., 46, *196*
McLuhan, M., 64, *196*
Menuhin, Y., 175, *196*
Messick, S., 147, 158, *196*
Mockros, C.A., 130, 132, *197*
Moos, R.H., 162, *197*
Morse, S.J., 6, *190*
Murray, F., 27, *197*

N

Norcini, J.J., 110, 113, *197*

O

Olson, D.R., 28, 29, 30, 49, 154, 155, 162, 163, *197*
Opper, S., 59, *194*

P

Parsons, M.J., 130, *197*
Pea, R., 122, *197*
Perkins, D., 28, 180, 181, *194, 197*
Phillips, D., 2, *194*
Piaget, J., 18, 20, 27, 59, 62, 63, 64, 81, 92, 99, 100, 115, 147, 148, 149, 150, 152, 165, *197, 198*
Piattelli-Palmarini, M., 154, *198*
Piirto, J., 9, *198*
Pipp, S., 6, 142, 156, *193*
Popper, K., 44, 45, *198*

R

Reis, S.M., 8, *198*
Rest, J., 135, *198*
Rimalt, I., 79, *200*
Robinson, R.E., 153, 155, 166, *190*
Rogoff, B., 4, 5, 8, 130, 164, *198*
Rolfe, L., 175, *198*

S

Salomon, G., 28, 29, 30, 32, *198, 199*
Schaie, K., 85, *199*
Scribner, S., 29, *199*
Selman, R.L., 114, 115, *199*
Siegler, R., 5, *199*
Silverman, I.W., 27, *199*
Simon, H., 122, 142, *189, 199*
Simonton, D.K., 184, *199*
Snyder, S.S., 63, 75, 78, 79, 80, 82, 94, 95, 98, 106, 110, 113, 117, *197, 199*

Sprinthall, N.A., 136, *199*
Sternberg, R.J., 5, 8, 9, 122, 142, *199*
Strauss, S., 10, 61, 78, 79, 99, 180, *199, 200*
Strother, C., 85, *199*

T

Taylor, J.H., 110, 115, 117, 118, 119, *200*
Thies-Sprinthall, L., 136, *199*
Thomas, L., 167, 170, 177, 178, 182, *200*
Torrance, E.P., 146, *200*
Turiel, E., 17, 18, 61, 78, 79, 99, 114, *200*

V

Voyat, G., 150, *198*
Vygotsky, L., 3, 114, 150, 162, 167, 170, 179, *200*

W

Waddington, C., 50, *200*
Walker, J.J., 110, 115, 117, 118, 119, *200*
Wallace, D., 161, *200*
Wallach, M.A., 146, *200*
Walters, J., 163, 166, *200*
Walton, R., 125, 127, 128, 129, 147, *201*
Werner, J., 99, *106*
Wertsch, J.V., 4, 130, *198, 201*
Wexler-Sherman, C., 147, *201*
Wilber, K., 156, *201*
Wilson, E.O., 46, 51, *201*
Wohlwill, J., 81, *193, 201*

Y

Yoshio, M., 31, *195*

Z

Zender, B.F., 114, *201*
Zender, M.A., 114, *201*
Zigler, E.F., 2, *194*

Subject Index

A

Accommodation (and assimilation),
    60–61, 62, 151, 153, 157 (*see also*
    Equilibration, Disequalibrium)
Aesthetic judgment and reasoning
    studies of, 130–132
Amplifiers (of human capacities), 28–31,
    64
Apprenticeship, 123

B

Bias index (*see* Transitions)

C

Child prodigies (*see* Early prodigious
    achievement)
Co-incidence (*see* Early prodigious
    achievement)
Computer programming
    research on, 133–135
    in Smalltalk, 134
Concrete operations, 42
Configurations, 77, 79, 82–85, 88, 90,
    94–95, 97, 98, 100
Consolidation (*see* Developmental theory)
Constructivist theory, 148–157
    vs. nativism, 154
Craftsman 8 (*see also* Education)
Creativity, 34–35 (*see also* Novelties,
    Transitions)

based on biological processes, 147–148
crafted vs. natural object recognition,
    153–154
definition of, 146
development and, 34–35, 147
essential factors, 147
insight and (*see* Novelties)
Crystallizing conditions, 164–166 (*see
    also* Environmental conditions,
    Early prodigious achievement)
Cultural organisms, 166–183, 185
    definition of, 169
Cultural incorporation, 39–40, 44–46,
    47–51, 52–53
Curriculum, 22 (*see also* Education)

D

Décalage (*see* Stages)
Development (*see also* Developmental
    theory, Early prodigious
    achievement, Education,
    Transitions, developmental)
    novelties in, 141
    existence of, 158
Developmental measures
    of teaching, 138–139
Developmental theory (*see also*
    Nonuniversal domains,
    Transitions)

Developmental theory (*cont'd.*)
  assumptions of, 20–22
  cognitive–developmental view, 15–20,
    59–63, 75–77, 92–93, 112
  co-incidence and, 7–8
  elaboration and consolidation, 80–84,
    85–88, 99, 114, 118, 119
  hierarchial integration, 21–22, 31, 36,
    63
  levels within fields, 19f, 31, 32, 34,
    63–64, 75–77 (*see also* Map
    drawing)
  invariant sequence, 19, 21, 32, 36,
    63–64
  stage vs. state, 75–77
  universality of acquisition, 21
Disequalibrium (*see also* Equalibration,
  Transitions)
  external disequalibrium, 62, 78, 80–81
  internal disequalibrium, 62, 80–81, 88,
    90
Domains (*see* Nonuniversal domains)

E

Early prodigious achievement, 166, 167,
  168 (*see also* Intelligence,
  Nonuniversal domains)
  as idiosyncratic development, 25
  crystallizing conditions and, 166
  descriptions of prodigies, 166, 172–183
  education and, 176–177
  environmental influences on, 161–183
  idiosyncratic achievement and, 24–25,
    33–35
  social structures of, 174–183
  transgenerational influence, 12, 169
Education (*see also* Curriculum, Early
  prodigious achievement,
  Instruction)
  art, 9–10
  craftsmanship as goal in, 123
  "gifted", 8–9
  levels of, 123, 124
Elaboration (*see* Developmental theory)
Elements, psychological, 90–101 (*see also*
  Transitions)
  deep reversion, 94, 98
  laggards, 94, 98
  leapers, 94–98
  movements in, 141
  novelties, 92, 95–98, 99–101, 102, 152,
    156

Environmental conditions, 26–35
Equalibration, 27, 61–62, 117, 149, 153,
  155, 157 (*see also* Disequalibrium,
  Transitions)
Evolution, 43–46

F

Formal Operations, 153
Friendship
  reasoning about, 114, 119
    Selman's five-stage sequence of, 115
  studies of, 115

H

Hierarchial integration (*see*
  Developmental theory,
  Nonuniversal domains,
  Transitions)

I

Individuality, 55–56
Informal education (*see* Education)
Instruction, 29–41, 34, 43, 49 (*see also*
  Education)
Insight (*see* Novelties)
Invariant sequence (*see* Developmental
  theory, Nonuniversal domains,
  Transitions)

L

Levels, developmental (*see*
  Developmental theory)

M

Map drawing, 63–75, 104–106 (*see also*
  Transitions)
  analysis of, 104, 119
  as cultural activity, 165
  levels of, 65–75
  modal level, 58, 77–78, 106, 108, 109,
    110, 111, 114, 116, 118 (*see also*
    Transitions)
  novelties in, 104, 106–108
  transitions and (*see* Transitions)
Medium, expression in, 30 (*see also*
  Amplifiers)
Metahobby, 33, 125–129
  juggling as, 125–130
Moral judgment and reasoning
  frequency histograms in, 110
  Kohlberg's stages of, 110–111, 118
  parental authority, 112–113, 119
  positive justice, 112–113, 119

Rest's Defining Issues Test (DIT),
135–139
correlation with OIT and TOPS,
136–138
Snyder–Norcini Study of, 110–111, 113

N
Nonuniversal development, 4
Nonuniversal domains (*see also* Cultural
incorporation, Developmental
theory, Transitions)
acquisition of, 4
cultural, 23–24, 28–31
developmental, 124
discipline-based, 24, 31–33
idiosyncratic, 24–25, 33–35
pancultural, 12
unique, 25–26, 35 (*see also* Universal-
to-unique)
vs. universal, 15, 22–35, 43
Novelties in thought, 40–42, 53–55, 58,
92–102 (*see also* Creativity,
Elements)
creative vs. noncreative, 25–26, 46–47,
54
egocentrism in, 42
in map drawing, 104, 106–108
insight, 54, 100, 107

O
Oversplicing, 85–89, 98

R
Radical nativism, 145, 157
vs. constructivism, 154
Resistances (*see* Stages)

S
Spontaneous acquisition, 20–21 (*see also*
Developmental theory,
Nonuniversal domains)
Stages (*see also* Developmental theory)
assumptions of, 16–20

décalage, 60, 65, 78, 92, 100
vs. levels, 18–19, 31–33, 34, 75–76
resistances, 92
structures as a whole (structures
d'ensemble), 18, 60, 62, 93, 99,
114
transitions between (*see* Transitions)
State, developmental (*see* Developmental
theory)
Structures as a whole (structures
d'ensemble) (*see* Stages)

T
Transitions, developmental, 16–20, 21,
22, 28, 36, 51–59, 92, 93 (*see also*
Creativity, Developmental theory,
Elements, Equilibration,
Novelties)
bias index, 79–80, 81–82, 87–88, 109,
111, 113, 118
chess as indicator of, 142
energetic parameter, 63
level mixture, 78–79, 90, 110, 112, 118
in map drawing, 58, 75–77, 81–82,
92–94, 98, 101–102, 109
phases of, 85–88, 89, 101
in juggling, 128–129
principles of, 88–89, 101
reversion, 94, 99–101, 108–110, 111, 118
stage mixture, 112
states of, 114

U
Universal-to-unique, 8, 22–26, 46–47,
51–53, 135 (*see also* Nonuniversal
domains)

V
Verification, 27 (*see also* Disequilibrium,
Transitions)